DOMINATING THE ENEMY

DOMINATING THE ENEMY

WAR IN THE TRENCHES 1914–1918

Anthony Saunders

SUTTON PUBLISHING

First published in 2000 by
Sutton Publishing Limited · Phoenix Mill
Thrupp · Stroud · Gloucestershire · GL5 2BU

British Library Cataloguing in Publication Data
A catalogue record for this book is available from the British Library

ISBN 0 7509 2444 6

Typeset in 10.5/13.5 pt Times.
Typesetting and origination by
Sutton Publishing Limited.
Printed in Great Britain by
Bookcraft, Midsomer Norton, Somerset.

Contents

Acknowledgements

This book could not have been written without a lot of help. I especially thank Mike Hibberd of the Department of Exhibits and Firearms at the Imperial War Museum for his continued assistance, for supplying me with most of the information from the List of Changes as well as answering a lot of questions. Beverly Williams, Assistant Curator of the Royal Engineers Museum at Chatham, went out of her way to answer my queries, searching out information from *The Royal Engineer's Journal*. The drawings from the *Journal* are reproduced courtesy of the Institution of Royal Engineers. The patent drawings are reproduced by permission of the Stationery Office. I have removed the labelling which, without the complete specifications, serves no useful purpose here. The Newton family kindly provided me with information about Lt-Col Henry Newton, and I thank his son, Mr H.A.B. Newton, and his grandson, Dominic Newton. I thank the staffs of Birmingham City Archive, the Dudley Record Office and the Worcester Record Office for their help. Dr Margaret O'Sullivan, the Derbyshire County and Diocesian Archivist, provided me with the information about Sir Arthur Conan Doyle and Herbert Frood. Mrs Joan Harper looked after me while I was in London visiting the Public Record Office, the Science Library and the Imperial War Museum. The Public Record Office staff were, as ever, very helpful when I was trying to track down elusive information. The staff at the Science Library and the British Library, which now houses all the patents, helped me on numerous occasions, including answering my sometimes unusual telephone enquiries. Derek Rackett, always an enthusiastic supporter of my endeavours, helped me by researching some of the memoirs for references to the devices that are described in this book.

Any mistakes are mine.

Introduction

This book is about weapons and equipment that were specifically devised for fighting in the trenches of the First World War. It is principally about the British search for solutions to the problems of surviving the trenches, dominating the enemy and defeating him. The enemy was not only the Imperial German Army, however, but the trench environment itself, which presented unusual and unexpected problems. Not all of the solutions were successful – many were not. Some were bizarre and some hopelessly optimistic. Many of these devices have not been written about before and yet they became as much a defining feature of the war as artillery, grenades, machine-guns and the trenches themselves.

Dominating the Enemy can be viewed as a companion to *Weapons of the Trench War, 1914–1918*, which looked at the development of grenades, trench mortars, bomb-throwers and flamethrowers. This looks at equally important trench warfare stores, some purely defensive, some offensive in purpose and some that were necessary tools for survival. Such devices included body armour, shields, wire-cutters, periscopes, periscope rifles, trench clubs and knives, muzzle and breech covers, and automatic rifles. The devices described in both books should be viewed as part of the same story. All came from the same sources: the public, professional engineers, soldiers at the Front, trench warfare departments and Royal Engineers. All were different approaches to the same problems – survival and domination. For this reason, American, French, German and Italian devices also figure in this story, although the emphasis is on British equipment.

The start of trench warfare on the Western Front in late 1914 caught the British Army unprepared. Not only did it not possess the necessary weapons and equipment to conduct this form of warfare but also the infrastructure did not exist to design, develop, manufacture or supply what the army needed – everything from grenades to breech covers to keep mud out of bolt mechanisms. The problem had to be resolved if the army was to survive in the trenches, let alone conduct offensive operations against the Germans on the other side of no-man's-land.

It was made worse by the lack of agreement over what was needed. The public, who responded to the army's dearth of suitable equipment by turning its mind to invention, had little idea of what was really required and even less understanding of what was workable in the trenches. Thousands upon thousands of devices, most of them quite useless, were submitted to the trench warfare and inventions departments that were set up to sift through these submissions and design new trench warfare stores. These included the Trench Warfare Department, the Munitions Inventions Department, the Trench Warfare Committee and the Munitions Inventions Panel. In addition, the Royal Arsenal at Woolwich, the Ordnance Board and the School of Musketry had separate inventions sections. There were others. The average rate of submission to the

Munitions Inventions Department alone was about a thousand every month from August 1915, when it was set up, until November 1918, when the war ended. These organizations tended to work independently, often unaware of what the others were doing. The consequence of this was an unnecessary expenditure of effort on the same or similar devices by several departments, each of which tended to come to a different conclusion about the usefulness of the same device. Although this was overcome to a large extent by reorganization and closer liaison as the war progressed, it was never entirely eliminated.

Yet despite this less than perfect arrangement, these departments accomplished remarkable things, although it has to be said that some of the devices left much to be desired. The task of getting something from the design stage into large-scale manufacture was not easy and the lead time could only be reduced by so much. Moreover, mass production as we understand it today did not exist. There were delays and shortfalls much of the time as well as technical problems.

Apart from the official channels, there were other means by which trench warfare kit found its way to the Front. The Edwardian entrepreneurial spirit went hand in hand with engineering inventiveness. Manufacturers and inventors took the opportunity to sell their wares through department stores like Selfridges, Army & Navy and Gamages to soldiers on leave and to their families to send out to them, even when a government inventions department had rejected the devices as unsuitable for the trenches. In the Second World War this would be seen as profiteering but in the First World War it was accepted as normal. Periscopes could be bought in department stores as well as trench knives, wire-cutters and even body armour, along with all manner of things that might conceivably be useful to a soldier in the trenches. Although the inadequate supply of effective equipment through official channels during the early years of the war encouraged private purchase, this was not the driving force. Private purchase by officers had a long tradition, and they were expected to buy their own equipment. And it was at officers that these products were aimed.

But there were problems associated with this commercialism. The inadequate supply of good optical glass, for example, was a constant thorn in the side of the War Office. This severely hindered the supply of good periscopes because they had to compete with other devices that required optical glass, such as gun sights. As a consequence, the infantry never got the best instruments and many commercial devices were woefully defective, often due to poor glass. That did not stop them being bought in large numbers, however. Many commercial trench knives were not sufficiently robust for combat use or were simply too exotic to be effective; body armour was sometimes more elegant than protective. Advertising in newspapers, popular magazines such as *The Sphere* and regimental journals all helped to promote the alleged usefulness and indispensability of many commercial devices, often making extravagant claims about their efficacy.

There was a third source of trench warfare kit – the Royal Engineers. From about mid-1915, Royal Engineer Workshops designed and made trench warfare equipment because of the inadequate supply of such things from Britain. These became sizeable organizations that could produce some devices on an industrial scale. They made practically everything needed for the trenches, from pumps and duckboards to mortars, from periscope rifles to trench clubs and daggers. Their equipment was well designed and well made for the most part. Unlike civilian inventors, the designers at the Workshops knew what was needed and what would work in the trenches. The devices were simple to make and simple to use.

The search for light, transportable automatic weapons to increase the infantryman's firepower was an oddity. Although by the end of the war the automatic rifle and the sub-machine-gun had made their combat debuts, showing the future of infantry small arms, they were viewed in Britain with considerable scepticism, where there was considerable opposition to automatic rifles. Tests had been conducted in the last years of the nineteenth century and they continued long after the First World War was over. The weapons were all rejected as having no advantage over the manual rifle.

I have used two main sources of information in preparing this book: Ministry of Munitions and War Office files held at the Public Record Office at Kew, and British patents that were applied for between August 1914 and November 1918 and subsequently published. For the chapters on armour and shields I have also referred to Bashford Dean's *Helmets and Body Armor in Modern Warfare*, first published in 1919. Dean, the Curator of Armor at the Metropolitan Museum in New York, played an important role in American research into body armour after the US entered the war in 1917, and his study is unique. It is based on his wartime work and includes information given to him by the Trench Warfare Department and the Munitions Inventions Department.

As with *Weapons of the Trench War*, it was not possible to look at all of the complete specifications, as there are simply too many of them. So once again the patent abridgements had to suffice in many cases. Until 1916, patents were numbered from 1 at the beginning of each year. To correctly identify these, the year must be added to the number, e.g. 1234/15. From 1 January 1916, the numbers became continuous, starting with 100,001. Because patents can be obtained in virtually every country in the world, it is, strictly speaking, also necessary to identify the country of origin; thus British patents have GB in front of the number. This is a modern requirement; British patents of 1914–18 did not have the prefix, largely due to British conceit and the fact that the British had the first modern patent system.

Patents are not generally appreciated as a valuable source of historical information. Although some of them are complex documents that run for several pages of incomprehensible detail, in which it is not easy to determine what the invention is, especially when compared with other similar patents, they are not the dry, pedantic legal documents they are often believed to be. They can also provide surprising insights into the inventors and the backgrounds of their inventions. These days, most inventions are the result of hugely expensive company or government research projects and the 'inventors' are companies and governments. But at the time of the First World War, the inventors were more often private individuals than big companies, and were rarely governments. There are precious few lone inventors left at the start of the twenty-first century because invention is now an expensive business. Moreover, if in some future war the public was ever inspired to invent, it is highly improbable that the results would be patented, simply because the cost of patenting is now prohibitively expensive, running into many tens of thousands of pounds (it is no longer enough to patent an invention in one country and patent agents do not come cheap). There is also the added disincentive of needing financial clout to pursue infringers, which is even more expensive than the lengthy process of patenting and has no guarantee of success: on the whole, it is the threat of expensive court action that deters infringers rather than the patent itself. This would deny future historians a valuable resource because there would be precious little in the way of an historical record of the inventive struggle.

In this respect, the patents of the First World War are unique. Although some of the patented inventions may have been unworkable, the published specifications provide an insight into the development of technical ideas during the war and thus into the problems of trench warfare.

CHAPTER I

Shields Against Fire – Defensive Loopholes

In the two decades before the outbreak of the First World War, many of the devices that came to be relied upon as essential for trench warfare were already known to the War Office. There was also a rise in the number of small-arms-related inventions, although there is little evidence to suggest the War Office took an interest in the latest patents by studying the newest abridgements. The majority of these were concerned with breech actions, barrels and sights but an increasing number related to hitherto largely untried devices. These were the instruments of trench warfare.

The bulletproof infantry shield was well known. The British Army had adopted a loopholed shield as early as 1902, although it had not been intended for general use. The effectiveness of infantry shields was demonstrated in Manchuria during the Russo-Japanese War of 1904–05, when the Japanese used them extensively. Particularly noteworthy was their advantageous use in the attack on Port Arthur. Body armour patents date from 1896 and 1907. Moreover, body armour had been used in the American Civil War and the Franco-Prussian War of 1870, if only on a limited scale and not entirely successfully. Again, the effectiveness of body armour was seen in Manchuria where it was used by both sides. Crude, locally made helmets had been used by the British during the siege of Ladysmith in early 1900, although they were reportedly ineffectual. Wire-cutter patents date from 1909. Wire-breakers intended to be attached to the service rifle had even been adopted by the army as early as 1912. The automatic rifle was more than two decades old. A periscope had been patented as long ago as the 1850s. The periscope rifle for shooting from below cover had been invented by 1900. And yet, prior to late 1914, the War Office showed little inclination to take these things very seriously as equipment for the infantry.

There was a good reason for this, even if it was a little short-sighted. All these devices were perceived as instruments of siege warfare, while, as far as automatic rifles were concerned, the British Army believed that there was no substitute for good musketry as inculcated in the pre-war army. The British Army saw a future European war as primarily one of movement, not of siege, and it trained and planned accordingly. Automatic rifles figured not at all. This was despite the warnings of the Russo-Japanese War and the more recent Balkan Wars in which trenches had featured prominently, suggesting that rapid movement might be quickly curtailed, denying a swift victory. These wars demonstrated that the firepower of modern small arms, the machine-gun and artillery made exposed infantry vulnerable to rapid annihilation. None of the European powers fully appreciated what this meant for a future war in Europe.

Nevertheless, the existence of these devices showed that some people had an inkling of what another war might bring. That is not to say that any of the pre-war patented devices would have worked effectively in the trenches of the First World War. Many of them certainly did not. For example, the Hale grenade, invented several years before the war in response to what had been witnessed in Manchuria, was a failure in the trenches, and a shield patented in 1911 failed to work quite as anticipated by the inventor. Indeed, some of the trench warfare devices used in the Russo-Japanese War did not perform well, certainly not well enough to be used in their original forms on the Western Front. This was partly due to the fact that in Manchuria most devices were improvised and lack of experience meant that trial and error was the only way of discovering what worked. Moreover, the industry to manufacture large numbers of workable devices did not exist. So between 1905 and 1914 the British largely chose to ignore this warning. But then so did France, Germany, Russia and Austria-Hungary for the most part. Improvisation inevitably reappeared on the Western Front during late 1914 and continued throughout 1915, on a far larger scale than in Manchuria, because the necessary equipment either did not exist or, if it did, the supply was quite inadequate to meet demands.

Prior to the First World War, British inventors were responding to a different impulse, one generated by war in South Africa, another conflict in which trenches and barbed wire had made their appearance, along with long-range rifle fire, machine-guns and modern artillery. But in South Africa, trench warfare as defined by the First World War had not occurred. As a consequence, the devices invented to cope with things like barbed wire and enemy small arms fire were, on the whole, naïvely conceived. It would take experience of the Western Front to teach those who became responsible for designing and testing equipment exactly what would work and what would not because, like in Manchuria, there was no previous knowledge on which to call. Sadly, many of the devices created by inventors keen to help the war effort were quite unworkable in trials, let alone in the conditions of the Western Front. For the most part, civilians had no background in the kind of devices they were attempting to make – they were amateurs in the Victorian sense.

And there was another reason. It is very easy to view decisions taken more than ninety years ago with the twenty-twenty vision of hindsight and accuse the pre-First World War British Army of short-sightedness but there was an important caveat to the practicability of such devices: they were unwanted additional burdens for the infantryman. Some devices, such as infantry shields, for example, were awkward and heavy. Consequently, soldiers tended to throw them away. They had done so in Manchuria. Some German infantry units were issued with portable shields for their advance through Belgium in 1914 but the infantrymen were sufficiently unimpressed with the additional burden that they quickly got rid of them. It is a universal truth that soldiers throw away anything they have no immediate use for, especially if it hinders them in what they are currently doing. And the heavier the device, the greater the chance of it being discarded. An unexpected hazard was also discovered. Some German infantrymen reputedly had their arms broken by the impact of bullets when carrying the shield, although this is probably apocryphal. Nevertheless, that sort of idea quickly gained credence, irrespective of facts.

German troops on manoeuvres, 1914. Note the pair in the centre lying behind a portable infantry shield. The Germans reputedly used a four-man shield like this, two men supporting the shield, one firing through the aperture and the fourth carrying grenades. (The Illustrated War News)

The portable infantry shield was originally viewed as a device of open warfare rather than of trench fighting but with the awareness that its use was limited to attacks on fortified positions. This was a fine distinction since trenches were often used in taking a fortified position. As an implement with which to protect rapidly moving infantry in the heat of battle, it left much to be desired simply because it got in the way, negating much of its supposed advantages. By their very nature, shields tended to be fairly large and heavy and were consequently not very portable, despite the hopes of their designers. One patent (GB 4,376/15) dating from March 1915, for example, describes a ridiculously impractical device, an enormous, rectangular, curved shield about 4 ft high perforated by various slots for eyes and rifle. The user was not only supposed to be standing when he used this but was also meant to walk along carrying this monster via supporting straps over his shoulders and 'distance pieces' attached to his belt (to keep it clear of his knees), his rifle poking out of a slot. It is doubtful if anyone other than the inventor took this very seriously. Quite apart from anything else, its size would have made it an unmissable target. And it is unlikely that anyone unlucky enough to have to wear one could do much more than hobble.

The Japanese model used at Port Arthur measured 19 in × 12 in, was 0.22 in thick and reportedly weighed 17.75 lb, which was no small weight but not untypical. The steel from which the Japanese shields were made was armour plate, supplied by Britain. The shield was rectangular, with the top corners sliced off at an angle, and had an oval loophole to fire through two-thirds of the way up, slightly offset from the centre line.

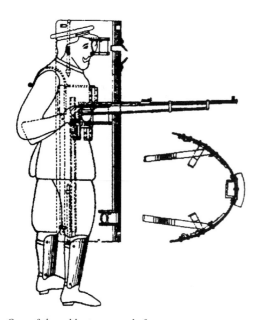

One of the oddest proposals for armour, a cross between body armour and an infantry shield. Note the ankle defences like medieval greaves. Mr Fontijn's patent GB 4,376/15.

To use armour plate was an obvious choice but this is not enough to prevent injury, even assuming that the plate stopped small arms fire. When a bullet strikes armour, depending on the angle of impact and the bullet's attitude, it may be deflected and ricochet off or it may disintegrate, causing the lead inside the bullet's jacket to splash. It is therefore important that the design minimizes this threat of injury to the user and other soldiers close by. In addition, a bullet striking the plate will tend to cause little pieces of the inner face of the plate to fly off (known as spalling) into the face of the user, risking injury to his face and eyes. This was one of the reasons why British tank crews were issued with steel goggles and mail masks. The Japanese inventor of the shield, Chiba Choksaki, overcame the problem of spalling by using a layer of hair, known as uralite, sandwiched between the steel plate and a layer of leather.

In 1916, a version of the Chiba shield was tested by the Munitions Inventions Department with a view to using it on the Western Front. It appears that the steel plate was of Japanese manufacture rather than of British origin; British armour plate was superior to Japanese armour because of better heat treatment techniques. The results were not encouraging. Although the shield was not penetrated at 100 yd by either British or German armour-piercing rounds, this was only achieved when two shields were placed one behind the other, with a 1 in gap separating them. Only the inner shield remained intact. And when several shots were fired at the same spot, the metal broke. Ordinary ball ammunition penetrated a single shield at 35 yd, although when the shield was set at an angle of 55° the rounds were deflected at 50 yd.

Right from the beginning of the war there was considerable interest in portable infantry shields and a number of designs were tried out by the Experimental Section at the School of Musketry and later the Trench Warfare Department and Munitions Inventions Department. The requirements for a portable shield were inevitably a compromise between portability and stopping power, which largely came down to a compromise on weight. Tests conducted during the war showed that a steel plate had to be at least 0.25 in thick to stop ordinary ball ammunition when fired directly at it from 50 yd but to prevent penetration by armour-piercing rounds the plate had to be at least 0.40 in thick and made of high-quality steel. There are many different types of steel and bullet resistance is a complex equation that takes into account the other materials alloyed with it, e.g. nickel, manganese and silicon, and in what proportion, as well as the heat treatment. The weight rose from 1 lb per 14 sq in for 0.25 in plate to 1 lb per 9 sq in for 0.40 in plate, so that a 12 in × 19 in shield rose in weight from 16 lb 4 oz to 25 lb 5 oz. If the bullet was reversed so that the blunt end hit the plate instead of the point, the steel had to be even thicker to prevent penetration (it was erroneously believed early on in the war that the Germans reversed bullets in their cartridges because of the nature of wounds caused by high-velocity bullets, with which few were familiar. For the same reason, accusations were brought by both sides during the war that dumdum bullets and explosive bullets were being used. They were not. Wound ballistics as a science did not exist at the time of the Great War. Consequently, many tests throughout the war were conducted with reversed ammunition.) Obviously, the bigger and thicker a shield, the heavier and less portable it was, but the degree of protection rose accordingly.

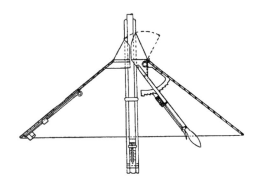

A rifle shield with clamping jaws operated by a lever patented by T.J. Gee in 1916 (GB 101,269).

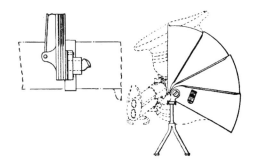

A rifle shield that folds like a fan, complete with bipod rifle rest, patented by C. Leven shortly before the outbreak of war.

There was also the not inconsiderable problem that while carrying the shield the soldier was unable to use his rifle. Neither could he easily see where he was going (hence the numerous apertures in GB 4,376/15). Moreover, he was poorly balanced by the extra weight that could not be evenly distributed around him, which made him less agile and more prone to falling over, especially on uneven ground. Even when using the shield for protection, the user was only afforded a limited arc of relative safety from enemy fire while at the same time his field of view was restricted. An enemy shooting from the side would have an accessible target. It was quickly realized that there were only certain circumstances under which a shield would be of practical value and that by necessity, such circumstances had to be of short duration. This was not an altogether surprising conclusion. The British Army had always viewed shields as specialist equipment for use in particular situations.

An alternative approach to strapping the portable shield to the infantryman's arms was to attach it to his rifle, so that it only gave protection while the soldier was aiming and shooting. There were some advantages to this approach, not the least being that the shield was smaller and lighter. But it meant that in open country the rifle could only be fired from the prone position as the additional weight made it too heavy and unbalanced to fire

MacAdam's armoured spade with loophole. (The Illustrated War News)

standing or kneeling. To use it while standing the soldier had to be in a trench so that it could be rested on the parapet, although that was not always what the inventor intended. The shield patented in 1911 (GB 23,075/11) was of this type. Invented by a Mr McDougall, the device was also, rather perversely, intended to double as the blade of an entrenching tool. The shape of the blade-cum-shield enabled the infantryman to attach it to the side of the rifle stock without it interfering with his line of sight along the barrel, yet it still concealed his face from the front. It was attached to the stock via hinged mountings that allowed the shield to recoil under the impact of a bullet. This feature evidently worked quite effectively.

It was tested by Capt Todhunter, the Experimental Officer at the School of Musketry, in March 1915. It is clear from his report that this test was not the first performed on the shield, which had evidently been improved on since an earlier evaluation. The shield had been made thicker and had been fitted with a loophole and a shutter. It stopped German 'S' (pointed or *spitzgeschoss*) ammunition at 75 yd while a thinner pattern was only effective at 220 yd. However, the shutter rivets tended to be loosened by the bullet impacts and bullet splash was 'very considerable', in addition to which, the area of protection was very limited. The thicker shield weighed 7 lb while the thinner one weighed 5 lb 2 oz. Todhunter concluded that use of the shield would not 'have any marked effect in the reduction of casualties'. Neither did he like the way the device was attached to the stock, which he described as 'objectionable' because it was weakened as a result. But as an entrenching tool he thought it was an improvement over the service issue. This can hardly have been reassuring for the inventor.

A similar idea was E. MacAdam's combined spade and shield, except that his shield was not intended to be attached to the rifle as the spade part remained fixed to the handle. A spike projected from the top of the spade and this was supposed to be pushed into the ground so that the spade could be used as a shield, which was provided with a loophole to fire through. The only drawback was that the handle had to be partially buried as well. It was not exactly a practical idea but MacAdam was granted a patent (GB 19,281/14). It was not taken up.

The belief that a shield attached to a rifle was the answer to protecting the infantryman gained quite a lot of ground from the opening shots of the war. It may be significant to note that the inventors of such devices appeared to have no experience of modern soldiering and consequently had little idea of what a rifle with a lump of metal

The GREENWOOD
BULLET DEFLECTOR
:—(PATENTED)—:

TO HELP THE TROOPS.

A Shield for the Soldiers.

Interesting Halifax Invention.

Above we give a sketch of an invention by Ex-Hon. Lieutenant and Quartermaster J.H.T. Greenwood, of Halifax. The idea is to protect the soldier with the rifle. The shield placed on the rifle would not weigh more than a couple of pounds, could be carried on the arm, and would be bullet-proof. It is claimed that it would assist in careful and deliberate shooting, and would greatly minimise the danger to troops in the firing line.

Inner View, Showing
: Sighting Aperture :

J. H. T. GREENWOOD, 28, Union Street, Halifax. Tele. 1069.

John Greenwood's advertisement for his patented rifle shield. The address and telephone number are his. (MUN 4/135)

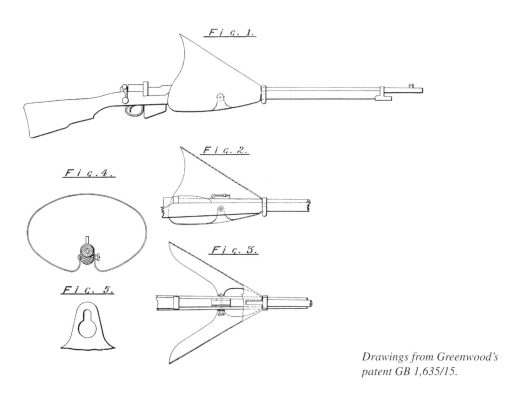

Drawings from Greenwood's patent GB 1,635/15.

permanently fixed to it would be like to use for more than a few minutes. One such inventor was dentist and 'ex-Hon. Lieutenant and Quartermaster' John Harrison Thompson Greenwood of Union Street, Halifax. He invented a conical shield for which he filed a patent application in February 1915, which was granted in September as GB 1,635/15. He also set about marketing his device with the aid of leaflets and a bundle found their way to the Ministry of Munitions. He believed that the invention would protect the rifleman 'from rifle fire, or from weapons used in hand to hand conflict [by which he meant bayonets], and . . . facilitate and improve the sighting of the rifle and increase its efficiency as a weapon of attack and defence'. Sadly, he was mistaken.

Shortly after Greenwood applied for his patent, Henry Lawson applied for one in respect of a similar shield. Like Greenwood he was successful and his application was accepted and granted as GB 3,801/15 in December. That did not mean it was practical, however. It was bigger and more substantial than Greenwood's and no doubt weighed much more. Lawson specified that it should be 0.25 in thick, indicating that he at least had some idea of what was required of a bulletproof shield. It consisted of two flat plates hinged together to enable the shield to be folded up when not clamped to the rifle. Slots in the plates formed a circular aperture with a vertical slot above it when the plates were opened out; these were to accommodate the rifle and allow the infantryman to see the foresight and thus aim at a target. The idea was for the two plates to be angled about the hinge to allow bullets to be deflected and for the shield to be set at about 20–30° from the vertical. Although this arrangement may well have protected the user, it would have been rather hazardous for anyone else close by. The lower edge of the shield was intended to be rested on the ground and act as a support for the rifle. Interestingly, Lawson's specification states that in defending a trench the most frequently wounded parts of the body were 'the fingers . . . the fore-arms, the eyes, and the head'. Quite where he obtained this information is not known but it certainly did not agree with the statistics gathered by the Trench Warfare Department. It is likely that he simply guessed. Unlike Greenwood, Lawson meant his shield to be used in the trenches rather than open country but like Greenwood's his invention was not taken up. It was unworkable and ineffective.

The problem with this type of shield was that it hindered ordinary use of the rifle, no matter what inventors may have claimed to the contrary. For a shield to be of practical use in the trenches it had to be built into the parapet and camouflaged. The Royal Welch Fusiliers knew this and, as Frank Richards explained, they concealed them 'as cleverly as we could, but in a day or two the enemy generally discovered them and would rattle bullets all around'. Merely to place one on the top was to invite immediate retaliatory fire from a sniper or a barrage of rifle grenades because it stuck out. To be useful, the shield had to be concealed from the enemy. Moreover, firing from such a position had to be done judiciously to avoid detection. German snipers gained intimate knowledge of the ground and immediately spotted any changes. They were very accurate shots and quite capable of putting a round through the aperture of the shield, as Edmund Blunden discovered when a sentry 'looking too faithfully through his loophole, was shot clean through the head', or even down the barrel of the rifle, if only by accident. Frank Richards described such an incident in late 1914:

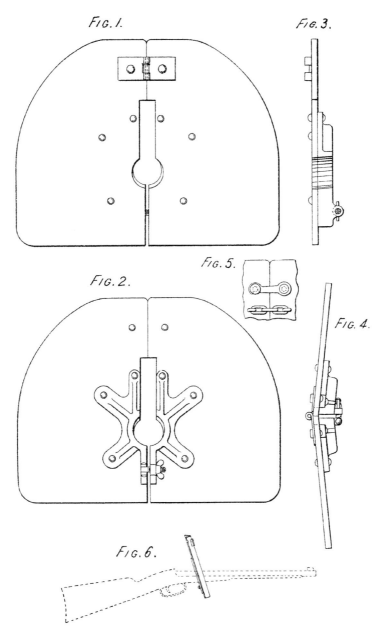

Lawson's rifle shield. Fig. 1 shows the outer face, while Fig.2 shows the inner face. Drawings from published specification GB 1,635/15.

A man named Blacktin was firing behind one of the plates. He had fired two rounds and was just about to pull the trigger to fire the third when he seemed to be hurled against the back of the trench, his rifle falling from his hands. A German sniper had fired and his bullet had entered the barrel of Blacktin's rifle, where it was now lodged fast, splitting the top end of the barrel the same way as a man would peel a banana.

This sort of thing was not one-sided. Ernst Jünger was on the receiving end from 'a harebrained Englishman who showed his head over the parapet of a trench 100 metres away . . . and got a succession of bull's-eyes on our loophole'. In the end the Englishman was silenced and Jünger 'got the plate behind which this mad fellow had kept appearing time after time with three shots of K ammunition, and sent it flying'. 'K' ammunition was armour piercing.

The shield also needed a shutter to close off the aperture when not firing from it. Neither Lawson nor Greenwood appreciated that and, interesting though their designs were, they were impractical for the trenches, irrespective of any capability to stop bullets. Shields that were attached to rifles were inherently impractical. In the trenches, shields of a different type were needed and they came to be used in quite specific ways which were not those envisaged by Greenwood and Lawson. By mid-1915, the fixed trench shield had become part of the standard equipment of the sniper. That did not stop other inventors trying their hands at rifle shields. In 1914, there were only two successful patent applications, while in 1915 there were five, including Greenwood's and Lawson's. By the end of 1916 there were another four. One of these was designed for the Villar Perosa sub-machine-gun. It included a simple ball-and-socket joint through which the weapon was projected and which could be rotated to allow a wide arc of aimed fire without moving the shield. But there were no more after this. Presumably, by the end of 1916, the futility of these shields was widely enough known to discourage inventors from pursuing that line of development. After all, none had been taken up by GHQ and none conformed to the requirements of a trench shield. The rifle shield was born of naïveté.

Although the rifle shield never found favour, the machine-gun shield did and from time to time various devices underwent trials with the Experimental Section, Royal Engineers (not to be confused with the Experimental Section at the School of Musketry). However, the mere use of a shield with a machine-gun

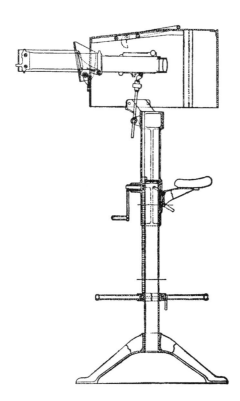

Austin's armoured turret for a machine-gun; it could be raised and lowered in a trench by the gunner. Capt Todhunter rejected it. Drawing from GB 13,346/15.

Segments of armour used to make observation posts. These are French. (The Illustrated War News)

tended to advertise the gun's presence and attract unpleasant attention from the enemy, a failing compounded by the fact that such shields usually didn't provide adequate protection. One such device was a fairly complicated affair that ran on rollers, allowing it to be traversed with the machine-gun. The Royal Engineers made about fifty of them which were used in the trenches but they were not a success because they were too large and unwieldy. A similarly complex device was patented by W.R. Ellison and H.L. Cole in 1915 (GB 12,195/15), which enabled the machine-gun to be traversed with the shield by means of a toothed track and gears. There were even more complicated devices than this. In October 1915 the School of Musketry evaluated a steel machine-gun turret on a pedestal that was raised and lowered by a crank, invented by a Mr Austin. The gunner rotated it with his feet.

An armoured observation post disguised as a tree. This one is German. (The World War 1 Document Archive)

Austin had already applied for a patent in September and this was eventually granted as GB 13,346. In theory it could be carried into the trench by two men but Todhunter considered that at least four were needed. The armour was proof against German 'S' ammunition at 15 yd but it had many faults, including poor ventilation, that needed to be put right before it became a viable proposition for the trenches.

Both the French and the British made limited use of steel cupolas as armoured observation posts. Some of them were camouflaged as trees; a fake was constructed behind the lines at the Special Works Park, Royal Engineers, and was made to resemble a specific tree at the Front. This was substituted overnight so that the Germans would suspect nothing. Sometimes the fake was made taller than the original to aid observation and the extra height had to be concealed by making the parapet higher where the new 'tree' was planted. The increased height of the parapet had itself to be concealed by gradually reducing its height at the 'tree' to that of the original parapet about 50 ft or so away – the graduation itself had to be unnoticeable. This made for a hard night's work, all of which had to be done silently. Some of the steelwork used for making these observation posts was French and consisted of short sections of tube bolted together. This was a full day's work in itself. A similar British shield, introduced in late 1916, was semi-cylindrical steel 'fitted with an upper plate, set at an angle, to provide head cover . . . and a hole . . . cut centrally in the top of the plate for observation purposes'. A 30 ft ladder was bolted to the top on the inside.

The so-called 'portable' infantry shield intended for the protection of the one man who carried it was short-lived. The alleged merits of its dubious practicality were finally laid to rest as the trench system grew like a fissure across northern France, starting on the Aisne in September 1914, eventually reaching north to the sea and south to the Swiss frontier, ending the war of movement. With the emergence of static warfare, the infantry shield was developed along different lines, continued interest in the rifle shield notwithstanding. It evolved into the fixed trench shield that was built into the parapet as a permanent feature. Another line of development led to the multi-purpose shield, which could be used as a portable one or worn as body armour. In a sense, the monstrous shield described in GB 4,376/15 was of this type but taken to an extreme that rendered it pointless.

The fixed shield was of more practical value and saw widespread use by all armies on the Western Front. Used from at least Roman times and known as a mantlet, this type of shield was still being used in later centuries by sappers during siege operations. It appears that the fixed shields of the Western Front were originally intended to be used in much the same way as the mantlets of the past. In other words, they were to be placed in suitable positions for a limited time and moved once the operation that required their use had ended. Such an operation might be wire-cutting, for example. However, there were problems with this. Soldiers who had to use them were unenthusiastic because they were even heavier than the so-called portable shields and they stood out like sore thumbs, making excellent targets as well as signalling to the enemy that the other side was up to something.

The British were probably the first to make extensive use of fixed shields, introducing them in late 1914. By 1917, there were 200,000 in the trenches. The British shield of 1914 and 1915 weighed 20 lb and had a loophole that could be closed with a shutter on

Wire cutting on the Italian Front, 1915, using a large shield. One man is supporting the shield while a second extends a wire-cutter on the end of a pole into the entanglement. (The Illustrated War News)

Austrian soldier, winter 1915/16, using a small shield to protect himself while cutting wire. Note the curve on the top of the shield and the puny wire-cutters. (The Illustrated War News)

some modified shields. It was very effective and would stop standard German ball ammunition at 50 yd. But its weight made it extremely unpopular. The British Army had adopted the 'Mk 1 Plate, Loop-holed' in 1902. It was introduced as a result of the war in South Africa, not the Russo-Japanese War, which it predated by two years. The shield was not intended for general use by the infantry, however, but was meant for the Royal Engineers, to enable them to conduct field engineering operations in relative safety. By October 1914, the plate was more widely available for trench use by the infantry. The Mk 1 was made of 'specially prepared steel, and has in the centre a 5-inch by 3-inch loophole'. It was bigger than the Japanese Chiba shield, measuring 2 ft × 1 ft and its weight was not supposed to exceed 20.5 lb. Thickness was not specified but it was clearly in the region of 0.25 in.

The Belgian Army used shields made in America, manufactured by Rosenwasser Brothers of Brooklyn, although it is uncertain when these entered service. It was 24 in wide, 31 in high and 0.29 in thick, and it had a pair of hinged legs at the back to keep it upright. Made of chromium-nickel steel, it stopped standard German ball ammunition at 6 yd and reversed rounds at 50 yd but it weighed a hefty 60 lb. On one side there was an aperture without a shutter to fire through and it was covered with canvas to stop light reflecting from the metal surface.

German shields of this type varied in size, thickness and weight. A shield introduced in 1916 weighed 30 lb, was made of 0.23 in thick silicon-nickel steel and measured 24 in × 18 in. It was reportedly capable of stopping machine-gun fire at 100 yd but was not proof against armour-piercing rounds. A more substantial shield introduced the same year weighed 50 lb and was 26 in long and 12 in high but was 0.42 in thick. Unlike the lighter model, which had a single hinged leg for support, this one was provided with hinged side panels to keep it upright and to minimize the effects of lead splash and ricochets. The front plate of both shields had outward-curving vertical edges for the same reason. The heavier model was proof against armour-piercing ammunition at very close range. The lighter shield had a 2 in × 6 in shuttered loophole off to one side and more or less halfway up, whereas the heavier model had only a 2 in × 5 in slot in the lower edge. Both types were used in large numbers on the Western Front. An improved version of the heavy model was introduced in 1917 and the vertical edges of this appear to have been given an even greater curvature.

Tests carried out on German shields by the Munitions Inventions Department showed that 0.42 in thick armour plate would resist penetration by British armour-piercing bullets at distances greater than 150 yd, whereas a 0.20 in thick shield was not penetrated by standard British ball ammunition at 100 yd. More worryingly, it was not penetrated by armour-piercing ammunition fired by the Lewis gun at the same distance.

Throughout the war, the Experimental Section of the Royal Engineers carried out numerous experiments with armour of various kinds to ascertain levels of protection against different sorts of ammunition. The Section concluded that it was possible to make 'parapet shields of practical weights' for snipers that were proof against small arms ammunition at 50 yd but that it was impossible to make shields or, indeed, any other form of armour that was in any way practical, which were proof against armour-piercing ammunition at the same distance. Nevertheless, the Section conducted many trials 'during the summer of 1917 to find material for facing loop-hole plates as a protection against armour-piercing bullets'. In particular, it experimented with Japanese shields covered with uralite, which proved to be one of the best protective coverings, but overall

French debris retrieved from trenches at Verdun, early 1916. Note the pile of shields in the centre and the two trench shields with side plates, centre right, which appear to be German. (The Illustrated War News)

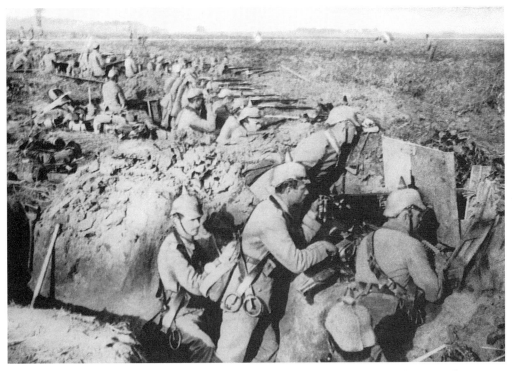

German trench, late 1914. The machine-gun crew are using a trench shield. Note the outward curvature of the sides to prevent bullet splash causing injuries. (The Illustrated War News)

the shields were simply too heavy. (This illustrates the duplication of work and lack of cooperation between departments, in this case between different organizations within the army – the School of Musketry and the Royal Engineers.) Work on parapet shields continued during 1918 but much of this was investigation into failures of shields in the trenches.

Maj Hesketh-Pritchard, a former big-game hunter who was given responsibility for developing British sniping on the Western Front early in the war, described the practicalities of various shields with loopholes supplied to the Front. Some of them were adapted by Royal Engineers to accommodate loopholes of his specification and were manufactured at the First Army Workshops at Béthune. Here, the Royal Engineers cut loopholes in 'standard plates by oxy-acetylene flame'. The Royal Engineers also cut the plates to size at Béthune and 'Every opportunity was taken in manufacture to make use of common and existing materials', which meant that not all the plates were made from armour. But it was done because of the shortage of materials and for quickness.

One of Hesketh-Pritchard's complaints about shields was that the size and shape of the loophole made it very difficult to use a rifle fitted with the British standard issue telescopic sights, which were mounted on the side of the rifle rather than on top. The modified loopholes overcame this problem. It was common practice for sniping positions to use three shields positioned to make a three-sided box facing the enemy parapet.

Sketch of British sniper in 1915 with three sniping plates set up in front of the parapet, each of which has a shuttered loophole; note that the shutter is on the inner face. Note also the supporting leg on the front of the central shield. (The Illustrated War News)

Hesketh-Pritchard observed that the side shields severely restricted the arc of fire open to the sniper because they prevented him moving very much. He recommended that the side shields should be angled at about 45° to the front-facing one to obviate this disadvantage. He was also of the opinion that although many shields 'could be indented for from the Special Works Park R.E. (Camouflage)' they were often of little use to the sniper for the simple reason that they did not blend in with the local surroundings unless the officer making the indent gave proper instructions on how to camouflage them according to where they were going to be used. He believed that the shields needed to be adapted to the local conditions so as not to stand out. By this he meant that the type of ground and what was behind the trench needed to be taken into account. There was good reason to go to a lot of trouble to conceal the shields. As soon as they were spotted, they were targeted by enemy snipers, trench mortars or rifle grenades and sometimes artillery shoots.

Sniping plates were sometimes absent from the places were they were needed most. At Stink Post at Ypres, Capt Hitchcock noted that

There were no sniping plates of any description, and our snipers had to 'chance their arm' and fire over the parapets. Whilst we were in the post, two of the Battalion snipers, 5970 Pte. Flanaghan, and 3784 Pte. Ward, were shot clean through the head. The former lived for just twenty minutes, the latter for about the same.

Throughout 1915 the infantry learned about how and where to position steel plates but they were not always put in the best places. Even in 1916 sniping plates were being badly located in parapets. Maj-Gen Capper, on a tour of inspection in the front-line trenches in October 1916, 'objected to the positions of some of the sniper plates' set up by the Leinsters and wanted them immediately repositioned.

On Boxing Day 1915, Gen Maxwell, who was on Haig's staff (Haig had only just taken over command of the BEF from Sir John French), wrote to the War Office on the subject of shields and body armour. This was in reply to an earlier letter from the War Office and was part of an already long-standing correspondence between GHQ and London about armour that spanned much of 1915 and continued into 1916. In this letter Maxwell restated his opinion that there was a definite need 'for a portable shield, proof against the German bullet fired at close range and at the same time of such weight as will allow of its being conveniently carried forward either as a whole or in sections'.

Maxwell's request for suitable examples was passed from the War Office to the Department of Munitions Design in the Ministry of Munitions, and from there it found its way to the Munitions Inventions Department and to the Trench Warfare Department, all of which were investigating armour. A Munitions Design letter sent to the War Office on 24 January 1916 in connection with Maxwell's, refers to 'composite shields capable of covering from 5 to 15 men', although whether this was quite what Maxwell had in mind is unclear.

It would seem that one of the outcomes of Maxwell's correspondence was the introduction in 1917 of another 'portable' shield. The British were sufficiently impressed with the German shield with side plates to want a version of their own. The Munitions Inventions Department conducted tests on suitable armour plate in December 1916 and orders were placed with four firms – Edgar Allen & Co., Thomas Firth & Sons, both of Sheffield, William Beardmore of Glasgow and The Miris Steel Co. of Holborn – to supply fifty plates each, plus an additional five for test purposes. The side plates were thinner than the front one and were fixed to it by brackets rather than hinges. Firth was only contracted to supply front plates while another firm, Fred Bradby & Co. of Deptford, was to supply the side plates for them while yet another, Dry & Co. of Westminster, was to make the brackets and assemble everything. And that was not the end of it. All the shields were originally intended to be fitted with leather covers but this was replaced by covers composed of woodite (a gelatinous material), which were to be made and fitted by W. Jenkinson & Co. of Moorfields at 7s 6d each. The Trench Warfare Supply Department was to take over responsibility for supplying the army in France. No doubt these eventually found their way to the Front.

The movable, as opposed to the portable, shield was one answer to the problem of manhandling heavyweight pieces of armour plate. This required wheels and, as unlikely as it may seem, the idea was not only taken very seriously but a large number of these devices were made in 1915. Some of them ended up in the Dardanelles, although it is doubtful if they were of much use. Not surprisingly, all the 'shields on wheels' required level ground if they were to be moved with relative ease or, indeed, at all. Moving them over ground broken up by shellfire or merely naturally uneven ground proved to be beyond human effort for all practical purposes. These wheeled shields relied for the most part purely on human strength and endurance. The origin of these devices was the Admiralty, although the original idea seems to have been American, dating from the Spanish-American War of 1898.

Some time after the outbreak of war and before the onset of trench warfare, the Admiralty asked Vickers and Beardmore to design and make wheeled shields. This was at a time when the Admiralty had an interest in the 'land ship' that was to

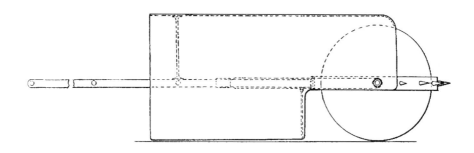

J.J. Oxley's mobile shield, as tall as a man, with a ball at the front instead of a wheel, a feature that was later adopted for garden wheelbarrows. Drawing from GB 101,827.

A mobile shield invented by Fred Wallis of Birmingham in early 1915 which he submitted to the War Office claiming that the 5 mm thick steel was bulletproof at 50 yd. It had enough loopholes for six men. The wheels could be removed and several shields joined to form a barricade. Compare this with Mr Griffen's device (overleaf). (The Illustrated War News)

become the tank. Their designs were tested at Wormwood Scrubs by RNAS personnel. They were evidently deemed workable enough to be shipped out to the Dardanelles and to the RNAS armoured car division in France. By the end of 1915, no one seemed to know what had happened to them; the Department of Munitions Design suggested it was possible that the RNAS examples might have gone with No. 15 Armoured Car Squadron to Russia. There was, however, 'a considerable assortment of Shields on Wheels in France with the 6th Division'. There were many different sizes and designs and these had been constructed under the supervision of a Lt Smith, who was serving in the RNAS Armoured Car Service which was attached to the 6th Division at the time. It is possible that his designs were based on a French model.

There were many problems with wheeled shields. They were unable to negotiate rough ground; they were too heavy to be pushed by one man if it was to give him adequate protection; anything larger than a one-man shield made too conspicuous a target; balance was a problem; and the user was always vulnerable to flanking fire even supposing that the armour plate was proof against armour-piercing rounds. The resulting designs and modifications were always unsatisfactory compromises.

A lot of suggestions and inventions were submitted for evaluation, including ideas from the public and serving officers. Some of these were looked at by the Munitions Inventions Department; others were examined by the Experimental Section, Royal Engineers. One suggestion was sent to Kitchener by a Canadian inventor who had originally sent his idea

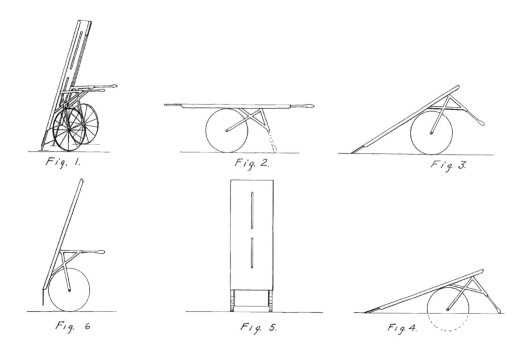

Mr Griffen's mobile shield, showing vertical rifle slits and foot defence. Drawings prepared by the Ministry of Munitions. (MUN 4/2749)

to the Canadian Militia Department. They informed him that his invention had merit but they lacked the time to evaluate it, advising him to send it to the War Office. Mr Griffen, the inventor, wrote to Kitchener on 21 May 1915 explaining that he was not a military man but he had an idea for a mobile shield. Disingenuously he stated that he no idea what thickness of steel would be appropriate but suggested ⅛ in thick nickel steel might do the job. He estimated that at this thickness his wheeled shield would weigh less than 100 lb, as though this was a mere featherweight. Griffen recognized that it had limitations, particularly that it needed even ground to be moved easily. He also claimed that it would be useful for making quick entrenchments and for 'sharpshooters'. His letter was duly passed on to the Munitions Inventions Department. It was turned down.

Another suggestion came from an officer at GHQ, France, and was evaluated by the Experimental Section, Royal Engineers. The shield was known as the Van der Weyden after the man who invented it. Unfortunately for him, however, the shield was constructed not so much for the purpose of evaluation but more to demonstrate the basic impracticality of wheeled shields. This it did admirably. Even with its weight reduced to 1 cwt (nearly 51 kg) it could not be pushed by one man alone, especially if he was wearing full kit, except on ground that was absolutely flat. The inventor claimed that it should be made so that it balanced like a wheelbarrow, allowing the weight to be over the wheels to make it easier to push, while at the same time affording protection. Sadly, no. The idea of pushing an armoured wheelbarrow was absurd.

French wheeled shield with side plates, propelled by muscle power. (The Times History of the War)

A partial solution to the immobility problem was found in the use of wide wheels. The French adopted this answer to one-man mobile shields and they were evidently used in large numbers during part of 1917 and into 1918 to protect individual men on wire-cutting duties in no-man's-land. It was basically a shield mounted on an axle with two hollow wooden wheels weighted with sand. A larger mobile shield used by the French and British in 1918 was akin to a three-sided metal box on wheels with a platform on which the user could lie with only his legs exposed. It was made entirely of steel, the armoured part being chromium-nickel steel. The front was V-shaped to deflect bullets. Like the French wooden-wheeled model, this one was also used for wire-cutting duties. It is hard to imagine how it was possible to move and steer such a thing with the feet and still cut wire.

Larger-wheeled shields, intended to protect anything from five to fifteen infantrymen at a time, were also built but were never used operationally. One such device built in 1917 was provided with rifle slits to enable the crew of five to engage enemy targets such as machine-gun positions. At least, that was the theory. It was propelled by the crew pushing on a pole attached to the shield. Although the combined effort of several men

Russian wheeled shields captured at the Second Battle of the Masurian Lakes, early 1915. These do not have side plates. Each shield covers six men and there are two rows of three loopholes. (The Illustrated War News)

Turkish mobile shields captured in the Dardanelles. Unlike the French shields illustrated on the previous page, these do not protect the lower legs and feet. (The Illustrated War News)

may have made it somewhat easier to move, it was still hard work. When, in April 1916, the Experimental Section at the School of Musketry tested a large portable shield intended to protect eight men, it was rejected because it was too heavy to move it on uneven ground and, being the size of a field-gun shield, it made a prime target for artillery. An even bigger shield was propelled by a gearing mechanism worked by

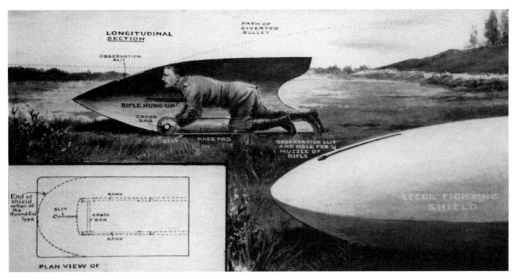

An impractical one-man mobile 'fort' invented by Mr H.J. Hedderwick of Glasgow in the summer of 1915. It weighed more than 200 lb. Such devices were incredibly naïve. (The Illustrated War News)

members of the crew turning two handles. This device was designed to carry a machine-gun and a crew of eight, who were provided with loopholes, although it was big enough to protect fifteen. It was conceived and constructed some time in 1915 and was still knocking around the Experimental Ground at Wembley in early 1916.

This ungainly thing was evidently the brainchild of the Department of Munitions Design and for some reason was called a pedrail. According to *The Shorter Oxford English Dictionary* a pedrail is a device with wide 'feet' fitted to the wheels of a vehicle to facilitate its movement over rough terrain, the word dating from 1902. This hardly described the device very accurately, unless whoever christened it had a sardonic sense of humour. The front shield was 5 ft high × 6 ft wide. It had 'wings' or side shields that extended for 10 ft on each side, increasing in height from 4 ft at the extremities to 5 ft where they joined the front shield. The angle of attachment of these wings could be altered according to circumstances. It weighed about 1.5 tons (Imperial measurement) and needed a minimum of three men to get it moving and keep it moving.

Clearly, manpower alone was just not enough to make mobile shields a viable proposition. What was needed was some other form of motive power. Horses were considered. Then someone had the bright idea of using a petrol engine. And the obvious addition to this was some form of traction other than wheels that could cope with broken ground. All these ideas were leading in one direction – to the tank. The development of the tank ended most of the work on mobile shields for infantry. After the tank, the mobile shield, whether propelled on wheels or by brute strength, was a dead duck, not that it was much of a flier to start with.

CHAPTER 2

Protect and Survive –
Body Shields

The public perception of armour has always tended to imbue it with almost magical powers to protect the wearer from harm. To some extent, this has stemmed from romantic ideas about what medieval plate armour could accomplish, particularly at the time of the First World War when the scientific study of armour was still in its infancy. It was an enthusiastic amateur, the barrister Samuel Rush Meyrick, who started the serious study of arms and armour in the 1820s, but from sculptures and illustrations not actual examples. It was not until the 1880s in Austria that scientific studies of actual examples began in earnest. It took until about the first decade of the twentieth century for the scientific method to become firmly established in Britain. A full understanding of the construction of medieval armour was yet to be achieved by the outbreak of war. The first 'complete' catalogue of the armour in the Tower Armouries was only published in 1910. Its author, Charles ffoulkes, was curator; by 1917, he had become head of the National War Museum, the forerunner of the Imperial War Museum.

It is hardly surprising, then, that commercial body armour at the time of the First World War was imperfect – commercial enterprises inevitably knew far less about the construction of medieval armour than curators of historic collections. (It is not clear when the word 'body' was first prefixed; medieval armour has only ever been called 'armour'. The prefix is unnecessary but it has become common usage. During the First World War, such armour was often referred to as a 'body shield', rarely as 'body armour'. However, in patent abridgements, but rarely in the specifications, it is consistently referred to as 'body-armour' as a distinct classification.)

Surprisingly, there was quite a strong connection between medieval armour and the body armour of the First World War. Both plate and so-called 'soft' armour of the Middle Ages suggested avenues for experimentation and some of the construction techniques used by medieval armourers, such as overlapping plates, were sometimes borrowed. For the most part though First World War body armour was designed by people who had no knowledge of old armour. It was, by necessity, far heavier and more cumbersome than medieval armour and was often less well designed and less comfortable to wear. (But, to be fair, the medieval armourers were superlative craftsmen and their metalworking was an art form in its own right, irrespective of any ornamentation; and armour was bespoke.) First World War body armour was probably no more effective than its medieval antecedents. There are no objective assessments of the effectiveness of medieval armour but armoured men-at-arms died just as surely as unarmoured men. And with the advent of plate armour came weapons to defeat it. It is no accident that medieval pole arms carried large tin-opener-like blades. Even with the introduction of the arquebus and the pistol, armour did not disappear from the battlefield although less of it was worn. Armourers attempted to make pistol-proof cuirasses and back plates, not always successfully as some surviving examples from the seventeenth century attest. It became so heavy by the time of the Thirty Years War (1618–48) that it was often discarded (three-quarters armour weighed 80–100 lb). Weight was always a problem with body armour of 1914 to 1918, an inevitable consequence of trying to make it bulletproof. Body armour was easily defeated by armour-piercing bullets and even by standard ball ammunition. Armour, from whatever age, has always been limited in what it can do for the wearer.

It is significant that the British produced a greater variety of body armour during the First World War than any other combatant nation. The fact that the public was becoming more aware of the nature of medieval and later armours when war broke out was probably a

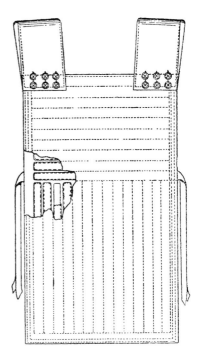

Countess Helen Mörner's body armour of strips of steel between layers of fabric. The gaps between the strips would have made this armour ineffective. Drawing from published specification GB 23,746/14.

major influencing factor. It is likely that Kitchener's call to arms played a part in encouraging the public. H.G. Wells had a letter published in *The Times* in which he called on inventors to do their bit and that certainly spurred them on to submit all manner of devices to the government. The Ministry of Munitions, after its creation in August 1915, was assiduous in its experimentation to find the most effective armour possible and had the full cooperation of the steel industry. Casualty rates were high even before the advent of trench warfare and, as the war progressed, Britain had an increasing manpower shortage and this may well have driven the Ministry's search. And yet Britain did not have a tradition of armour-making – the finest armours had always come from Spain, South Germany and North Italy.

There is no doubt that body armour was enthusiastically supported by many, including the famous and the influential. Sir Arthur Conan Doyle was very interested and went so far as to invent a form of soft armour. Haig was another. He was in constant communication with the War Office and the Army Council about trench warfare devices and body armour figured regularly in his correspondence. Winston Churchill as Minister of Munitions took a keen interest in body armour and sent memoranda to the head of the Munitions Inventions Department on the subject. Lloyd George, when Secretary of State for War, expressed the view in the House of Commons in July 1916 that body armour did not detract 'from the valour of a man'. His statement suggested that there had been voices raised expressing doubts about the value of armour, whether a man wearing it was in some way less courageous than a man not wearing it. Men did not wear armour because they were cowards. They wore it to prevent unnecessary injury and for reassurance in a hostile environment. In some ways, armour tended to embolden men and spur them on to take risks they would not otherwise have taken.

Whatever the underlying reason for the British fascination with body armour there is no doubt that civilian inventors tended to believe, even if they did not always express it explicitly, that they were producing the antidote to bullets, and spoke of 'bulletproof' and 'puncture-proof' with a beguiling faith. It is unlikely that many of them were aware of the realities of the trenches or the nature of war injuries, indeed, of what really made effective body armour, until well into the war or until they approached the Trench Warfare Department or the Munitions Inventions Department. Consequently, many of the early designs had little scientific basis. Some were downright dangerous. During the war, at least eighteen commercial models were available from department stores, where the on-leave soldier could purchase his body armour labelled with such reassuring descriptions as the 'life-saving waistcoat', the 'Wilkinson's Safety Service Jacket' and the 'Best' body shield. And British soldiers bought them in considerable numbers. Despite the fact that some models of commercial armour were decidedly poor in their ability to protect the wearer, all of them seem to have saved someone at some time. The companies that made them received enthusiastic testimonials to tell them so.

Advertisements for body armour in journals reinforced the notion of invulnerability with enthusiastic claims of impregnability. 'Wear it and survive' was the message. Reality was somewhat different, despite encouraging mentions of government tests that supposedly demonstrated the powers of the armour being advertised. 'Development of Weapons used in Trench Warfare', a lengthy Ministry of Munitions report written in 1919, stated that:

> From experience gained from experiments it would appear that it is only possible to provide efficient protection to the individual soldier from shrapnel and splinters. Up to the time of the Armistice steel had not been produced, with sufficient resisting power and lightness, to provide efficient protection against rifle and machine gun fire to the individual.

The writer might have added that practical experience at the Front corroborated this conclusion.

The Ministry of Munitions was always keen to find a steel panacea to shell fragments and small arms fire. It even had a special committee that looked at body armour and nothing else. Much money was spent on research and testing. The government also bought large quantities of commercial body armour. In the end, the British Army in France was supplied with enough body armour of various types to equip about 2 per cent of the front-line troops. Armour was never worn all the time, of course, nor was it intended for general use. For one thing, it was too heavy and too uncomfortable. It was only used under specific circumstances. Typically, bombers on raiding parties, sentries, members of patrols, soldiers on wire-cutting duties and some medical personnel wore armour, although it would be a mistake to assume that they always did. The curious thing is that men who bought their own armour were prepared to carry the extra weight around, ready for when they might need protection. It must have been an inconvenient and uncomfortable additional burden. Their toleration of it demonstrated their faith in the life-preserving powers of their armour.

In some ways, body armour was unpredictable in its ability to stop projectiles injuring the wearer. There were many factors that influenced whether someone would be killed, injured or escape scot-free. Some bullets flattened or mushroomed on impact with steel (known as setting up), which could cause a more serious injury to the wearer than if he had been unprotected. To some extent, a propensity to set up was a consequence of the type of steel used to make the armour, whether there was another energy-absorbent layer made from a non-metallic material adjacent to the steel, as well as of the construction of the armoured garment. Although a great deal of research carried out by inventions departments on different steels and different constructions of armour tended to show what might work and what definitely would not, in the end the effectiveness of body armour came down to probabilities not certainties. Whereas a rifle or machine-gun bullet might well penetrate body armour at a given distance if it struck the armour squarely, another bullet at the same range but striking at a different angle might be deflected. Projectiles came in all shapes, sizes, speeds, angles of impact and attitudes, and this made for a complex equation.

By about the middle of the war, it had been discovered that at least 60 per cent of injuries were caused by projectiles travelling at low to medium velocity. In other words, they were mostly caused by shrapnel from artillery shells and trench mortar bombs. Some reports suggested that the figure was as high as 90 per cent. It was certainly true that different statistics could be gathered from different parts of the Front. This may have been due to different ground characteristics as well as to differing belligerence of enemies. There were, for example, 'live and let live' sectors that tended to be much quieter than others. Wounds attributable to rifle and machine-gun bullets, which travelled at high velocity, accounted for around 35 per cent.

It is surprising that, given the desire to find effective armour, very little statistical information was available to ascertain which parts of the body were most vulnerable. Records were kept but the information was not organized in such a way that really helped. The figures came from casualties admitted to hospitals for treatment and hospitals did not necessarily record the right sort of information from the armour designer's point of view. However, it seemed clear that about 50 per cent of injuries were caused to the head, neck and torso, although statistics did not always back this up. The other 50 per cent were to the hands, arms, legs and feet. These figures did not include men who had died in the trenches, of course. Abdominal wounds, those to the head and those to the upper chest tended to be fatal, as did those that severed main arteries, such as the femoral arteries in the groin and upper thigh areas, so that the wounded man quickly died at the scene. Thus, when fatal injuries were taken into account, the true figures would have been rather different and it became clear that the head, upper chest, abdomen and the groin were the most vulnerable areas. That is not to say that wounds to the extremities could not be fatal, especially when caused by rifle or machine-gun bullets. Because of their high kinetic energy, high-velocity bullets can set up shock waves that are transmitted through the body's fluids if a large proportion of that energy is given up on impact; such shock waves can break bones and cause damage to internal organs.

The Trench Warfare Department prepared a number of body charts (excluding the head and extremities) with dots on to show the location of about 1,000 entry wounds. From these they concluded that the most dangerous region was the front of the chest approximately 1 sq ft around the area of the heart and the large blood vessels. Penetrating wounds here tended to be fatal, 'especially from the front where little protection is afforded by bone, equipment, &c'. And the wearing of armour made little difference to lethality. This was not used as an argument to dispense with armour, however. Although the number of injuries from bullets may have been only marginally reduced by armour, injuries from shrapnel could be significantly reduced. It was this possibility, realized quite early on in the war, that persuaded experimenters in the Trench Warfare Department, the Munitions Inventions Department and others that body armour was worthwhile.

No doubt it was commercialism that led many inventors to patent their armour. The market was large and it prevented rivals from copying their designs with impunity. During the course of the war, more than thirty patents in respect of armour intended to

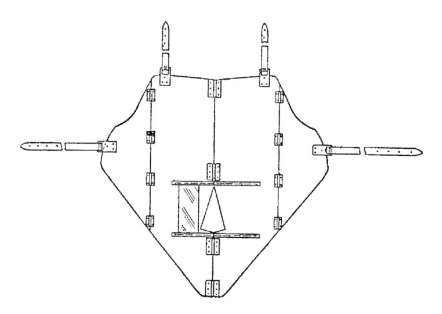

T. Roberts's body shield of hinged plates, complete with rifle aperture (the triangle) and sliding plate to close it and keep the armour rigid. He patented this in 1916 (GB 104,617) but hinged plates did not make good armour.

protect the trunk were successfully applied for in Britain and subsequently granted. Six applications were applied for in 1915, fourteen were filed in 1916, but there were only four successful applications in 1917 and in 1918. During the same period, there were ten successful applications in respect of helmets, four of them in 1916, including the Brodie steel helmet which was adopted by the British Army. All these armour inventions were tested by the Trench Warfare Department or the Munitions Inventions Department in addition to experimenting with designs of their own. Some of the inventions were the result of work carried out in cooperation with the Ministry of Munitions.

Not all the patented inventions were concerned with steel plate as armour. Nor, indeed, were all the government experiments. Six of the specifications described armour that contained little or no steel at all as the main puncture-preventing component. The advantage of so-called 'soft' armour was that it did not cause bullet splash or ricochets, nor was spalling a problem. But then, neither did it stop rifle or machine-gun bullets.

Soft or yielding armour is far older than plate armour, going back about a thousand years before the birth of Christ. In the Middle Ages, padded or quilted armour (called a jack) was worn beneath plate but it was also intended to absorb some sword blows alone, as was Chinese silk armour. Soft armour in the First World War was designed to absorb the impact of projectiles travelling at low to medium velocity. It could sometimes even stop pistol bullets. The British used two types, one designed by the Munitions Inventions Department, the other a commercial design. The commercial one was the invention of Wilfrid Hill and Joseph Percy Wilks, which they patented in 1916 (GB 104,699). Wilks was a draper from Uttoxeter, while Hill was an industrial chemist at the Chemico Works in Birmingham. Their armour was known as the Chemico Body Shield.

The Chemico Body Shield weighed about 6 lb and was a lot more comfortable to wear than steel armour, despite being 1 in thick (although it would have been unpleasantly hot in warm weather), and it was inexpensive at about £3 15s. It was in the form of a waistcoat that buttoned up the right-hand side (so that the opening faced backwards for a right-handed man, an idea that may have come from the fencing jacket, which the waistcoat resembles) with an optional 'apron' covering the groin, attached to the waistcoat by buttons. It had quite a complex construction, described in two patent specifications. According to the first complete specification filed at the patent office on 28 July 1916, the

> invention comprises a bullet-proof or like garment . . . involving a base or cover of flexible material to which layers or flaps of flexible material are attached at their one edges so that the said layers overlap one another without being adhered together, and in which the arrangement is such that not less than a plurality of thicknesses of the flap element occur all over the surface which it is desired should be puncture-proof.

The flaps were made of pieces of rectangular, tough, close-weave fabric and were arranged like overlapping fish scales, about twelve double thicknesses being ideal at any point; each piece was folded and almost covered the piece immediately beneath it. This

*George Lynch demonstrating
gloves made from his
patented (GB 6,900/15)
barbed-wire-proof fabric.*
(The Illustrated War News)

formed a base substrate. This layering was designed to absorb impact energy by giving or yielding. (It is worth noting that scale armour is ancient, the scales often being made of leather or metal but this, of course, had been a defence against swords not bullets.)

A second layer of these scales, impregnated with an undisclosed resin, was combined with the base substrate. In addition, some or all of the scales or layers had a zigzag mesh of wires secured to them, the zigzags of one layer going in a direction 90° to those in the layers immediately above and below. The zigzagging ensured that the wires were not in tension and could act elastically under impact. The wires consisted of a core of 'fine steel springy wire', which was loosely, spirally wound with a narrower gauge wire. Other arrangements besides zigzags could also be used.

About seven months later, in February 1917, the two inventors filed another patent application for an improvement to their armour (GB 110,093 was an 'addition' to the earlier one and was accepted in October 1917). This added 'a layer or layers of covering or protecting material applied to the outer or free edges of the flaps or layers'. It was not until this specification was published that the complete structure of the Chemico Body Shield took shape – their earlier patent made no provision for an outer cover. This took the form of two or more layers of calico between which was packed waste pieces of calico, silk, cotton wool or similar materials, and the layers were quilted together in the manner of a medieval jack.

The Chemico Body Shield was not used in large numbers. No doubt it suffered from the same problem as other soft armours of the period: they deteriorated in the wet and muddy conditions of the trenches. It was not the only armour invention to make use of resins. There were other patents, including George Lynch's filed in 1915 (GB 6,900/15) and H. Siswick's filed in 1916 (GB 109,343), which described the use of hardening resins. Lynch was a well-known war correspondent who had covered the South African War for the *Illustrated London News*. He was evidently inspired to invent by what he saw in France and filed no fewer than five different applications, which were eventually combined in the one patent. It was a 'puncture-proof material . . . composed of wool or cotton wool impregnated with . . . resin and enclosed in a waterproof or other fabric covering for making uniforms'. It was evidently available 'as leggings, knee-pads, waistcoats, overcoats, airmen's jackets and helmets, sheets, and sleeping-bags', was 'waterproof and warm' and moreover 'the British and Russian War Offices are using large quantities of it'. It was known as the SOS fabric.

Siswick's, on the other hand, was similar to the Chemico Body Shield but without the fish-scale layers. The Coir Tyre Company got in on the act in 1917 and claimed to have invented a form of non-metallic armour. This was in fact a variation on the structure of a pneumatic tyre (GB 115,912), and was nearly rejected by the Patent Office as a consequence, but it took the form of sheets rather than tyre-shaped mouldings. Although the complete specification suggested the possibility of using a backing of metal or even wood, their invention was perhaps the earliest form of plastics armour, although whether it was ballistically useful is another matter. Moreover, rubber was not readily available for things like armour.

In September 1915, E. Sherring filed a patent application. The specification (GB 12,957/15) described a composite structure of 'layers of materials in close contact and bound together', the edges of which 'faced towards the direction in which the shock is received'. Again, the idea was for the edges to absorb the impact by yielding. The layers consisted of metal plates alternated with asbestos, cork, natural rubber, gutta-percha (coagulated latex, harder and more crystalline than natural rubber) or leather. Even bristles could be bound in between the metal plates. The range of materials that could be used in any armour invention was perhaps not as wide as some specifications suggested. It was the patent agent's duty to try for the widest possible legal protection for an invention. Consequently, many materials were included in a specification when in reality only one or two of them were actually used by the inventor. But the widest cover prevented a rival from circumventing a patent simply by using different materials.

However, that is not to suggest that many, if not all, of the materials had something useful to add to a layer-type armour; to some extent it is the layering rather than the composition of the layers that makes the armour effective. And there is no doubt that some unlikely materials were seriously looked at for body armour. A case in point is asbestos, an improbable material since it is not elastic and will not give under impact but is also too weak to prevent penetration. There are several patent specifications that list asbestos as a layer material, although in some cases it was intended to be used as a fibrous reinforcement in gutta-percha or a similar material.

One invention that did intend asbestos to be used as something more than a reinforcement (although there appears to have been no patent for it), was the brainchild of Sir Arthur Conan Doyle. In 1916, he approached Herbert Frood, the founder of Ferodo, which made asbestos-based articles, including brake linings, in the hope that he would develop the idea into something workable. Herbert Frood was an energetic entrepreneur and always keen to take up and pursue ideas. He took up Conan Doyle's and enthusiastically worked on asbestos compositions from which he developed an asbestos fabric. On 9 August 1916, Frood noted in his minute book that 'F.F. die pressed from ¼ to ³⁄₁₆' and 'Boiled in Blk [black] Wax with 20% Carnuba [sic]' was sent to Conan Doyle. Frood is supposed to have tested the materials with a shotgun. Although his asbestos material may well have passed his shotgun test this was no guarantee that it would stop shrapnel or rifle and machine-gun bullets. Nevertheless, Frood informed Conan Doyle of his success and the invention was duly submitted to the War Office. It was most likely tested by the Munitions Inventions Department. Whatever Frood's and Conan Doyle's expectations, the material clearly failed to impress and it was not taken up.

The Munitions Inventions Department believed early on that soft armour had something to offer. The danger with steel armour was that it might splinter causing fragments to be driven into the wearer's body. Worse, there was always the chance that a bullet might mushroom on impact and still penetrate to cause a massive wound. And when the armour was made up of small plates, it could become deadly. Ernst Jünger described an incident during the German retreat to the Hindenburg Line in March 1917. A British attack was repulsed and an 'officer, though he wore a steel shirt under his uniform, was accounted for by a bullet point-blank from Rheinhardt's revolver that drove a whole steel plate into his body'. Soft armour suffered none of these disadvantages; bullets passed through it without being deformed. Although an inability to stop bullets might seem like a perverse advantage for armour to possess, it was nevertheless of great importance since a propensity to set up bullets on impact ensured that wounds would be worse than they would have been without the armour.

All sorts of fibrous materials were tested by the Munitions Inventions Department, including hair, silk, flax and cotton, as fabrics or as padding, quilted together into various forms of armour. Even sisal and hemp were tried. Both these fibres are used in rope-making (at least, they were until nylon and polypropylene came along). Unlikely as it may seem, the experimenters had good reason for trying rope; some fifteenth-century helmet liners had been made from coiled rope. Tests were carried out in a 'fragmentation hut' at the Wembley Experimental Ground, in which grenades were exploded. As well as these materials, balata was also used in some experiments. Balata is a coagulated latex similar to gutta-percha but from a different tree. In the end, silk emerged as the best material.

In fact, silk turned out to have astonishing ballistic properties. An experiment using pads of silk and the steel plate that was to be used for shrapnel helmets, obtained from Firth of Sheffield, showed that the silk was more effective at stopping shrapnel than the

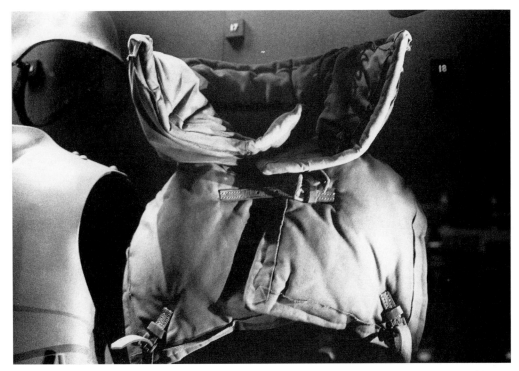

Silk neck armour devised by the Munitions Inventions Department and on display in the Imperial War Museum. (Author)

steel. Weight for weight, silk was much more effective then manganese steel when it came to stopping projectiles travelling at low to medium velocity. In *Helmets and Body Armor in Modern Warfare*, William A. Taylor, the armour specialist in the Munitions Inventions Department, is quoted as noting that 'silk weighing 10.8 oz. per sq. ft. is proof against shrapnel at 800 foot seconds [800 ft/s], whereas steel to give the same resistance would weigh about 20 oz'. Although silk was superior to manganese steel when it came to relatively slow-moving projectiles, it had the disadvantage of being prone to deterioration after prolonged exposure to water. Moreover, being a natural fibre, it was particularly appealing to the many rats which lived in the trenches.

In 1915, as a consequence of their experiments, the Munitions Inventions Department came up with a form of soft armour to protect principally the neck but which also covered the upper chest and upper back. It was nearly 2 in thick, weighed 3.25 lb and had a high collar that reached beyond the ears so that it looked like some outlandish fashion statement. This neck shield was fastened in place by straps. It had the same stopping power as the steel helmet. The shield consisted of about two dozen layers of Japanese silk and was padded with waste materials like the Chemico Body Shield. It was covered with canvas and muslin or drill. To ensure that it kept its shape the shield was stiffened with wire. Tests showed that it was very effective at stopping shrapnel and even 230-grain pistol bullets travelling at 600 ft/s. So much faith was put in this neck armour that each division was issued with 400 of them; bombers used them to protect themselves not only from enemy grenades but also from their own, especially the Mills, which produced large and lethal fragments that could travel much further than any man could throw one. It turned out to be not quite so useful as anticipated, however. The materials rapidly deteriorated in the trenches so that the armour lost its shrapnel-stopping abilities. Moreover, it cost more than £6 and the silk was hard to come by.

Despite the potential benefits of soft armour, it was not really suited to the conditions under which it would be used and consequently was never likely to have supplanted steel armour. Steel body armour came in a wide range of constructions, from single plates to strips or small plates attached to a flexible backing, from large overlapping horizontal bands to combinations of plates of various sizes and shapes complete with overlapping apron plates. The one-piece steel breastplate was the simplest but not necessarily the most effective form of armour. It had to be shaped to the body, if only partially, which was not as simple as it sounds. To ensure that the resulting curvature did not weaken the steel, the skills of a medieval armourer were required if the metal was to be cold-worked. And such skills had long since vanished. Consequently, such body armour tended to be crude, sometimes being made of rolled steel, which was not ideally suited to provide protection. For steel to be useful as armour it had to have the right composition and the surface had to be heat treated to harden it.

Steel is iron with carbon in it. It can be alloyed with other metals such as chromium (which makes stainless steel), nickel or manganese, for example. To be useful as armour, it has to be very hard but not brittle. Hardness is relatively easy to control but ductility is much more difficult. This is directly related to which metal is alloyed with the steel and in what proportion. Medieval armour was made in a labour-intensive process of heating and hammering out a metal ingot, folding it over and repeating the process countless times before shaping and tempering it. This produced a structure of alternating hard and soft layers. Although William Taylor did not believe that laminated steel of this sort was any better at stopping bullets than a solid plate, the problem of hardening the outer surface without making the steel brittle remained. And the problem with a solid steel plate was that it was heavy because the metal was necessarily thick to stop projectiles.

So the search was started for a strong but ductile steel that could be used in thinner sheets as body armour. The British already had Sir Robert Hadfield's manganese steel, which was hard and tough. Hadfield had patented the manufacturing process in 1883. Working with the Munitions Inventions Department, he developed a manganese steel that contained 10–17 per cent manganese, but preferably around 13 per cent, and 0.9–1.4 per cent carbon – the manufacturing process of the steel and the armour plate is described in GB 124,817, GB 125,157 and GB 133,131. Hadfield was the chairman of Hadfields Ltd, a major steel company founded by his father in 1872, and was well known for his many mettalurgical inventions. He was knighted in 1908 and made a baronet in 1917. Unlike other steels used for body armour, Hadfield's manganese steel required no annealing after it had been shaped and thin sheets could be stamped into the required shape by a hydraulic press, thus enabling rapid production. This was because of what happened to the steel when it was quenched in cold water during its manufacture; other steels tended to become brittle when quenched, which made them unsuitable for stamping, whereas the colder the quenching water, the greater the ballistic strength of manganese steel. It was this remarkable property that made it an ideal material for body armour and especially the shrapnel helmet.

The Munitions Inventions Department conducted exhaustive tests with German ammunition, including reversed ammunition, firing at steel plates at various ranges. The department looked at the effect of bullet yaw, which causes keyhole-shaped penetrations (called keyholing) and promotes tumbling when a bullet enters a material denser than air, and bullets fired at several plates placed one behind the other, with and without spacing between them. Placing two plates back to back with no space meant that they behaved like a single plate and if a bullet penetrated the first it also penetrated the second. The department also looked at the possible benefits of springs to cushion impacts; this showed that no spring had time to react because of the speed of the bullet. Many of these tests were supervised by William Taylor at the School of Musketry in Hythe.

In 1919, Taylor summarized the results of the tests with manganese steel, which were still incomplete. He explained that 'a large number of rounds of ordinary German "S" ammunition and German "K" armour-piercing ammunition' were fired from various ranges up to 1,200 yd at steel plates 18 in square (or at least, charges were reduced to give the equivalent energy of a bullet striking from the longer ranges to allow rounds to be fired from much closer because it was extremely difficult to hit such a small target at extreme range). Shrapnel bullets 'loaded to give various striking velocities' were also fired at the plates. All the bullets were recovered and examined to see what damage was done to them on impact, and register cards were placed behind the plates to indicate the kind of wound that would result when a bullet penetrated a plate. The tests were carried out at Claremont 'where there are facilities to obtain velocities of the bullets by chronograph'.

Gauge	16	12	10	6
Thickness (in)	0.064	0.104	0.128	0.192
Weight per square foot (lb)	2.60	4.24	5.22	7.84

German 'S' bullet
  no penetration velocity (ft sec)
  penetration velocity (ft sec)
	1,246 (cracked)
	1,322
		1,545 (cracked)
		1,545 (just through)
			1,673
			1,870
				2,126
				2,217

German 'K' bullet
  no penetration velocity (ft sec)
  penetration velocity (ft sec)
	675 (estd)
	700 (estd)
		875 (estd)
		900 (estd)
			915
			1,026
				1,254
				1,276

Shrapnel bullets (41 to lb) proof at velocity (ft sec) (estd)	1,350	1,900	2,200	2,900
Approximate range proof against 'S' bullet (yd)	800	650	500	300

Normal impact of German ammunition on 18 in manganese steel plates (from 'Development of Weapons for Trench Warfare', 1919)

The results demonstrated that when a high concentration of manganese was combined with a low carbon content, as outlined above, a thin plate of only 0.036 in (just less than 1 mm), the thickness of the steel helmet, always deformed under impact; when the velocity of the projectile was above 850 ft/s it was almost certain to penetrate after causing an indentation about 1 in deep. However, a propensity to deform so deeply was hardly an advantage for body armour since the wearer would still be injured by an impact, even if nothing penetrated. This tended to make thin plates of manganese steel unsuitable for body armour, other than for helmets of the Brodie design.

It had been intended to conduct similar tests with the plates set at various angles to the vertical to ascertain the effect of different angles of impact of pointed 'S' rounds. However, problems over the supply of suitable plates meant that only some of the proposed tests were completed before the end of the war. In September 1918, Admiral Bacon, then head of the Munitions Inventions Department, reported that although shrapnel was relatively easy to deflect it was more difficult to deflect 'S' ammunition. He concluded that it would not be feasible to make a plate hard enough and thick enough to deflect 'S' bullets, since the thicker and harder manganese steel became, the greater the chance of it shattering on impact. On the other hand, although thinner plates did not shatter, they deformed under impact and thus failed to deflect the bullet.

A plate of 18-gauge manganese steel was arranged at an angle of 60° to the normal, i.e. 30° to the line of fire. It was pierced at all ranges up to 1,000 yards by 'S' ammunition. The same plate could probably be proof against normal fire at 1100 yards; so that the difference between normal and 60° fire was only equivalent to 100 yards in velocity – a truly interesting fact.

(Admiral Sir Reginald Bacon had a distinguished career before becoming head of the Munitions Inventions Department in January 1918. He had been Captain of HMS *Dreadnought* on its commissioning voyage, Director of Naval Ordnance and Torpedoes 1907–09, retiring to become managing director of the Coventry Ordnance Works 1910–15. He commanded the Dover Patrol from 1915 until the end of 1917 when he was sacked, somewhat unfairly, because of his failure to stop U-boat movements in the Channel.)

Steel armour made of a single plate was not comfortable to wear, especially as it was not tailored to the individual. There was also the problem of keeping it on. This was usually solved by using shoulder straps, sometimes adjustable, so that the weight was borne on the shoulders, and with side straps that met round the back of the wearer to keep the plate against the body and prevent it bouncing up and down with movement. Such a breastplate was described in GB 3,663/15, applied for in March 1915. A similar breastplate was described in GB 11,012/15. Invented by F.C. Hunt, it had 'spring bands' at the sides that went round the body of the wearer. A more uncomfortable method of keeping it on is hard to imagine. That the top edge of the breastplate was 'turned outwards . . . to deflect an upwardly glancing blow' indicated that inventors were finally beginning to realize that there was more to armour than simply placing a thick piece of steel plate in front of the body. Hunt went on to develop his body armour to include an additional set of four plates, joined along their edges by 'resilient strips' and attached by two leather straps to the inside face of the main shield, so that the chest and abdomen had additional protection (GB 105,785, filed in November 1916). However, if Hunt believed that by simply placing additional plates over the chest area would provide additional protection, he was labouring under a misapprehension.

There were some relatively successful armours of the single-plate type, however. One was an abdominal shield designed by Gen Adrian (who also designed the French Army's steel helmet). This was used by the French in limited numbers in 1917; about 100,000 were made. It weighed only 2 lb and was shaped to fit the abdomen, its lower edge having a deep downward curve, while the top edge had a gentler upward curve. It had a blue-grey cloth cover that matched the French Army uniform. The shield was fitted with a woven belt and a pair of

Verdun, 1916. General Adrian's body armour modelled by a French grenadier. He wears a breastplate, an abdominal guard and three apron plates that cover his groin and upper thighs. He is brandishing a rectangular shield and wears an Adrian steel helmet. (The Illustrated War News)

hooks that fixed on to the service belt. Although it was reasonably successful in preventing injury it was not popular. Adrian later added a one-piece groin shield and two one-piece thigh shields, all of which could be joined to the abdominal shield, but these were liked even less and usually cast aside because the whole ensemble made movement too difficult. Not discouraged, Adrian then designed a breastplate to be attached to the abdominal shield. When combined with a small throat guard (a gorget), the whole lot weighed 5.5 lb, which evidently proved to be too much of a burden for the soldiers to countenance, although it was remarkably effective at stopping shrapnel from grenades. About 3,000 breastplate-gorget shields were made but it is not clear how many of these found their way to the Front.

More successful than Adrian's shields, although used in smaller numbers, was an invention by a French engineer, Amand Daigre, which he patented in Britain in 1917, GB 116,362. (Remarkably, the application was accepted on the same day it was filed at the Patent Office, 17 June.) This was not simply a steel breastplate like those described above but a form of composite armour that used steel as a component. Even this idea was not new, since patents dating from 1896 and 1907 described similar but less sophisticated

Verdun, 1916. This French sentry wears Amand Daigre's body shield. Later shields were shorter and had a squarer lower edge. He also appears to be wearing a Favre face shield and steel goggles as well as the Adrian helmet. (The Illustrated War News)

armour. It was considerably heavier than Adrian's armour, weighing 21 lb, but it was designed to be a multi-purpose shield that could be both portable – there were arm straps provided – or fixed, as well as body armour. To wear it as body armour, strong adjustable straps with hooks and a substantial belt hook were needed; these engaged rings on the back of the shield. That soldiers were prepared to use this as body armour when they objected to Adrian's is something of a mystery. The possible explanation is that it was very effective and could be relied upon. Most of its weight was due to a chromium steel plate 0.275 in thick, 23 in tall and 14 in wide, which was roughly rectangular in shape with a curved lower edge and a large rectangular cut-out in the top right-hand corner to enable the rifle to be brought to the shoulder without the armour getting in the way.

An aluminium U-section frame went round the edges of the steel plate. It was wider than the thickness of the plate, and both frame and plate were sandwiched between two layers of a resilient material (woodite). A denser woodite filled the gap between the frame and the plate. The frame had projecting lips and these, combined with the infill material, were designed 'to stop any splinters [lead splash] from a projectile which after the shock [impact] are driven parallel to the plate and still possess considerable residual kinetic energy'. The whole thing was encased in a tough, close-weave blue cloth that prevented wear and tear to the layers of woodite. This armour was capable of stopping German ball ammunition at very close range, even when the round was reversed. However, like all body armour, it was not proof against armour-piercing ammunition except at long ranges. Approximately 65,000 Daigre shields were manufactured, being produced at the rate of 2,000 a day. Each one cost about £5 10s.

Daigre conducted numerous tests on the shield, as did the French equivalent of the Munitions Inventions Department. Analysing the results, he formulated a theory about how his body armour worked. A fundamental aspect of the armour was its particular use of two layers of resilient material to sandwich the steel:

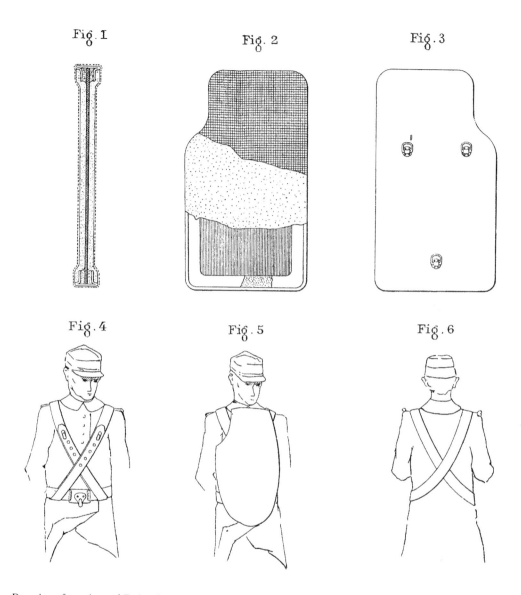

Drawings from Amand Daigre's patent, GB 116,362, showing its construction and the method of wearing the body shield. Figs 2 and 3 show an infantry shield, while Fig. 5 shows the body shield, although Daigre intended the infantry shield to double as the body shield. Both forms existed.

The elastic or plastic material is chosen . . . to offer with a small volume a comparatively high degree of resiliency and resistance, and so that it may be cast under pressure or compressed in order to obtain a compact mass capable of presenting to projectiles striking it a high elastic resistance and of neutralizing, by absorption, the greatest part of their kinetic energy, thus deadening the blow.

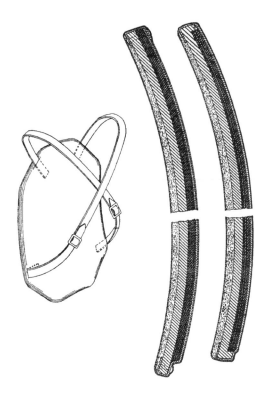

The Correli body shield as shown in GB 108,801. Like Daigre's armour, this included energy-absorbent layers. The steel layer is sandwiched between them.

Although woodite was used as the resilient material any one of a number of alternatives could have been used, including natural rubber and synthetic rubber. Neither of these were really viable simply because they were in short supply and needed for other essential war uses. It is difficult to be certain what woodite was but perhaps Daigre's specification gives a description. It appears to have been a mixture of 'glues or gelatines and glycerine', which was reinforced with fibrous materials, animal, vegetable or mineral. When making the shield the woodite was moulded or cast on to the steel plate and to the fabric covering so that the cover was impregnated with the material.

According to Daigre's conclusions, the resilient material played a major role in stopping projectiles. He thought that, on impact, a high proportion of the kinetic energy of a bullet was absorbed by the outer resilient layer, the energy being converted to heat. The heat generated was enough to soften the bullet, which aided its deformation and disintegration, and further impeded its progress until it hit the steel plate. Because of the bullet's rapid deceleration, this plate resisted penetration and stopped the bullet. Impact with the steel plate set up vibrations, aiding the disintegration of the bullet, the vibrations being absorbed by the inner resilient layer so the wearer felt very little. Should the bullet fragments penetrate the steel plate, however, the inner resilient layer stopped them. This is more or less how composite armour works, although modern composite armour is constructed from different materials, including ceramics and man-made fibres of very high tensile strength such as Kevlar.

A similar approach was adopted by Arthur Corelli, managing director of Cammell, Laird & Co. of Sheffield, the steel manufacturing and engineering firm. Patented in 1917 (GB 108,801), it consisted of an 'anti-splash or anti-rebound composition . . . interposed and compressed between two plates', which were 'curved to conform to the shape of the front of the body'. The outer thin plate, which was preferably buffalo hide, was intended to be penetrated by a projectile and was placed over a resilient layer. By bending back the edges of the outer plate to engage the rear of the main plate, the resilient material was compressed in place and the outer plate secured in position. The sandwich material proposed consisted of 'alternate layers of tough linen, felt and canvas' each layer being impregnated with 'liquefied Swedish or vegetable pitch'. Interestingly, the specification suggested that an alternative to this was compressed asbestos, raising the possibility that Herbert Frood may have contacted Cammell Laird with his bulletproof asbestos fabric. And there is another patent (GB 108,244) in which asbestos figures as a major component. Here it is apparently used as a fire-retardant layer that might, in combination with the steel, make the body armour more bulletproof. Another alternative was woodite but impregnated fabric layers were evidently cheaper. Before covering the armour with a waterproof fabric, medicated wool could be used as padding on the inner face to make it more comfortable to wear. This was not the only patent to suggest medicated wool as a padding; it was proposed, in all seriousness, that the cover could be ripped open to get at the wool so that it could be applied to a wound in the event of the armour failing to stop projectiles and an injury being sustained.

The Corelli body shield was 11 in × 16 in and weighed 17 lb, so it was no lightweight. Although it was designed to cover the vital organs it was simply too heavy to be seriously considered for widespread front-line use as far as the British were concerned. Nevertheless, its ballistic characteristics were quite impressive. It was capable of stopping standard German ball ammunition at 10 yd and it could withstand six impacts by such ammunition within a 6 in circle. The main steel plate was evidently a special alloy but there are no details of its composition.

There were other heavy body shields. All were considered but all were turned down, including the Roneo-Miris body shield that was 22 lb of 0.3 in chromium-nickel steel plate, proposed in March 1916. Then there was one designed by Cols Treeky and Close. This weighed a mere 18 lb. The Munitions Inventions Department turned this down too. There was no virtue in so protecting a man that he became immobile, like some kind of human pillbox.

CHAPTER 3

Life Savers and Portobanks – More Body Shields

One of the enduring images of the Western Front is the helmeted German soldier clad in body armour. This figure represents the brutalization of the war and it is significant that he is German and not British. Because of this image, body armour has become associated with the dastardly German infantryman and is far more familiar than British body armour which, although more widely used, is hardly mentioned by anyone. It is as though only cowards (not to mention losers) wore body armour but brave and honourable men (and victors) did not. This image is disingenuous propaganda that has come about since the end of the war and had no currency at the time.

German body armour did not appear on the Western Front until mid-1917, although the German helmet had appeared in 1916. In June and July 1917, a number of examples of the armour were captured as were several documents relating to its use. These documents described the *Infanterie Panzer* (infantry armour) as proof against small arms ammunition at 550 yd but was mainly intended as protection against 'shrapnel bullets, splinters of shell, which strike with great force'. The armour was to be 'worn according to requirements, either on the back or on the chest. The position which a man has to assume when on the defensive in trench warfare will often make it necessary for him to wear the armour on his back.' This no doubt referred to sheltering during bombardments when access to a dugout was not possible. The armour came in two sizes and was to be regarded as trench equipment to be handed over to a relieving unit. The

German body armour, 1918. The top abdominal plate should be lying flat. He is probably carrying something underneath that prevents it falling correctly, consequently reducing the effectiveness of the armour. The distinctively shaped German helmet can be clearly seen. (The Illustrated War News)

armour was not supposed to be used by attacking infantry, simply because it was too heavy, but was intended for the protection of sentries, machine-gun teams, 'garrisons of shell holes' and soldiers manning listening posts.

Examination of captured armour showed that it was ⅟₁₁ in thick, weighed 22 lb 10 oz and was painted grey. The armour comprised three components, a breastplate, shoulder pieces and three belly plates. The breastplate was curved to fit the shape of the body with an outward turn at the top to protect the throat. The shoulder pieces were also curved, measured 4.5 in × 9 in and were riveted to the breastplate. These not only protected the shoulders but were how the armour was suspended on the wearer. Protection of the shoulders was rather more important than at first realized and both the French and Italians experimented with shoulder armour. French epaulette armour designed by Gen Adrian was remarkably successful and hundreds of thousands of sets were issued. It consisted of steel plates weighing only a few ounces that were slid between the layers of the tunic. They were hardly noticed by the wearer but afforded excellent protection against aerial shrapnel bursts from which the balls could enter the body through the shoulders and penetrate vital organs. These plates were made from the offcuts left over during the manufacture of the Adrian steel helmet. The Italians used large, curved shoulder defences that looked like medieval pauldrons, only much cruder. They were joined at the back by a strap and worn with a small one-piece breastplate to which they were attached at the front.

The three overlapping belly plates of the German armour were attached to each other and the breastplate by two webbing straps. The uppermost plate was 17.25 in wide and 6 in deep, a curved rectangle. The middle one was slightly smaller at 13.75 in and slightly less curved, while the lowest one was almost flat, approximately D-shaped with the curve pointing downwards, 7.125 in deep and 10 in wide across the top edge. The overlap was 1 in. To prevent the plates from rattling, pads of felt were attached to the webbing straps.

This turned out to be the small size; the larger armour weighed about 24 lb. Later captured examples showed that the thickness of the plates varied from 0.140 in to 0.131 in according to the size of the armour, with the thicker plates on the smaller armour. These were all thicker than the first captured examples. Unlike the British, the Germans used silicon steel that contained some nickel. It was very hard and tough but they had problems finding enough nickel for all its other uses (it was also used in vehicle springs and gears, for example) so the nickel content in the armour was lower than it might have been.

Although the Germans issued large numbers of this type of armour (for example, one battalion of the 95th Infantry Regiment was issued two per company in June 1917), it was no more popular than British or French heavy armour. Later captured documents listed criticisms. It made shouldering the rifle to aim and fire difficult and bombers found it tricky to throw their grenades. Carrying ammunition while wearing the armour was next to impossible. When the wearer was forced to crawl, the sides of the breastplate dug into the armpit region, which was painful. German Headquarters recommended that it was removed when under attack because it restricted movement too much and made the wearer more vulnerable. Interestingly, Ludendorff recommended that troops about to go into the line should be made familiar with the armour beforehand so that they knew its strengths and weaknesses.

Because of these shortcomings, a number of modifications to the armour were recommended. These included reshaping the breastplate to prevent it digging in and changing the way the shoulder pieces were attached to allow some adjustment. This would then accommodate different shapes and sizes of individuals and make the armour more comfortable. In addition, padding of the shoulder pieces was also recommended. Having to wear the armour for any length of time proved tiring and hard on the shoulders and it tended to slip off if the wearer had to jump about or crawl. Straps on the ends of the shoulder pieces that could be attached to rings on the breastplate were suggested. It was also recommended that hooks should be added to the outside of the breastplate so equipment could be hung on them. To allow the armoured soldier to bring his rifle to bear, aim and shoot without the butt slipping from the breastplate, it was suggested that a short vertical bar be added to the outside of the armour on the top right. Armour captured by the British in May 1918 showed that some of these modifications may have been implemented.

However, the captured armour seemed to only consist of the breastplate, which was longer in the body than the earlier armour. This suggests that the overlapping apron plates and the shoulder pieces had been discarded. Moreover, the plate had various layers of fabric, front and back, which the earlier armour had not. The outer surface had two layers of felt covered by eight layers of strong canvas, while the inner surface had four layers of canvas. The canvas layers were 'sewn together round the edges of the plate, and further secured to the plate by three pieces of thick steel wire passing through all the thicknesses of canvas and felt'. These additional, non-metallic layers may have been used for the same reason that the Daigre and Corelli armours had resilient layers – to absorb the energy of impact and to prevent splash and spalling. There was a rectangular recess in the top right-hand corner, similar to the one on the Daigre shield, to allow the rifle to be brought to the shoulder. There were four canvas loops on the inside of the plate which appear to have been arm straps. It is not clear whether this breastplate was a variation on the armour of 1917 or something different. It was evidently even heavier than a complete set of the earlier armour as it weighed 24 lb 4.5 oz. The steel was also twice as thick at 0.281 in.

Tests showed that the armour was made of high-quality steel alloyed with various undisclosed additional metals. Its resistance to armour-piercing ammunition was good. It was proof against standard ball ammunition at 250 yd; out of three hits on the armour, none penetrated. But at 200 yd, two out of three rounds penetrated. The brief summary of the tests concluded that the steel 'does not appear to be better as a bullet-resisting material than other German plates of softer steel and less complex composition. The softer shields would probably be less liable to break up after repeated hits.' Breaking up was a potentially serious problem with all body armours.

The only other form of armour that the German army was known to use was a small but heavy face shield for snipers. This covered the whole face and was tied to the head with leather straps. It was 0.227 in thick and weighed 13.25 lb, although there were reports of similar shields weighing as much as 17 lb. Although it was provided with a forehead pad, the very idea of having such a heavy weight tied to the head seems more like a form of torture than effective defensive armour. It was approximately rectangular with a reflex curvature so that the central part was bowed to accommodate the face while

German sniper's face shield demonstrated at the School of Musketry, September 1917. (IWM)

the outer edges turned outwards. This outward turn was continued at the base of the shield while the top of it was bowed inwards to follow the curve of the upper part of the head. A recess was cut into the lower right-hand side so that the rifle could be brought to bear and there were tiny eye slits 0.7 in long and 0.3 in wide. It was evidently proof against standard ball ammunition at very close range but was pierced by armour-piercing rounds at 200 yd. The shield was not issued in very large numbers. Because it appeared that the shield would stop anything, one of Hesketh-Pritchard's officers offered 'to put one on and let someone have a shot at him. This I [Hesketh-Pritchard], of course, refused to countenance for a moment, and lucky it was, for the first shot went clean through.' Even when the bullet did not penetrate, it seems likely that anyone wearing one would have suffered concussion from an impact.

Like most of the armies of the First World War, the Italian Army was keen to find a form of body armour that would provide adequate protection against small arms fire as well as shrapnel. There is photographic evidence that the Italians made use of the fixed trench shield as a portable defence when attacking. Before the advent of steel defences, Italian soldiers evidently improvised shields from filled sandbags which they wore across their chests when attacking, and there is some evidence to suggest that the Germans did likewise from time to time. Even before the Italians entered the war in May 1915, it is evident that they had been taking note of the armour in use on the Western Front. It is also clear that there was some degree of cooperation between the Munitions Inventions Department and the equivalent body in Italy (as, indeed, there were exchanges of ideas between the British and the French). Examples of many different Italian body armours were tested by the Munitions Inventions Department. Some were ordered for use by the British Army on the Western Front.

Left: *an Italian soldier equipped for wire-cutting duty in late 1915, wearing a breastplate, shoulder defences, a three-piece abdomen and thigh defence, gauntlets and the Adrian helmet. The wire-cutter on the end of a pole was invented by P. Malfatti and patented in Britain in June 1916 (GB 106,334).* Right: *a close-up of the breastplate and shoulder defences worn with a special helmet of thicker steel by a captain in command of a company of engineers.* (The Illustrated War News)

Ansaldo et Cie of Genoa manufactured body armour that could also be used as a portable shield. And, like the German *Infanterie Panzer*, it could be worn on the back. It came in four sizes that ranged in weight from 16 lb to 22 lb. This was a single-piece breastplate with integral shoulder pieces, curved to fit the torso (most of which it covered). To keep it on, the shoulder pieces had leather straps that diagonally crossed the back and were buckled to shorter straps on the sides of the plate near the lower edge. For use as a shield, it had two rotating legs, pivoted on the ends of the shoulder pieces, which were used to keep it upright and seemed to have been clipped to the front of the plate when not required. There was a loophole on the right-hand side, closed by a sliding plate on the 1917 model while the 1918 model had a rotating closure plate. This was probably introduced because the rivets of the guides for the sliding plate may have popped out when hit. The armour was made of 0.25 in thick chromium-nickel-vanadium steel and was proof against standard ball ammunition of 2,500 ft/s at 100 yd. Curiously, there appears to have been no padding or resilient material on the inner face to prevent spalling. Photographs of Italian soldiers modelling the body armour show them looking far from comfortable in it. In particular, the lower edge looks as though it cut into the top of the thighs if the wearer knelt or did anything other than remain upright in it.

In October 1916, R. Fariselli of Astori in Milan filed a patent application in Britain (GB 105,513) for an armoured waistcoat that had three pockets on the front into each of which a steel plate could be slipped. This method of carrying the plates apparently made the waistcoat more comfortable than other forms of steel armour. The two top pockets were on either side of the chest, extending into the third pocket that covered the whole of the abdomen. This was divided up the centre and closed with buttons. Different thicknesses of plate could be used according to circumstance because the plates were not fixed to anything, but it is doubtful whether this would have been a feasible proposition in the field as it would have necessitated keeping numerous plates of varying thicknesses near the front line.

The Fariselli armoured waistcoat. Note the pockets for the steel plates. The lower pocket, buttoned up the front, is the width of the garment. Drawing from GB 105,513.

A sample of this armour, which used 0.3 in thick chromium-nickel steel and weighed 17 lb, was tested by the Munitions Inventions Department. It was proof against Austrian Mannlicher service ball ammunition at 20 yd but was penetrated by Mauser ball ammunition at 200 yd. The Munitions Inventions Department were sufficiently impressed with it to suggest that it might be serviceable in France and 200 were ordered for trials. It is unclear whether it performed any better than other forms of armour already in use. There was another similar body armour developed by Frati of Milan. According to French tests, this was very effective indeed although it was only about ⅕ in thick. But it was not much lighter as it weighed 15.5 lb. Another Italian armour, went further in its use of multiple steel plates. This was the Gorgeno-Collaye armour, which first appeared in 1916. It consisted of a waistcoat of tough material to which were attached numerous rectangular steel plates in three columns. Each plate overlapped the one below and its neighbouring plates in the adjacent columns and was separately covered in the same material as the base garment.

The use of several plates rather than relying on a single breastplate became a more popular approach to body armour as the war progressed. This was less to do with increasing the wearer's ability to move easily in it and more to do with increasing the degree of protection. It also had the added advantage of being easier to shape the smaller plates. The increased mobility that came with the use of multiple plates was a fortuitous bonus, although the weight of such a coat of plates was generally just as great as the one-piece armour – but some were considerably lighter. With multiple plates it became necessary to make them overlap to ensure that there were no gaps between which a shell fragment or a bullet could penetrate. This type of armour was nothing new. It was one of the most common forms of armour used between the fourteenth and seventeenth centuries

Franco-British armour with separate upper chest and neck defence. Made up of small squares of steel joined together with rings, it was not as effective as overlapping plates. He is also wearing Xylonite Goggles (see pp. 66–7) and a steel skullcap. (IWM)

The Lanciers body armour with overlapping pockets of steel plates. (IWM)

when it was known as a coat of plates or a brigandine – in France it was called a *cuirassine* – and had been popular because of the freedom of movement it allowed. These started to appear on the Western Front in 1915. Surprisingly, the Germans do not seem to have even experimented with this type of armour although they must have captured examples of it.

The Gorgeno-Collaye armour may have been an early model of an armoured waistcoat of the multiple-plate type known as the Lanciers, which was made and sold in France to both French and British soldiers. The two armours bear so strong a resemblance that they may actually be one and the same. The name is an interesting choice and may owe its origin to the *cuirassine* of old; cuirassiers were heavy armoured cavalry of the sixteenth and seventeenth centuries while First World War cavalry were called lancers. This same armour was also referred to as the Franco-British cuirass although this name is more usually associated with an earlier multiple-plate armour. At 8 lb, the Lanciers was somewhat lighter than the Fariselli.

The earlier Franco-British cuirass had a quite different structure, being made from a large number of small interconnected steel rectangles attached to a waistcoat of similar shape to that of the Lanciers. This, too, was made and sold in France but it was also sold in Britain. The advantage of using a construction of such small plates was flexibility and ease of movement. It consisted of eight columns of plates, each one being connected to its neighbour by eight steel rings, two on each side. The cuirass was fairly good as a defence against shrapnel but was useless against bullets. Not only was the steel of low quality but the plates did not fully overlap so bullets could easily penetrate between them, as indeed could shrapnel. Each plate, in effect, acted independently of the others and the rings allowed a plate to be pushed into the body when struck. Despite these shortcomings it was bought in large numbers by British soldiers at around £6 a time. In British shops it was called the 'life-saving waistcoat'. No doubt its lightness was influential as it weighed only 'a few pounds'. There was also a separate bib or upper chest and throat guard constructed in the same way.

The designer and manufacturers of the Franco-British cuirass are unknown. However, there were two similar armours that appeared around the same time and it is possible that it originated with the designer of one of these. The most likely candidate is John Berkley of Newcastle who made various items of body armour and whose 'armoured waistcoat' had a similar shape to the base garment of the Lanciers and the Franco-British cuirass. Of course, he may simply have plagiarized the idea. At the end of May 1916, Berkley filed a patent application (subsequently granted as GB 105,822) in respect of his waistcoat, which was

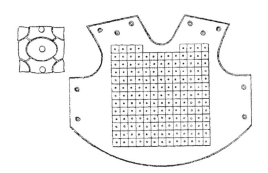

Berkley's patented Flexible Armour Guard of 1916. The small circles are eyelets for laces (but other fastenings could be used). The inset figure shows an alternative to the square plates.

known commercially as the Flexible Armour Guard. It consisted of a canvas base garment with a front and a back. Around twelve columns of small steel plates were centrally attached by rivets to both front and back so that the body had all-round protection, although other methods of attachment were also described. As with the Franco-British cuirass, none of the plates overlapped. Neither was the steel of high quality. Berkley's armour weighed 3 lb but there was also a heavier model at 4 lb that used thicker plates. As a defence against bullets it had little practical value; tests showed that when one of the plates was struck by a pistol bullet it was driven backwards with enough force to penetrate flesh. The British officer shot by Jünger's companion was probably wearing one of Berkley's Flexible Armour Guards. About its only virtue was that it was easy to wear.

Thomas Randolph, director of Wilkinson Sword, designed a similar armoured garment around the same time as Berkley. He filed a patent application and was subsequently granted a patent (GB 103,915). This, like Berkley's, was made up of small rectangular plates (preferably forty-eight, although why he should have fixed on this number is unclear), which did not overlap. Randolph even stated that they should not even touch edge to edge but that there should be a small gap between them to facilitate easy movement. Curiously, he seemed to believe that other 'armoured articles of wear have not been a success mainly because the armouring has been visible either from the inside or outside of the garment'. Quite why visibility should have made a difference he did not elucidate. The protective capabilities of armour were not influenced by whether the steel plates were concealed by fabric or not. The plates of his jacket were positioned between the outer fabric and the lining, the two layers of material being sewn together around each plate. Although his motives may have been worthy, his understanding of body armour was flawed. Nevertheless, it sold well under its commercial name of Wilkinson's Safety Service Jacket. It was lightweight, weighing only 3 lb, the recommended thickness of the plates being a mere $\frac{1}{16}$ in, hardly adequate to stop shrapnel, let alone bullets, although he claimed that it would 'stop spent bullets and shell fragments'. An advertisement claimed that a 'Sheet of Wilkinson's "Special Bullet-Proof Steel"' was not penetrated by bullets from a '.455 Service Revolver fired at 20 yards'.

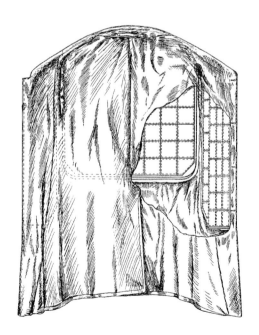

The Wilkinson Safety Service Jacket, showing construction. Again, these are abutting plates. It could be bought from all good department stores. Drawing from GB 103,915.

The idea was for the Wilkinson Safety Service Jacket to be worn in place of the standard uniform tunic which the garment externally resembled. Wilkinson's motive was not so much commercial as a desire to do away with the need for an extra garment, although the Safety Service Jacket was far from cheap at about £10 a throw. It is clear that the jacket was intended only for officers and the cost would have ensured that only officers could afford one. He did not consider what it might be like to wear a 3 lb jacket day in, day out although he may have been aware that no one wore armour all the time and an officer was likely to have more than one tunic. Interestingly, the specification mentions the well-known use of thin sheets of aluminium in 'overcoats, police-caps and the like' in place of rubber to make them windproof and waterproof. It is not clear whether this was part of the Wilkinson jacket.

It is evident from the complete specification that Randolph was aware of the Franco-British cuirass and the Lanciers and that his invention was meant to be an improvement over them. He may also have been aware of the Star body shield that was made from horizontal bands of chromium-nickel 'rustless' steel, riveted together, supplied from Whitworth. A breastplate and a backplate were available and these could be strapped on quite easily. However, their coverage was limited; neither plate was body-shaped so there was inevitably quite a large part of the torso that was unprotected. Each one weighed less than 3 lb and the breastplate could be bought on its own for about £2 while the pair cost a little over £4. An improved version of this was apparently invented by J. Pullman (GB 105,699, filed August 1916). Externally, it looked like the Star but its construction was quite different.

Pullman's body armour was made up of rectangular steel plates that were interlocked horizontally by tongue pieces so that they not only overlapped but were hinged together to give the armour flexibility. The tongue pieces were alternately male and female and the plates were in pockets formed between the inner and outer fabric layers of the shield. The pockets were made by tucking the outer fabric layer under each plate and securing it

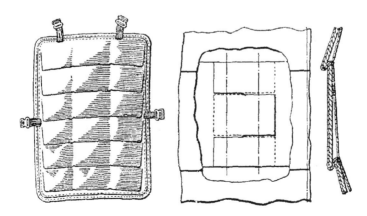

Pullman's armour of interlocking plates as shown in GB 105,699.

A group of RAMC personnel wearing Dayfield Body Shields at an Advanced Dressing Station during the Battle of Messines, June 1917. (The Illustrated War News)

to the inner one. These securing points formed what were, in effect, fabric hinges but just how well they would have stood up to normal wear and tear let alone rough treatment in the trenches is open to question. This idea of fabric 'hinges' was repeated in a number of armours, including the Lanciers.

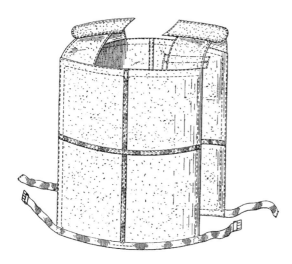

The first Dayfield Body Shield, as shown in GB 5,196/15. The drawing shows the shoulder defences.

One of the most widely used and best-known body armours of the war was the Dayfield Body Shield. It was also one of the first and went through various changes as it was developed between early 1915 and late 1917. There appear to have been at least three different versions devised by different people, although the name remained the same. The name Dayfield was derived from the names of the original inventors, Frances Dayton

A British officer wearing a body shield constructed from small plates, about mid-1916. Unusually, he is wearing it over his tunic. (The Illustrated War News)

and Ernest Whitfield. Their relationship is a mystery. In the patent specifications they filed at the Patent Office in 1915 (April, September and October), they are described as a gentlewoman and a gentleman respectively, which means they had independent means and were neither in trade nor in business. How they came to invent a form of body armour is unknown. Their first patent application (known as a provisional specification) was filed on 6 April 1915; this was only concerned with armoured protection for the front of the body. It consisted of four convex steel plates enclosed in pockets, created by placing the plates between two layers of fabric and stitching them together in the gaps between the plates – like the Wilkinson jacket – the shape of the plates allowing them to follow the curvature of the body. They evidently discovered that having gaps was not a good idea and in their second provisional specification filed five months later this defect was remedied by the use of metal strips to cover the gaps. It also included provision for a similarly constructed shield to cover the back, the two shields being joined together by straps round the waist and over the shoulders, while adding dished 'steel epaulettes' to the shoulder straps. Three weeks later, the complete specification was filed and the patent was granted on the 17 April 1916 (GB 5,196/15).

The Munitions Inventions Department evaluated the Dayfield but the fact that the plates did not overlap, even though the joins were covered by strips of steel, together with the lack of protection to the abdomen and the thighs, meant that it did not provide adequate cover. Nevertheless, the Dayfield could be bought in shops in Britain and a number of them seem to have been sent out to France for troop trials; correspondence between GHQ and the War Office shows that various body shields were sent out to France from time to time. Haig was keen to have effective body armour supplied to his troops and on 26 December 1915 Gen Maxwell, writing on Haig's behalf, made it plain 'that some form of light protection for the body against splinters of shells and grenades would be valuable for men taking part in trench warfare'. This statement also makes it clear that no such defence yet existed. On 9 August 1915 Maxwell had already expressed the view that 'the provision of satisfactory body armour capable of resisting the German bullet fired at short range is not practicable in view of the weight entailed'. Steel armour capable of stopping bullets weighed at least 10 lb per sq ft and this meant that such body armour was simply too heavy. The British Army was not looking for bulletproof armour but shrapnel-proof armour. That did not alter the fact that the armour could have no gaps in it and it had to cover all the vital areas.

Maxwell listed three essential requirements of a body shield as envisaged at GHQ. It had to be capable of providing 'all-round protection against splinters burst within a few yards of the wearer'. The armour had to allow the wearer unhindered movement of his arms and not interfere too much with moving around generally. It had to be light enough not to tire the wearer if he had to keep it on for long periods, especially if he was engaged in activities of an 'arduous nature such as throwing grenades'. He relayed the opinion that 'something of the nature of a leather jerkin covered with metal plates might be suitable'. Who formulated this idea is not known but it clearly had Haig's backing. But the premise was flawed. It may have been in response to this idea that John Berkley invented his Flexible Armour Guard. It is quite possible that the idea of a leather jerkin with metal plates gained currency because of GHQ's support for the idea, and designing something to fulfil a known requirement along lines that were already considered favourable was not a

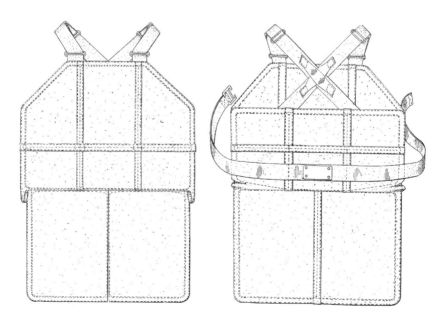

Front and back of the second Dayfield, invented by David Anderson in 1916, showing the additional aprons and the reshaped plates.

bad approach. The Munitions Inventions Department was conducting experiments with 'a protective garment or apron (fore and aft) made from plaques of 18-gauge hardened steel, weight about 2 lbs per sq. ft', in January 1916. It provided 'fairly satisfactory protection against the smaller splinters of grenades when burst within a few yards of the wearer'. But the final garment was going to weigh about 15 lb. It was too heavy.

The Design Department of the Ministry of Munitions and the Munitions Inventions Department were both looking into the problem of body armour (with some degree of cooperation – they were within the same Ministry, after all) and the designers of the Dayfield were asked to modify their body shield in the light of its obvious shortcomings. This led to at least three independent lines of development, none of which included jerkins. By January 1916, the Dayfield had been modified to include armoured protection to the upper thighs using two additional steel plates, one for each thigh, each being 'flexibly connected to the body shield and arranged to hang loosely in front of the thighs'. What this amounted to in practice was attachment via folds or pleats in the fabric enclosing the steel plates. The number of plates in the front and back parts of the armour was increased from four to six in each and their size was accordingly reduced, again, to increase mobility for the wearer. In addition, a curved groin plate could be attached. Curiously, although this was still referred to as the Dayfield Body Shield, the patent

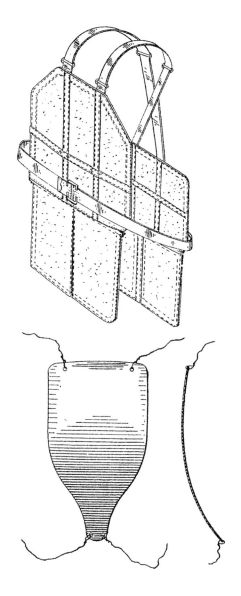

The upper drawing shows the relative position of the front to the back of the complete Anderson Dayfield, while the lower drawings show the groin protector.

applications filed in January, April and July 1916 were all in the name of David Anderson, an engineer, who appears to have no connection with Dayton or Whitfield, apart from having used the same patent agent.

These were for the same body armour as that described in GB 5,196/15 but 'specially adapted for the use of bomb throwers', the specification adding that it 'admits of the wearer readily using his arms for throwing bombs or other purposes'. These modifications were clearly in response to the requirements listed by Maxwell in December 1915. The specifications also included a 'tail-like extension' consisting of a couple of steel plates to protect the back of the thighs and the buttocks as well as protection for the front of the thighs. Again, the thigh protectors, front and back, were added because of specific requirements from the Munitions Inventions Department. To make it more comfortable to wear and to make it less of a hindrance to movement, a number of refinements were added. These included cutting the outer corners off the upper front plates so that they did not interfere with the arms and rounding the corners of all the plates so that there were no sharp bits to stick in anywhere. In addition, the edges were all rounded off and padded with extra material. The plates were also slightly dished so that they would follow the contours of the body. Because of the flexibility of the armour due to the use of 'abutting plates' rather than overlapping plates, enclosed in fabric, together with the waist straps, the Dayfield now more or less wrapped round the torso.

The patent specification was drafted as the armour was being developed – hence the two provisional specifications – whereas the drawings were not made until the complete specification was drafted. By this time, the form the Dayfield was to take at this stage of its development had been settled. Comparison of the patent drawings in GB 103,140 with photographs of the Dayfield show almost identical devices. The shoulder straps, which now crossed on the wearer's back, the side straps and all the buckles shown in the drawings are the same as those in the photographs (drawings were not always drafted from actual examples).

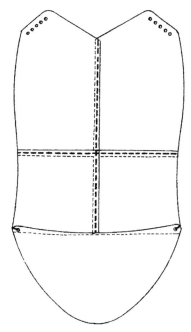

Beedle's simplified third Dayfield. The plates overlap slightly. Unlike the previous Dayfields, this had no fabric covering.

In the meantime, in March 1916, while these modifications were being worked out, William Beedle filed a patent application for body armour (GB 104,911). This is also identified as the Dayfield Body Shield and there are photographs that clearly show the armour illustrated in 104,911; the Imperial War Museum has an example. Yet this bears little resemblance to either the early or later forms of the Dayfield described above, apart from the backplates. The whole point of Beedle's invention was to make inexpensive armour. Beedle, who was an engineer like Anderson, had the same address as Frances Dayton; it is likely that Frances Dayton was Beedle's wife and had used her maiden name in the original patent. This does not explain, however, how Frances came to be involved with armour in the first place.

Beedle's body armour not only consisted of fewer and larger plates but these had no fabric covering. It had four plates in the front and another four at the back. The back four were more or less square while only the lower two of the front section were this shape. All were curved to fit the shape of the body. The upper front plates were longer and met to form a V-neck at the top with the outer corners cut off at an angle. The plates overlapped and were riveted together, although the complete specification suggested that lacing was better because it allowed the plates greater freedom to move in relation to each other. The front and back were supported via shoulder straps. Finally, below the four front plates, a D-shaped apron plate was suspended, which would not get in the way of the wearer's legs when he moved or sat down. The provisional specification mentioned that the plates could be enclosed in pockets – like in the other forms of the Dayfield – but this was not included in the complete specification. The Beedle-based Dayfield was evidently known as a simplified form of the Body Shield and it weighed about 4 lb whereas the heaviest form of the armour, the Anderson version, weighed between 14 lb and 18 lb.

On 24 January 1916, the Secretary of the War Office replied to Maxwell's letter of 26 December 1915, advising him that 1,000 Dayfield Body Shields were 'on order which comply generally with the conditions laid down . . . and further investigations are proceeding'. At the same time, he indicated that another body shield was under development but that the final design had yet to be settled. When it was ready, samples would be sent out for trials. The Dayfields were sent out to France in February. Following these trials, GHQ requested 50,000 Dayfields and by October 7,000 of an initial order for 10,000 had been sent out. There were by now about 20,000 body shields of various types in France. The Dayfield was used by bombers, members of patrols, garrisons of craters and sentries, much like the German Army later used its body armour. In the end, the Dayfield was found to be too cumbersome, a common problem with body armour, and it was used less and less frequently. A light form of the Dayfield was also used by the Canadians. This reportedly weighed 5.5 lb (7 lb with a groin plate and shoulder armour) and was known as the New Featherweight Shield, which may have been based on the Beedle armour. However, it proved to be too light and did not have enough stopping power. And yet, the ideal weight for body armour was determined to be no more than 6 lb.

In late August, after GHQ had also trialled 'a consignment of special body shields' developed by the Munitions Inventions Department and the Design Department that had been sent out in June, it decided that it preferred these to the Dayfield. General Maxwell informed the War Office that troop trials with the body shield had gone well. But the armour needed some modification if it was to do its job properly without impeding the wearer. Despite the rigour with which body armour, and indeed all manner of trench warfare devices, was designed, tested and modified in Britain, there was no substitute for trials on the front line. What the soldiers themselves felt about testing new and untried equipment can be imagined, especially when it was often so heavy. There are quite a number of references to new equipment in memoirs and none of the authors or their companions viewed new kit as something to applaud. New equipment was mostly greeted with suspicion and scepticism. This had grown from bitter experience of new equipment that had not only failed to live up to expectations but had proved to be dangerous to the user.

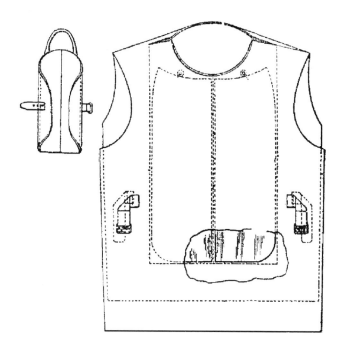

A. Taylor's armoured waistcoat containing two steel plates and a layer of asbestos. The small figure on the left is an example of arm and leg defences of two hinged, curved steel plates, lined with asbestos. Drawings from GB 108,244.

The Munitions Inventions Department body armour was perhaps an exception. Maxwell recommended three improvements following the summer troop trials:

(a) The waist strap should be lowered and another added higher up so as to prevent the corner from opening out when the shields are strapped on.

(b) The braces require to be shortened; as, at present, even when adjusted to their shortest they are too long.

(c) The top corners of the back piece catch the arm in the action of throwing. It is noted that the stamps for these shields have already been made, but if possible the top corners of the back piece should be hollowed out to obviate this objection.

When these recommendations had been implemented, he wanted to provide 400 of the body shields for each division. It became known as the Experimental Ordnance Board body armour or EOB for short. Why it was not given a name that reflected its origin within the Ministry of Munitions is not clear. It may simply be that the Ordnance Board was still the final arbiter. It is evident that the modifications were carried out and the body armour was supplied in large numbers to the troops in France during 1917, presumably on the basis that Maxwell indicated.

The EOB was one of the more lightweight body armours of the war at 9.5 lb, though that was heavy enough. It had three steel plates, each of 18-gauge manganese steel, a breastplate, a backplate and a plate to protect the groin area, all of which were shaped to conform to the contours of the body, and would withstand shrapnel and even rifle bullets provided the shots were fired from a long way off. The plates were padded to make the armour more comfortable to wear and were contained in fabric covers. Unlike other body shields, the plates were separate pieces and were joined by straps and buckles.

There were two other body shields that resembled the Dayfield and may have evolved from it. One was the Best Body Shield which also resembled Pullman's armour. However, there is insufficient information about the Best to be certain if the resemblance is superficial or whether there was a stronger connection. The Best appears to have consisted of three parts, a front shield, a back shield and a liner shield for the front. The manganese steel plates were body width and arranged in a single column in each shield, each plate overlapping the one beneath, the bottom plate being D-shaped. The armour was quite narrow and consequently the amount of protection it offered was significantly reduced but it only weighed about 6 lb and could be folded into a small package for easy transportation.

The other body shield was the so-called BEF; this was a commercial product and not one developed by a government department. The name was obviously chosen to give it some sort of credibility with potential customers. It was made in Willenhall in Staffordshire and cost about £5. Made of manganese steel, it weighed 7.5 lb. The BEF was better than the Best Body Shield because it afforded better coverage of the vital areas of the body. It consisted of a large breastplate flanked by two smaller plates to which an abdominal shield was attached by buttons, and a backplate made up of a column of plates. The abdominal shield, which also covered the groin area, was made up of several overlapping plates, the lowest of which was D-shaped. Like the Best, it could be folded into a relatively small package, making it easy to carry around. It was claimed to be one of the most effective body shields available to the British soldier.

The Best Body Shield was perhaps named because the manufacturer believed it was its best model. The same firm also produced the Lanciers, or at least a version of it, known in Britain as the Military Body Shield, as well as two other body shields, the Portobank and the Army & Navy, the latter for the department store of that name. The Portobank appears to have been available in a number of versions; breastplate only (2.25 lb), with backplate (4.25 lb), and both with and without fabric covering in the form of a waistcoat (3 lb and 4 lb respectively). It offered only limited protection as it did not cover the abdomen but was light and cheap, ranging in price from approximately £1 to £4. When in the form of a waistcoat, it consisted of several layers, including felt between the steel and the outer fabric covering, and surgical wadding and antiseptic lint on the inside. The Army & Navy was similar but had some sort of protection for the abdomen and groin.

The name Portobank conjures images of the mountebank, if only because the two words sound similar, and mountebank, in some ways, sums up the commercial approach to body shields. All these body armours highlighted three flaws that were not resolved until the advent of more modern composite materials: excessive weight, lack of comfort and inability to stop bullets. But a lot of body armour was nevertheless worn in the First World War.

CHAPTER 4

Armoured Shovels and Tin Hats

It is curious that one of the first proposals for a shield should end up, albeit in another form, as one of the last proposals of the war. This was the armoured entrenching tool, first proposed by McDougall, who had patented his invention 1911 and which was tested at the School of Musketry at the start of 1915. By 1918, the concept was being considered again by the Trench Warfare Subcommittee. In its deliberations, it appears to have been unaware of the earlier proposals (for there had been more than one) or the obvious irony. The logic behind it was simple. Some form of body armour was still needed and rather than making it available to a few to undertake specific tasks it was proposed to make it available to all. An obvious way of achieving this was to take an item of equipment that most front-line soldiers carried when attacking and make it serve two purposes. And since the entrenching tool was carried by troops in the attack so that they could dig in when necessary this became the obvious choice.

One of the first body armour patents of the war was for an armoured entrenching tool, granted to E.W. Jackson, who filed his application in November 1914 (GB 21,863/14). Unlike MacAdam's armoured spade-cum-shield, the blade of Jackson's tool was detachable and could be clipped to the belt and held against the body with a strap. It even had a loophole so that it could be used as a fixed shield as well. It was not taken up and yet the proposal of the subcommittee was not so very different from Jackson's invention. The main difference was that the subcommittee intended to modify a shovel that was now carried because it was bigger and more useful than the much smaller standard entrenching tool. However, they also considered the latter.

In August 1918, when Winston Churchill was Minister of Munitions, the subcommittee was set up at Churchill's instigation 'to consider and advise upon possible improvements to the existing service stores used in trench warfare, and to devise new stores to meet requirements, or anticipated requirements, in the field'. The Trench Warfare Subcommittee (which is not to be confused with the Trench Warfare Committee created in 1916) included representatives from the Trench Warfare Department and the Munitions Inventions Department with various advisory members 'as required, from Departments concerned in Service Stores'. Appointed members included Brig-Gen A.M. Asquith, Lt-Col Henry Newton and Lt-Col O.F. Brothers from the Trench Warfare Department and Maj A.L. Oke as the sole representative from the Munitions Inventions Department. The advisory members represented the Master General of Ordnance, Director of Inspection of Small Arms Ammunition, Controller of Munitions Design, and the Research Department of the Royal Arsenal at Woolwich, among others. The subcommittee had a short life, just three-and-a-half months, by which time the war was over. During its brief existence it looked at body armour and the armoured entrenching tool.

The committee arrived at three possibilities for an armoured entrenching tool:

(1) Utilising the present Entrenching Tool and helve without any modifications, with the addition of a shovel to form a breast plate [sic] when not in use.
(2) Using a helve with a screw joint with the present entrenching tool head adapted so that the helve may carry a shovel, and double headed pick or entrenching tool head.
(3) An entirely new entrenching tool, of which the shovel forms a breastplate on the line of design M.I.D. 2240.

The second option was very similar to Jackson's invention. Much time and effort went into preliminary experimentation and the results were promising but the final experiments were not carried out because the Trench Warfare Department was being gradually closed down as trench warfare gave way to open warfare.

It is clear that the experiments did bear fruit of a sort, however. The experimental work was carried out with the full involvement of Sir Robert Hadfield and his company who supplied the steel blanks from which the shovel blades were stamped and subsequently heat treated. He requested that samples of the shovel blades be sent to him for examination and firing tests to determine whether the steel had deteriorated as a result of working it in the course of making the blades. In February 1919, his test report had yet to be delivered to the Munitions Inventions Department, which had taken over the work of the Trench Warfare Department. The curious thing is that Hadfield, with someone called A.G.M. Jack, had filed a patent application for an armoured shovel in October 1918 (subsequently granted as GB 133,165). The shovel would appear to be the very same one tested by the committee, possibly the design identified as MID 2240. It is entirely possible, of course, that the idea had originated with Hadfield.

At around the time the subcommittee had been set up, an RAMC captain called Walker had suggested that the heart could be protected by putting a steel plate at the back of the box respirator which was now worn by everyone. Gen Asquith submitted the idea to Churchill, who was enthusiastic about it. Churchill had clear ideas about what tests were necessary and how they should be conducted, set out in a detailed memo that he passed to Adm Bacon for implementation:

I am greatly interested in this proposal, and I regard it as of high potential importance. A number of gas masks should be fitted with armour plates of the highest quality but of varying strengths according to weight. These should be placed on dummy targets and fired at from 300 to 1,000 yards range. If possible the dummies should sway about backwards and forwards, from side to side during the firing. Merely taking a steel plate and shooting at it at right angles at close range does no justice to the effect of armour. Many bullets are spent or half spent in war. Others have ricocheted. The overwhelming majority do not strike a piece of armour at right angles either horizontally or vergically [sic]. Every deviation from the normal increases the value of the plate. It would probably be a truer guide to the value of a plate always to fire at it 15-deg. from the normal.

The fact that the mask has to be worn in this ready position affords a most convenient reason for fitting this plate over the most fatal surface. . . . The steel plate should in practice be easily removable from the . . . box respirator, so that troops wearing this in ordinary work behind the lines or on ordinary occasions in the trenches would not be inconvenienced by the additional weight. It could be . . . inserted for an attack . . .

Please proceed with the utmost energy upon these studies, bringing into play all the latest information which General Swinton has brought back from America . . . I wish to be kept fully informed.

4.9.18.   (Sgd) W. C.

Despite this endorsement from Churchill, the subcommittee decided that it was not as good an idea as the armoured shovel and the proposal was dropped.

American interest in body armour increased as soon as the United States entered the war in 1917. Gen Pershing, commander of the American Expeditionary Force, was very keen to supply his troops with armour and the American government obtained samples of more than thirty different body shields for testing in the US by the Ordnance Department. None proved satisfactory, however. Consequently, the Americans set about devising their own body armour. The US government engaged Bashford Dean, Curator of Armor at the Metropolitan Museum, New York and an acknowledged world authority, to develop armour for the American troops. From 1917 to 1918 he served as a major in the Ordnance Department in order to undertake the project. It was the details of this work to which Churchill had referred. Dean was in close contact with the Munitions Inventions Department, the Trench Warfare Department and Sir Robert Hadfield as well as the Inventions Bureau in Paris. Despite the fact that the United States did not have fighting troops in France until the summer of 1917, and these did not participate in the fighting for some time after this, back in the US a major research programme into armour was underway.

A shoulder defence that also protected the upper chest was made of manganese steel and sent out to France for trials in 1918. Manufactured by the New England Enamelling Company, it was reportedly very effective and would have seen widespread use had the war continued. This lightweight armour (1.5 lb) was unlike any used by the European armies and like much of American body armour used vulcanized sponge rubber padding. This was on the lower edge of the chest defence to cushion any impacts. It was even shaped over the right shoulder in such a way that it would not interfere when the wearer brought his rifle to bear. Another shoulder defence was also tried out in France but it covered too small an area and was subsequently dropped. Various body shields were tried out, including that designed by Dr Guy Otis Brewster of New Jersey, which included a breastplate supported on a complex metal frame, using spring mountings at the shoulders to not only cushion impacts but to hold it away from the body. However, extremely effective though it was, the breastplate alone weighed 40 lb and the complete

Dr Brewster wearing his 110 lb body armour while a US soldier shoots at him. The huge, angled breastplate and massive helmet can be clearly seen, although the picture has been retouched. The dark 'mouth' on the helmet is, in fact, the eye slit and the light 'nose' is one of two shutters that rotate over the slit. The dark line along the top is no more than heavy retouching, as is the curved line at the base of the helmet which, in fact, rests on the breastplate. (The Illustrated War News)

armour, which also included a massive helmet like a medieval jousting helm, weighed 110 lb. It was quite impractical. Interestingly, Brewster had been working on body armour for about ten years and he had so much faith in his massive body shield that he was prepared to wear it while someone fired a Lewis gun at him.

The Metropolitan Museum armour workshop developed a more practical form of armour in February 1918. This consisted of a breastplate, two overlapping waist plates and a thigh shield for each leg. Not surprisingly, considering its origin, it resembled medieval armour. However, it weighed 27 lb and tests showed that it was uncomfortable and tiring to wear for any length of time. Another design was devised in France, made up of multiple plates, but it had too many disadvantages to warrant taking it beyond the experimental stage.

Much work was also devoted to light armour and several experimental models were constructed by the Engineering Division of the Ordnance Department. All were much more complex than those in use by European armies and all clearly showed the influence of Bashford Dean, particularly where the whole-arm defences were concerned. These were obviously adapted from medieval armour. The Ordnance Department even considered the armoured box respirator but with two plates instead of one. American businessmen were just as keen to be involved and a number of commercial body shields were produced. Some of these were based on commercial models on sale in Britain, including the Featherweight (the US version was called the Selecta), the Franco-British and the Dayfield. Whether these were ever used in France by the American Army is not known. Others were quite complex, one making use of coiled springs to cushion impacts, for example, while some were bizarre, like the glass armour submitted to the Ordnance Department by someone called Szmyt. It is interesting to note, however, that the idea of coating armour with a hard enamel was seriously considered as it would enhance the ability of the armour to deflect bullets. (Some modern composite armours use ceramic 'tiles' that are designed to break on impact and by so doing absorb some of the kinetic energy of the projectile.) There was also pneumatic armour, which was devised independently by several different inventors, and armour that used ball bearings to deflect projectiles by moving under impact.

The Americans sent out 35,000 pieces of leg armour to France, this armour covered the front of the leg from the shin to just above the knee and each guard weighed 12 oz. But the American Expeditionary Force decided not to use them. One American firm went further and made guards for the entire leg but these were so uncomfortable that they were discounted as a viable proposition. The Americans were not alone in experimenting with this sort of armour, the French having tried out leg defences in 1916. However, no army made much use of leg or arm defences and concentrated on protecting the vital areas of the body which, of course, included the head. The steel helmet was undoubtedly the most widely used form of body armour and had been adopted by all armies by 1916.

Gen Adrian is credited with introducing the first steel head defence of the war, a hemispherical skull cap that was worn beneath the French kepi. Adrian was renowned from his colonial service days as someone who cared about the well-being of his men. The idea for the skullcap allegedly came from a chance remark made by a wounded man who claimed to have escaped death because he had his metal mess bowl on his head when he was struck by a projectile. Why he had it on his head is not explained and there is no evidence to suggest that other soldiers took similar action under fire to protect themselves. A more likely inspiration was the steel *secrèt* worn beneath hats by many soldiers in the sixteenth and seventeenth centuries. The skullcap, weighing only 9 oz, was tried out in December 1914. It was an immediate success and inspired Adrian to devise a helmet that was based on both the French fireman's helmet and the cuirassier's helmet. By March 1915, 700,000 skullcaps had been issued. A few months later, the helmet replaced it.

Whereas the skullcap was 0.197 in thick, the helmet was 0.0277 in thick and weighed 1 lb 11 oz. It was supposedly designed by the artist Edouard Detaille, famous for his military paintings, but he had died in 1912 so clearly he was not the designer. The helmet came in three sizes and was fitted with a liner of leather and felt so that it was cushioned against the head. Elegant though the design was, it was far from simple to manufacture and required seventy operations merely to mould it into shape. Nevertheless, it was made in huge numbers, one manufacturer producing 7,500 a day in 1917. Another manufacturer was reputed to have made more than 3,000,000 in a little over two years. To make them on such a scale required a manufacturer to use 200 presses. It was also used by the Belgians and the Italians with some slight modifications.

Unlike the later British helmet, the Adrian was made of mild steel, heat treated to be half-hard; fully hardened steel did not lend itself to the moulding processes. Although it was considerably lighter than the British helmet, the ballistic value of the Adrian was not nearly as good which was not helped by the numerous holes that were punched into it during the complex manufacturing process. Various alternative models underwent trials but the Adrian helmet was never supplanted. Jean Dunand developed a number of helmets, only one of which interested the French Army, a heavy model with a face guard intended for sentries, but it does not appear to have been used. Dunand's helmets elicited much more interest from the Americans when they arrived in France in 1917. All of Dunand's helmets were fitted with visors, something which he felt was crucial, no doubt, because his brother had lost an eye earlier in the war, but they were all problematical. AEF Headquarters was sufficiently impressed with Dunand's designs to ask for 10,000 helmets to be made in the US for troop trials in France. However, the shape of the helmet proved too difficult to press in manganese steel and they were never made. Dunand redesigned the helmet and a Paris company undertook to make samples which were then submitted to AEF Headquarters and eventually to the Ordnance Department in the States. The helmet was liked but the visor was not and the Americans asked for a Polack visor instead; there was a possibility that it might become the standard US helmet if the Polack was fitted. However, it did not. The Belgians used the Dunand shape as the model for a design of their own.

Visors greatly interested the French. They were investigated by the French Inventions Bureau, which included Gen Adrian and Maj Polack among its members. Polack designed many different visors of different shapes, with different eye apertures, different methods of attachment and hinging, and in different metals. The earliest experimental design dating from early 1916 was made of zinc but later models were made of manganese steel. A form of the visor with a series of long slits in front of each eye was eventually adopted and used fairly widely by the French Army late in the war. All Polack's visors were shaped with a nosepiece whereas Dunand's were curved plates that wrapped round the face and were pierced with apertures like little slots that extended all the way round. The problem with puncturing a visor with slots was that it inevitably became weakened and would not withstand bullets at any range. However, they were only ever intended to protect the wearer from small splinters.

None of the Polack visors was patented in Britain but Jean Dunand filed an application for a visor that was apparently intended for use with the British helmet. This was filed in September 1916 and consisted of a visor with one large aperture that could be closed by a slotted shutter. It may well have been tested but it was never used. The face shield offered better protection than a visor and the French experimented with one at Verdun. Invented by M.C. Favre in 1915, it was patented in Britain (GB 6,585/15). It weighed 10 lb and was made of chromium-nickel steel. The shield was a complex shape that covered the face from the eyes down and extended to the upper chest on which it rested. It was held in place by straps that went over the head and round the neck. Like the German face shield it was intended for snipers.

The earliest British face shield was invented by John Berkley in 1915 and was simply a steel plate in a flattened V-shape to fit across the face and was attached beneath the peak of the service cap. It had two short vertical slots, each intersected by three small horizontal slits to see through. It was never used. The incidence of eye injuries seemed to vary from army to army so that the statistics do not agree but the British determined that 50 per cent of eye injuries were preventable and that a visor or mask of some kind would be effective. However, the number of eye injuries compared to those inflicted to the head and torso were small. Nevertheless, various experiments were conducted with masks, face shields and similar devices and one or two emerged as potentially useful.

GHQ was keen on shields to protect the eyes from 'minute fragments of shell and stone . . . which might cause blindness if lodged in the eye'. Two types of eye shield were sent to France for trials. One was a mail (often incorrectly referred to as 'chain mail') mask invented by King George V's eye-specialist, Capt Cruise RAMC. Connected to the rim of the helmet, it was pulled tight against the tip of the nose and the cheeks. It was evidently quite effective but very uncomfortable, heavy and noisy, added to which it unbalanced the helmet and obscured vision. During 1916 and 1917 it was manufactured in large numbers but the soldiers did not like it and rarely used it. In fact, GHQ withdrew it and asked for a number of improvements to be made. These were evidently carried out and trials were conducted in France. A similar mask was issued to some tank crews to avoid injury from spalling when the tank was hit by small arms fire. They were no more popular with tank men than with infantrymen.

A curious criticism of the mail veil was that it caused giddiness due to the eyes having a problem refocusing through the holes if the eyes or the helmet moved. This kind of claim was not uncommon with all visors, irrespective of the nature of the apertures. However, fencers use masks with lots of tiny apertures not dissimilar to those of a piece of mail and dizziness caused by looking through them is unknown. The eye does not see individual holes, merely a fuzzy mesh which the brain soon ignores. It may be that the smallness of the holes and closeness of the mask to the eyes caused the problem with the veil. However, it is possible that claims of dizziness were merely excuses to avoid wearing it. There is no question that some forms of aperture were less easy to see through than others but the problem here was one of obscuration.

A different approach to protecting the eyes was splinter goggles. Various types were produced during the war, all of which were basically the same, consisting of a metal band that went across the face level with the eyes, the areas adjacent to which being pushed out into large oval or circular protrusions perforated with slits. Unlike the slits in visors, these were so narrow that none of the eye was visible from the outside. Although the slits varied somewhat between different goggles they essentially conformed to the same pattern of a long horizontal slit intersected by a shorter vertical one near the nose, resembling a crucifix on its side, with a subsidiary slit above and one below the horizontal one. These were angled as though radiating from the same point near the nose. In September 1915, F. Della Valle and C. Benazzi filed a patent application for a pair of goggles like this (GB 101,629). The French manufactured goggles of almost identical construction and the British produced goggles with only slight differences, the main one being the thickness and shape of the band. Made of manganese steel, the British goggles, known as Xylonite Goggles (*see* p. 48), weighed 5.5 oz and could be bought in the same shops as other forms of body armour. During trials in France, Xylonite Goggles were shown to be extremely effective but, because it was hard to see through the tiny slits, it was almost impossible to use the rifle. GHQ rejected them. Curiously, Xylonite is a tradename for celluloid. It is interesting to note that bulletproof glass consisting of layers of glass and celluloid – laminated glass – was used in airmen's goggles later in the war but was never considered for infantry goggles.

Goggles had the advantage of being held in place by straps and a buckle. Visors needed to be attached by some hinge arrangement that often weakened the helmet at the attachment points. Although the French used Polack visors in the later stages of the war, the British tended to rely solely on the helmet introduced in late 1915. Its shape did not afford as much protection as the French pattern but it was made of better steel and was remarkably effective, so much so that the Americans chose it over the French pattern when they entered the war. Millions were produced on both sides of the Atlantic, being churned out by some companies at the rate of 10,000 or more a day.

The 'tin hat', as it was quickly named by British soldiers, although it was sometimes called the 'battle bowler', was created by John Brodie, an engineer who worked in London. Not only was the shape of the helmet his design but the impact-absorbing liner was his invention too. In August 1915, he filed a patent application for the helmet, the liner of which was a fundamental part; it was granted one year later and became GB 11,803/15. It is not clear from his specification whether he was referring to the French skullcap but he probably meant the Adrian helmet when he said that 'existing steel

Workers at a factory in Britain packing Brodie steel helmets for dispatch to France, spring 1916. (The Illustrated War News)

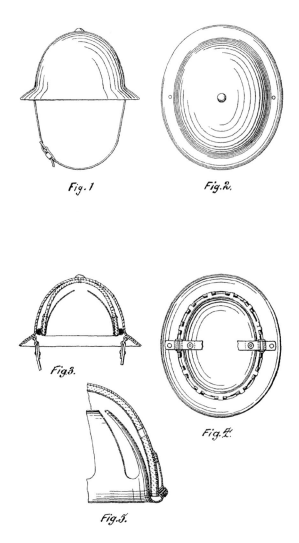

Fig. 1

Fig. 2.

Fig. 3.

Fig. 4.

Fig. 5.

Drawings from John Brodie's patent, GB 11,803/15, showing the liner that spaced the helmet from the head and helped to absorb impacts. Fig. 5 shows the construction of the liner.

helmets designed to protect the head against wounds caused by the impact of rifle bullets, shrapnel bullets, shell splinters . . . depend upon the thickness of the metal of which the helmet or head shield is made'. He went on to say that with existing helmets 'the method of fitting them on the head has the disadvantage that the force of a relatively small impact is transmitted direct to the skull and may easily produce concussion of the brain or at any rate a severe bruise'. And there were problems when it came to removing a damaged helmet from a man wounded in the head if it was perforated by a ragged hole 'because the metal gets imbedded in the head'. There was also evidently the problem of frostbite in cold weather. Brodie's helmet and liner overcame such problems.

Unlike the liner in the Adrian helmet, Brodie's liner ensured that the steel shell of the helmet was never in contact with the wearer's head. In effect, it was a hat within a hat, the inner hat being the liner. It was flexible and adjustable and spaced from the shell by rubber pads. Thus, in theory, it was possible for the steel shell to be quite severely dented before the wearer was hurt by an impact, whereas the same degree of indentation to the Adrian helmet would almost certainly result in death. However, the Adrian tended to be penetrated by an impact that would only dent the Brodie. As Brodie's specification states:

The lining acts as a buffer to prevent concussion of the brain by external impact and to prevent injury to the frontal, parietal or occipital bones of the cranium by any indentation or penetration of the helmet. This buffer or anti-concussion lining is by means of studs spaced away from the helmet shell so that a free space or air gap is left between lining and shell, and therefore the helmet may be subjected to a considerable force of impact or even be indented or penetrated without injury to the wearer.

The liner used in the Mk 1 helmet was described in an entry in the List of Changes dated 22 October 1918 (this was, of course, retrospective). It was 'principally of canvas American cloth and buckram. A narrow lining of cordite cloth, in which is inserted a row of ½-inch by 1-inch tubular rubbers which serves as a ventilating course and buffer is also provided.' Later helmets used a different liner with a drawstring-adjusted net. This

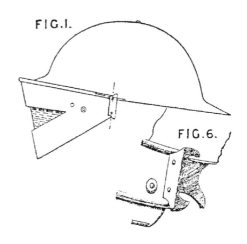

Dunand's visor for the Brodie, proposed in September 1916.

may have been the liner described in GB 105,348 granted to Sir Robert Hadfield and A.B.H. Clerke, which they applied for in February 1916.

One particular advantage of the Brodie shape was that it was possible to stamp it in one operation from manganese steel, which had been adopted at the suggestion of Sir Robert Hadfield. This was unlike the French Adrian helmet which was not only far more complicated to make but ballistically far weaker – the Brodie was twice as strong. It was heavier and thicker than the Adrian, weighing around 2 lb (it ranged in weight from about 1 lb 11 oz to about 2 lb 3 oz) and being 0.036 in thick. It came in one size only as the liner allowed for adjustments to fit individual heads. The Brodie did not have the sartorial elegance of the Adrian as it looked like an upturned bowl but the British soldier took to it with sardonic humour. It is uncertain whether Brodie devised the helmet off his own bat or whether he was asked to come up with something by the War Office or one of the inventions departments but, once he had devised his helmet, it was quickly recognized as a potential life-saver. Robert Graves observed that the number of head wounds fell after the issue of helmets, whereas Edmund Blunden felt that helmets were a sign of worse things to come. Capt Hitchcock thought 'They were very cumbersome and heavy, but one got used to them after a time.' But not everyone immediately took to them. Guy Chapman described how the first steel helmets

were doled out first to the snipers; and, as fate would have it, Gerrard, a charming intelligent boy . . . was at once killed. A fragment of shell tore through the steel and pinned his brain. Thereafter the helmet was condemned with one voice. No man would wear one, except under the direct orders and observation of an officer, and the trench store was gradually put to other uses. They were found to make admirable washing basins, were not to be despised as cookpots, and could be put to all kinds of uses not contemplated by their designer, often of a nature not to be recorded.

It is not hard to imagine what that was. Helmets have always been put to such uses.

The Brodie remained largely unchanged from its adoption in October 1915 until the end of the war, although the early version did not have the separate rounded rim capping which was later applied to the helmet to prevent injury from its sharp untrimmed edge. The chin strap was also changed to avoid throttling the wearer if the helmet was knocked backwards by an explosion or impact, and the liner was altered as noted above. Brodie recommended that the helmet was painted 'in rainbow colours so as to make it invisible to the enemy' but it was usually simply painted khaki, sometimes with sand sprinkled on it to roughen the surface to prevent the sun reflecting off it. The Germans often painted their helmets in splinter pattern camouflage. A hessian cover was also often used both by the British and the Germans. The Brodie cost about 10s to make.

From its first appearance in late 1915, the steel helmet was issued according to circumstance from trench stores. Capt Dunn, the Medical Officer of the Second Battalion, Royal Welch Fusiliers, noted that 'Steel shrapnel helmets, for use of bombers in sap-heads, were first issued' in late October 1915. The sight of a party of Argylls sporting the new helmet inspired ribald comments from the Royal Welch adjutant who thought they looked ridiculous. In February 1916 steel helmets were still being issued for special occasions, such as a raid to oust Germans from a mine crater that dominated the British line. But by March, the Royal Welch were issued with helmets simply because they were in the line. By then, the number of helmets manufactured was becoming large enough to equip many of the front-line troops but it was to be the summer and the opening of the Battle of the Somme before the tin hat became standard issue and everyone wore one; about a million had been made by then.

When the United States entered the war, the first 400,000 Brodie helmets for the US forces came from Britain, the initial batch arriving in France in July 1917. By November, the helmets were being manufactured in the US, the first 100,000 of which were sent to France in crates but after this the helmets arrived there on the heads of the men who were going to use them. By the end of 1918, US companies had made 6,500,000 helmets. All but 200,000 were made in manganese steel of the Hadfield formula. The Brodie was only ever viewed by the Americans as an expedient. They had every intention of designing their own helmet that would provide better protection than the Brodie which left parts of the head exposed. In the space of about eighteen months the Armor Committee of the American Council of National Research, which included Brewster among its members and was chaired by Bashford Dean, experimented with more than fourteen different designs, apart from looking at Dunand's models. Of these, the Liberty Bell was being seriously considered when the war ended. According to Dean, this looked like 'the dome-like hat of a Chinese fisherman'. In fact, the Americans did not adopt a new design until 1941.

Brodie filed another two applications in November 1917. One was for additional armour to protect the frontal and parietal bones and increase 'the distance between the fore part of the helmet and the wearer's face'. It consisted of an

adjustable anchor-shaped piece of manganese steel placed within the helmet, the shank portion . . . of which extends from the top of the helmet, and passes over the centre of the skull, while the side portions . . . curve over the front of the skull and cover the sutures between the parietal and temporal bones.

This became GB 120,606. The second application, which became GB 120,607, was for a visor. Although the specifications both refer to his first patent, the drawings illustrate a helmet similar to Dunand's designs rather than the familiar Brodie design, and the visor is also very similar to Dunand's. In fact, it would appear that the Belgian Army used these helmets and visors on a limited basis and was known as the Weekers model.

A few inventors were responsible for some odd helmets. One invention, devised by L. Soren (GB 118,251) was a Brodie-style helmet with 'an external detachable cushioning device' which consisted of 'curved overlapping spring tongue members' attached to a central disc. It is not clear quite what this was supposed to achieve. Others were helmets-cum-weapons, truly odd affairs. One was so bizarre that you wonder whether the inventor was playing some sort of practical joke, especially when you see the drawings – they illustrate the head of someone with a strong resemblance to the Kaiser. The helmet illustrated closely resembles a German *Pickelhaube* and was not only meant to house a semi-automatic pistol, which was fired by the shooter blowing through a tube, but the top of the helmet was removable and could be used as a cooking utensil.

The inventor of this eccentric device had the oddly appropriate name of A. Pratt. But so convinced was he of the merit of his invention that he filed not one but two patent applications, the first in July 1915 (granted as GB 100,891) and the second in May 1916 (granted as GB 106,461 as an addition to the first one). The second specification did away with the cooking bowl and added incredibly complex machinery for loading and firing the pistol.

The German helmet, with its distinctive coal scuttle shape, was first used at Verdun in January 1916. 'Coal scuttle' was a term of derision adopted by the English but the helmet was based on a fifteenth-century helmet known as a sallet. It was perhaps the most effective helmet of the war (it is noteworthy that the current American helmet is very similar in shape). It was designed by Professor Friedrich Schwerd who started experimenting in the summer of 1915. The shape afforded more protection than any other helmet used on the Western Front, providing cover for the neck as well as the

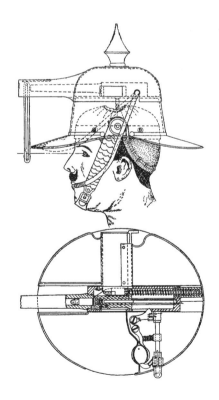

Perhaps the strangest invention of the war, Pratt's helmet gun as illustrated in his patent, GB 100,891, which he applied for in July 1915.

A captured German helmet with additional armour used by snipers. Slots in the shield engaged lugs on the side of the helmet and a leather strap kept it in place. (The Illustrated War News)

whole of the head. It was made of silicon steel that contained some manganese and nickel and varied in thickness from 0.040 in at the crown to 0.045 in at the brim and weighed 2 lb 6 oz. However, the ballistic strength of the helmet seemed to be variable; this was probably due to variations in the composition of the steel as well as stresses introduced during manufacture. The lining included pads that rested against the forehead and the sides of the head to make wearing it more comfortable.

In 1918, the helmet was modified to be deeper and less curved. It was slightly heavier than the earlier model at just over 3 lb. The liner was also altered to use cheaper materials and to take a wound dressing. After the dressing had been used the helmet sat more deeply on the head, which is clearly seen in some photographs where soldiers look as though their helmets are too big for them. There were variations on the standard helmet, including one in which curved spaces adjacent to the ears were cut out to allow the wearer to use the earpiece of a telephone. This has also been referred to as the cavalry model although there is nothing to suggest that it was specially issued to the cavalry.

No helmet was bulletproof, although it was not unheard of for a bullet to penetrate and follow the curvature of the helmet on the inside and exit the other side without causing serious injury to the wearer. Brodie helmets tended to dent if the bullet had travelled some distance, was partially spent or impacted at an angle. German helmets tended to be punctured when hit by bullets. During the Battle of Cambrai in 1917, Ernst Jünger was hit in the head by a 'shot of a far-distant rifle' which 'pierced my helmet and grazed the skull'. His helmet had 'two large holes in it', entry and exit holes. But often a rifle bullet would penetrate the front and kill the wearer – in the same action, the man next to Jünger was shot through his helmet and killed. It was because of this likelihood that the Germans used an additional shield that could be attached to the front of the helmet, slots in the supplementary armour engaging lugs on the outside of the helmet. The plate had a strap that passed round the back of the helmet to keep it in place. The Austro-Hungarian Army used a similar supplementary shield for their helmet which was itself very similar to the German one. The plate was shaped to conform to the curvature of the front of the helmet and was 0.23–0.24 in thick. It was heavy, weighing about 6 lb, and consequently it was not easy to wear as it overbalanced the helmet. It was disliked and only occasionally used by snipers.

CHAPTER 5

Vigilant with a Glass Eye – Periscopes

Domination of the enemy parapet became a British priority in 1915. The decision to adopt an aggressive policy had far-reaching consequences, not all of them good. It led to raiding, the raising of effective British snipers and the search for other means to take the fight to the enemy. Raiding, which at first was conducted by volunteers rather than by men told off for the task, also led to unnecessary casualties among the experienced men who tended to be the volunteers – despite the old army adage about not volunteering for anything – and they could not be replaced. The steady loss of these men would come back to haunt the British Army later in the war. But the most pressing problem was enemy snipers who were taking a steady toll.

Almost from the start of trench warfare in late 1914, German snipers had made British parapets dangerous places. Exposure of a head above the parapet often resulted in a sniper's bullet cracking past if it did not hit the unfortunate individual which more often than not it did. Great care had to be taken when moving along the trenches, which were not always deep enough for a man to stand upright without showing his head to the enemy, and those places had to be crossed quickly and at irregular times. Capt Hitchcock noted in May 1915 that the trenches at Armentières

> appeared to be very formidable; they were duck-boarded, and the parapets and paradoses were completely revetted with sand-bags. The parapets were 6 feet high, and the wooden fire steps being 1½ feet in height, gave a fire position of 4½ feet. Owing to the low-lying nature of the terrain the trenches were breast-works.

The trenches at Ypres had parapets that were much lower. German snipers were

An early tubular periscope being used by the 10th Hussars at Zillebeke, January 1915. (IWM)

quick and sharp. They did not allow anyone to make the same mistake twice and certainly not in the same place. GHQ feared that the soldiers were developing a defensive, cautious mentality which they would be unable to shake off.

It became apparent that to dominate the enemy parapet it was first necessary to make the British one safe or, at least, to stop the enemy dominating it. To turn the tables was no simple matter as there were all sorts of problems to overcome. Not least among them was the state of the British parapets themselves. There had been a tendency to impose pre-war regularity in their construction because the army liked neatness – but neatness spelt danger. A smooth line meant that anything breaking the orderliness of it was easily spotted by German snipers. So the neatness had to be undone and the parapets made untidy and uneven. Steel loopholes were added, but were not always camouflaged at first, to enable British snipers to fire back. But there was still the basic problem of how to observe the enemy safely. To cautiously raise your head above the parapet to take a look was foolish but many did it. Raising it quickly and looking for a couple of seconds before dropping out of sight again was much safer because it gave the enemy sniper less time to see you, aim and fire, unless you were unlucky enough to pop up just where he was looking. But you could not do it twice and 'many a day-sentry had been drilled through the head' recalled Frank Richards. As a method of observation it was all but useless. An alternative was to send a patrol out into no-man's-land at night to lie camouflaged in a shell crater (or in the long grass before shellfire had churned up the ground) to watch the enemy during the day, returning after dark the following night. But this needed skills that the average soldier did not possess. It required specialized training. And it did not provide immediate information.

The obvious solution to the problem of observation was the periscope. The periscope became the eyes of the infantry in the front-line trenches. Without periscopes, a battalion was blind. Dunn reported that when his battalion went into the front line in May 1916 the Germans had the upper hand and had shot down every one of its predecessor's periscopes. The 2nd Royal Welch Fusiliers counted themselves as an aggressive battalion so they set about restoring the balance with rifle grenades and sniping carried out under the grenade barrages. Within a matter of days, the number of German periscopes visible along their parapet had been 'thinned' so much that the Royal Welch were able to put up their own periscopes without them being shot at. 'Counting periscopes as points', recorded Dunn, 'the Battalion was easily the winner' in the contest. And this was no idle achievement. It mattered. The periscope was a symbol of dominance; whoever had the most above the parapet tended to be master. Capt Hitchcock noted that, while inspecting a sap, Maj Gen Capper found a sentry standing 'head and shoulders above the parapet' quite unconcerned about the danger. Capper 'told him not to expose himself, and asked: "Have you not got a periscope?"' to which the sentry replied, 'Sure, what good would it be sir? Aren't they just after breaking two on me?' It was a continual struggle.

This apparently simple device was merely a couple of mirrors arranged to reflect light from a distant object to someone below ground level. Or rather, that was precisely what it was not. A periscope is a precision instrument that requires good optical glass for its mirrors, lenses and prisms, among many other considerations, if it is to be of any value.

Learning how to make prisms. There are twenty-three in the holder, bound in place with plaster of Paris for polishing. (The Illustrated War News)

Learning how to make lenses at the Northampton Institute. This worker is polishing twenty lenses. (The Illustrated War News)

This was a major problem. It was no good using just any old glass to make the optics. The optical quality had to be high to avoid distortions and chromatic effects as well as clouding – all such defects made the glass useless for meaningful observations. The manufacture of optical glass called for specialist skills, and the Germans were masters. Before the war, British optical instruments had relied almost exclusively on German glass because it was the best in the world. With the outbreak of war, the supply was suddenly cut off and the government was faced with a crisis. The need for high-quality optical glass grew enormously as the war progressed because it was needed for all optical gear related to artillery as well as telescopic sights for rifles, gunsights for aircraft, field glasses, periscopes, camera lenses for taking reconnaissance photographs and other specialist purposes.

At the start of the war, British glass was not nearly good enough. Moreover, the technical problems associated with suddenly having to manufacture the glass on a large scale had to be addressed. Experts from industry and university professors became involved in the search for a solution. In 1916, a committee made up of representatives from industry, the Ministry of Munitions, the services and learned societies, including the Royal Society, was given the task of researching optical glass and its manufacture. Although ameliorated by technical advances, the problems never entirely went away, however, and British glass was never as good as German glass. The difficulties in producing optical glass were a major cause of the delays in supplying good quality periscopes to the army in France.

There was more to a periscope than its optics. Although various early periscopes consisted of little more than mirrors without an enclosing box, it was very difficult to see anything meaningful with this sort of instrument. There was also the question of size. By about the middle of the war, the maximum length for an infantry periscope was set at 24 in, and it was considered essential that it should have a removable 12 in spike at the base so that it could be fixed into the side of the trench. Most early periscopes had to be held in both hands so wobbling was inevitable, which not only made them more conspicuous but also made observation difficult. Snipers were quick to shoot out the top mirror so there was also the danger of glass splinters falling into the eye of the observer. A canvas or leather carrying case with a sling was necessary. The outside of the instrument was required to be painted khaki, not because it was a military colour, but because it helped to make it less conspicuous. All the metal parts had to be dulled for the same reason.

The shortage of optical instruments for the trenches came to the attention of MPs. Alfred Tobin MP learned of it from an artillery officer on leave. He subsequently made an appeal in the Press for members of the public to send him any 'periscopic field-glasses' they might have. He would then forward these to the appropriate authorities for artillery observers so that they did not have to raise their heads above the parapet – many of them had become casualties while doing this. Bearing in mind that a periscope was not the sort of thing the average household possessed, it seems unlikely that he achieved much with his appeal. However, he no doubt received all manner of unsuitable devices from well-meaning people. In 1915, the problem was so acute that the government seriously considered exchanging rubber for German optical instruments, something that

The sort of simple box periscope that Alfred Tobin MP wanted the public to send in. This one contained mirrors and was made by Ross. It is too short to be of practical use in the trenches. (The Illustrated War News)

the German government was willing to go along with. The British government wisely changed its mind and it never happened. Instead, all British firms involved in making optical instruments were required to submit their entire stocks of instruments for evaluation. Those that passed were marked accordingly and compulsorily purchased. By the beginning of January 1917, this had produced only 583 periscopes, not exactly a resounding success. The shortage meant that there was a brisk trade in periscopes in department stores, opticians – from whom you could also buy armoured goggles – and gentlemen's outfitters, all selling equipment that had been rejected by the Ministry of Munitions. New businesses sprang up to make optical equipment, often based on the inventions of enterprising individuals. But none of this helped to solve the ever-present problem of where to obtain good optical glass.

The German Army was equipped with trench periscopes before the start of the war. It also had a massive mast periscope with eight telescopic tubes that could be extended by a winch to 82 ft and had to be steadied with guy ropes. The device, which weighed about a ton, could be hidden behind obstacles such as trees or buildings. It saw action during the advance on Ypres in 1914 but it did not have widespread use after the start of trench warfare as it was not exactly suited to the trenches. Something more handy was needed. The first British periscopes were improvised at the Front from pieces of mirror.

A German observer looking into the eyepiece of the 1-ton mast periscope, August 1914. (The Times History of the War)

The lower end of the mast periscope. The left-hand tube is part of the periscope, while the right-hand tube is the mast, which can extend to 82 ft. (Author)

The mast periscope extended at Crystal Palace, 1920. The ring at the top is the upper mirror holder. (IWM)

Sometimes shaving mirrors were used and sometimes the Royal Engineers devised simple mirror periscopes. Often these were no more than a single mirror set at an appropriate angle on a post and fixed to the trench. Frank Richards recalled the introduction of periscopes to the Royal Welch Fusiliers in February 1915. These were 'little mirrors stuck up on the back of the parapet' with which the daytime sentries watched the enemy positions while sitting on the fire step. These sorts of 'periscope' were very crude and of little practical value because the field of view was far too small. The sun also tended to glint off the glass and give the game away so that the observer would get a sniper's bullet, a rifle grenade or a mortar round or two for his trouble.

One of the first periscopes to be issued to the infantry was the No. 18. Strictly

The simplest 'periscope' was a single mirror with a shade. This one is attached to a stick stuck into the parados. (The Illustrated War News)

The No. 18 bayonet periscope in action. However, this is clearly a posed shot behind the lines – note the two men peering over the parapet. The helmets are covered with hessian and the observer's rifle has a Mk I breach cover. (IWM)

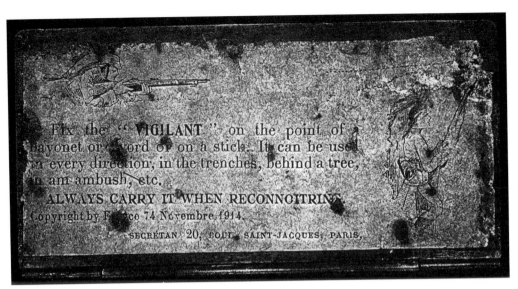

The box for the Vigilant complete with label, if a little worn.

speaking, this was not a periscope as it was no more than a mirror mounted on a metal frame with a clip that fitted over the blade of a bayonet. The mirror was only 3⅝ in × 1⅝ in, but the whole thing weighed a mere 3 oz, and it had a hinged cover to prevent sunlight glinting off the mirror. The idea was to hold the mirror above the parapet while sitting on the fire step with your back to the enemy. It must have caused many a cricked neck. A single-mirror model, intended to be attached to the rifle butt, tested by Capt Todhunter at the School of Musketry in June 1915, was turned down for this very reason.

The No. 18 appears to have been first issued in the summer of 1915 and was produced in considerable numbers. The Second Army Workshops, set up by Capt Henry Newton in spring 1915, turned out 200 a day, whereas it only made fifty box periscopes a day. The difference in scale was probably due to how easy the bayonet periscope was to make. Demand always exceeded supply. It was still being made and used in 1918. In the third week of March 1918, 2,343 were held in stock at the Hazebrouck Workshops of No. 2 Workshop Company. In 1917, the device was also manufactured in Britain by Selfridge & Co., the London department store.

Selfridge had probably been making the periscope from at least early 1916, if not before, when a G. Baker filed a patent application for essentially the same device (GB 101,826). A similar periscope, known as the Vigilant, was on sale in France from as early as November 1914. This was patented in France and made in Paris. The Vigilant differed only slightly from the British bayonet periscope: the Vigilant clip was open-ended whereas the British clip was closed. Clearly, the Vigilant and the No. 18 were one and the same. The Vigilant came in a small hinged box on the lid of which was a label that stated in English 'Fix the "Vigilant" on the point of a bayonet or sword or on a stick. It can be used in every direction, in the trenches, behind a tree, in an ambush, etc' and in capital letters underneath was added 'ALWAYS CARRY IT WHEN RECONNOITRING'. Such salesmanship suggested that if you used the Vigilant you could save yourself from harm, much as the advertisers of body armour implied with their slogans. The label also stated 'Copyright by France 74 Novembre 1914'. This appears to be a mistranslation. On the mirror cover was printed 'Secrétan Paris Breveté SGCC'. *Breveté* is the French for patented so the translation should read 'French patent 74'.

There were other British patents related to simple periscopes besides Baker's. R.J. Cracknell's device (GB 673/15, filed January 1915) used a single mirror. It was no more than a Y-shaped wire frame with a mirror positioned in a holder. The 'handle' of the Y could be inserted in the parados or a spike could be attached so that it could be pushed into the trench wall. Most simple periscopes, however, used two mirrors. The Ocentric rifle periscope, a commercial instrument, consisted of two mirrors fitted with clamps for attachment to a rifle, one near the muzzle, the other lower down near the

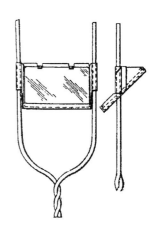

A simple trench 'periscope' invented by R.J. Cracknell in January 1915. The mirror holder slides on the frame.

magazine. The mirrors were about 7 in × 3 in and together weighed 11 oz. With the waterproof canvas case it cost 4s 6d. The idea was to raise the rifle above the parapet but the unshaded top mirror would have been so conspicuous that it is likely to have attracted a sniper almost immediately. The makers claimed that it was possible to use the rifle as normal with the mirrors attached but they must have been a hindrance. It was an unnecessary one at that, since there were other periscopes available that did not need to be attached to something else in order for them to be used effectively. According to an advertisement for the Ocentric, 'All military men are demanding a periscope which is no trouble to carry and yet of a size to be thoroughly practical for trench work and scouting.' Whether this device was 'thoroughly practical' is open to question. The makers evidently saw the device as a multi-purpose tool as they also suggested that it would be 'quite useful for heliograph signalling, or to fix to a chair or doorpost when shaving'. Charles Carrington tried using a periscope mirror as a heliograph to signal to a passing British aircraft when a barrage was getting a little too close for comfort. He did not succeed.

The Ocentric may have been invented by Arthur Adams. He applied for a patent in December 1914 and his specification, GB 24,743/14, describes a very similar device to the Ocentric. A collapsible, hinged rod supported the mirrors but, since the invention principally uses two independently mounted mirrors, the Ocentric comes within the scope of the patent. Thus, if Adams did not invent the Ocentric, its designers infringed his patent. Adams, who wrote his own provisional specification, stated that existing box periscopes, irrespective of whether they were collapsible or not, had 'a certain bulk and length . . . consequently they are not of a very portable nature'. In his complete specification, drafted by a patent agent in June 1915, lazy-tong periscopes were specifically excluded from his patent. Adams & Co., manufacturers of photographic equipment, produced many optical instruments for the army but not the one described in GB 24,743/14.

THE "OCENTRIC"
RIFLE PERISCOPE

All military and service men are demanding a periscope which is no trouble to carry and yet of a size to be thoroughly practical for trench work and scouting.

The "Ocentric" RIFLE PERISCOPE is made to meet such requirements, and is quite the <u>strongest</u>, yet <u>lightest</u> and <u>most compact</u> instrument now made.

Rifle Showing Mirrors Attached.

The whole apparatus is packed into a flat water proof canvas case $7\frac{1}{2}$ ins. long × $3\frac{1}{4}$ ins. broad and the total weight is only <u>11 ounces.</u> The case is provided with a loop at the back for fastening to belt.

No trouble.

No leaving it behind in a scramble.

Easy to fix and remove.

Rifle can be sighted and fired with periscope still attached.

Mirrors may be fitted as illustration, or bottom mirror fastened to "pistol grip" for observation over tall obstructions.

Can be fitted to any board or pole.

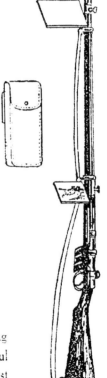

Should appeal to all military men, for mirrors being provided with clamps, would also be found quite useful for heliograph signalling, or to fix to a chair or doorpost when shaving.

PRICE IN CASE 4/6 COMPLETE.

An advertisement for the Ocentric rifle periscope, which appeared in The Sphere.

Many of the early commercial periscopes were indeed 'no trouble to carry' as they were collapsible. Some of them were quite ingenious but whether they were truly effective as optical instruments for observing the enemy is another matter. The problem with collapsible periscopes was mirror alignment. If one mirror was out of alignment with its partner, not only was the field of view distorted but the chances of random reflections from the sun were increased. To get the best from an instrument, the alignment of the optical components had to be fixed and steady. However, to a large extent, the optical deficiencies of any instrument used in the trenches were swamped by inexpert usage; to get the most from a periscope, the user had to be trained, and the more complex the instrument's optical system, the more important that training became.

During the course of the war as many as thirty periscope patents were granted, although not all of the instruments were collapsible. Most of the applications were filed in 1915. Typical of the collapsible instruments was the periscope invented by Edgar Duerr. Duerr applied for a patent in early January 1915 and filed another application in May. The periscope was based on the lazy-tong principal with a top and bottom mirror. The original device was marketed as the Lifeguard periscope and sold by F. Duerr & Sons

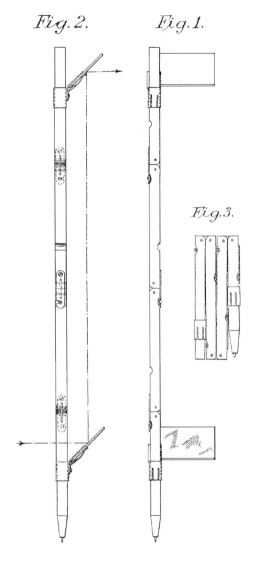

Fig. 2.   *Fig. 1.*

Fig. 3.

Drawings from Arthur Adams's folding periscope patent, GB 34,743/14. The mirrors are gripped in the holders by spring arms to enable them to be removed when the instrument is folded but it meant that alignment could never be precise.

of Manchester, better known for making jam than periscopes. The first application was published but no patent was granted because Duerr failed to pay the sealing fee, despite an advertisement in *The Sphere* in March which claimed that it was patented. 'Save a British Life – and weaken the Enemy' went the slogan. The Lifeguard extended to 2 ft and weighed 22 oz; closed, it was only 2 in deep. The mirrors, made from the 'best British thin plate glass', which was not saying much, measured 4⅜ in × 3½ in; the

Demonstration of a collapsible box periscope called the Ork-Oie (hawk eye!). Note how it folds flat in the picture second from left, bottom row. Compare this with William Youlten's patented collapsible box periscope. (The Illustrated War News)

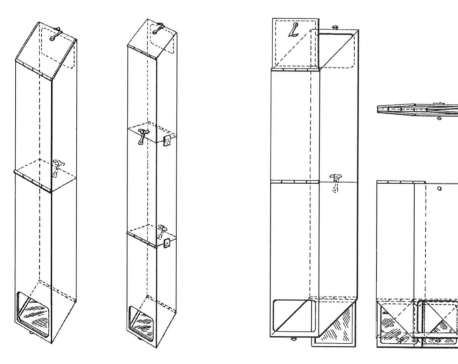

William Youlten's invention, a hinged and folding periscope that can be made flat, described in GB 110/15, shown here extended for use, the one on the right having three folding sections instead of two.

The two-section periscope folded flat. The top right-hand figure demonstrates just how thin the flattened instrument is, enabling it to fit into a pocket. Rigidity of the extended instrument might have been a problem after a lot of folding and unfolding.

silvering was 'protected by watertight aluminium cases'. The steel frame was coppered and nickel plated to make it rustproof. It cost 12s 6d, including a spare mirror, or 15s with the waterproof canvas carrying case.

Duerr's second application became GB 6,926/15. The difference between this and the first application was slight but significant. The first application described two parallel sets of tongs only joined at the ends by the mirror holders. This lacked rigidity when extended. GB 6,926/15 overcame this problem by inserting several U-shaped pieces to join the two tongs. In effect, there were no longer two separate tongs but a number of much shorter, paired tongs joined in series. By using this method of construction, the mirrors always remained aligned when the periscope was fully extended and the instrument was easier to hold. About a month before Duerr's first

A Scottish officer using Duerr's lazy-tong periscope in the Balkans, 1915. (The Illustrated War News)

application, David Sunderland, a consulting engineer, had filed an application for a periscope that worked on the same principal but was less robust and its bottom mirror holder was more complicated. It is likely that Duerr failed to pay the sealing fee because he knew that the patent would be invalid in light of Sunderland's application.

There was quite a variety of collapsible periscopes but none were adopted by the army. A. Cuthbert filed a patent application for one in February 1915 (GB 2,345/15). It was merely a hinged frame of metal rods with mirror holders. Although it had pieces to keep it rigid when open, it is doubtful whether the periscope would have been of much use. An even simpler periscope was invented by H.R. Taylor (GB 4,397/15) which was a telescopic arm made up of a number of flat casings that fitted inside each other, with a hinged mirror holder at the top and another at the bottom. To enable the user to see anything at all, it was necessary for the uppermost casing to have a square window in it. There was also the added refinement of hinged 'fixing legs' with which it could be fixed to the side of the trench. Since there was no means for fixing the mirror holders in the open position, the inventor having apparently relied merely on the stiffness of the hinges, mirror alignment would have been a serious problem.

Others were not much better. There was J.T. MacCallum's periscope which, again, was a simple metal frame with hinged mirrors. His patent specification was published as GB 5,239/15 but he failed to pay the sealing fee. Then there was the device invented by R.D. Batten which, like Sunderland's and Duerr's inventions, used the lazy-tong idea

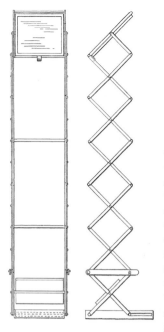

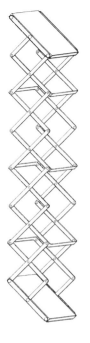

Sunderland's lazy-tong periscope, GB 24,284/14. Note the locking bar to keep it open, just above the lower mirror holder. Compare this with Duerr's Lifeguard periscope.

The drawing from Duerr's patent, GB 6,926/15, showing the U-shaped links to give it rigidity when opened up. It had no lock to keep it open, however.

(GB 5,633/15). The mirror holders were more complex yet the whole thing was less robust than the earlier devices and it lacked rigidity. All these devices had one thing in common: the optical pathway was not enclosed in a box. This did nothing for their usefulness as optical instruments. Some inventors tackled the problem of making a box periscope collapsible. F.E. Moody invented one using the ever-popular lazy-tong approach combined with bellows to enclose the optical pathway and the mirrors. Another approach was adopted by William Youlten, an architect from Hove in Sussex. Basically, the box collapsed much like a cardboard box can be made flat, then it was folded in half by means of hinges. This was the subject of GB 110/15, one of several patents granted to Youlten in respect of periscopes and other optical devices. Youlten, it seems, later formed a company called Periscopes & Hyposcopes to manufacture them.

It is hardly surprising that folding and collapsible models were popular and sold well: they could be conveniently packed away in a canvas case attached to the belt when not needed. All of the collapsible models were bought in department stores, opticians and gentlemen's outfitters. Shops like the Army & Navy even had a Weapon Department which sold everything from periscopes to trench knives, from personalized steel helmets to wire-cutters. A sales assistant tried to persuade Siegfried Sassoon to buy a prismatic periscope when he was on leave in London in June 1916. He declined because of the impending Somme offensive, reasoning that he would not need one as they were going to be advancing. A year earlier, Robert Graves had been sent a periscope by his mother who had bought 'a little rod-shaped metal one' with only a tiny top mirror 1 in square, which would have allowed him to see very little. A sniper shot it out at 400 yards.

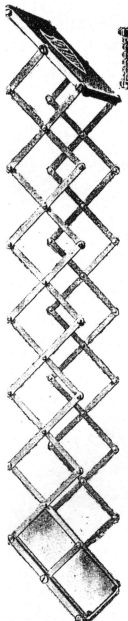

Periscope closed to 4½ ins. square by 2 ins., for the Pocket or Belt Case.

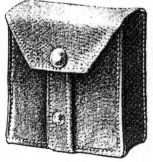

Packed in Khaki Case for Belt.

"Save a British Life
—and weaken the Enemy."

THE

"LIFEGUARD"

Patent Collapsible

Pocket Periscope

is a scientifically constructed instrument fulfilling every possible requirement and entirely superseding the cumbersome makeshifts hitherto offered.

Light, Strong, Compact, Invisible, and Efficient.

It weighs only 22 ozs., measures 4½ ins. square by 2 in. thick, and IN-STANTLY extends, with a single movement, to 2 ft., ready for use, without the slightest adjustment of any kind, raising the line of sight any desired elevation from 6 to 20 in., giving clear cover from rifle fire of 1 to 15 in.

Perfectly Rigid in any Position.

Exceedingly durable—the frame is made of tough steel, practically unbreakable, heavily coppered and dull nickel plated to render it rustproof. The mirrors are best British THIN PLATE glass (replaceable). 4⅛ in. by 3½ in., giving perfect reflection : the silvering protected by watertight Aluminium cases finished dull black.

Order now for yourself, or your friend at the front.

| Price, complete with spare mirror and polishing cloth, in cloth-covered leather-board box. Post free **12/6** | Price, complete with spare mirror and polishing cloth, in strong khaki collapsible waterproof case for belt, packed in box. Post free **15/-** |

Purchase price refunded without question if not approved on receipt.

F. DUERR & SONS

MANCHESTER, S.W.

ALSO FROM OPTICIANS, MILITARY OUTFITTERS, STORES, Etc.
For Trade Discount Apply on Trade Heading.

Periscope extended to 2 ft. ready for use.

Postage and packing free in the United Kingdom. Postage and packing 6d. extra to France, Belgium, Egypt, New Zealand, and Canada.

An advertisement that appeared in The Sphere *for Duerr's Lifeguard. The periscope illustrated is Duerr's first version of the device without the U-shaped links. Although claimed to be patented, it was not; his specification was published but he failed to pay the sealing fee so no patent was granted.*

A French box periscope with wide mirrors, 1915.
(The Illustrated War News)

The British Army was issued with a wide variety of periscopes during the course of the war but always had problems getting enough of the right sort. The War Office believed that the infantry were not bright enough to learn how to use anything but the most simple of instruments. This meant that they tended to be supplied with mirror periscopes rather than prismatic or magnifying periscopes which were, in any case, considerably more expensive. Magnifying periscopes were the preserve of artillerymen as far as the War Office was concerned; they needed fewer of them and were less likely to lose or damage them. The problem with magnifying periscopes was that they were provided with an eyepiece which only allowed the use of one eye for observation whereas mirror periscopes allowed the use of both eyes. Any instrument that allows the use of only one eye needs instruction in its use, whether it is a telescope, microscope or periscope. It is not just a simple matter of closing one eye and staring through the eyepiece with the other. The War Office's opinion on the matter did not stop requests from GHQ for magnifying periscopes for the infantry. For the most part, however, the infantry had to make do with non-magnifying mirror periscopes like the No. 18 and the No. 9, a box periscope issued at much the same time. It is difficult to be certain when any periscope was first issued but it would appear that the No. 9 was being supplied to the troops by the summer of 1915.

The No. 9 Mk I periscope was made of wood and had a rectangular cross-section. It was hinged in the middle with a catch to fasten the two halves together when it was extended. The distance between the centres of the mirrors was 22 in and the whole thing was 25.5 in tall; folded, it was only 14.5 in tall but still considerably larger than the collapsible periscopes. In its canvas case with two spare mirrors, it weighed 5 lb 10 oz. There was a glass screen with a movable metal shutter in front of the bottom mirror which protected the user's eyes from glass splinters if the upper mirror was hit by a sniper's bullet. Without such protection, the splinters were often deflected by the angled lower mirror into the user's face. It also had a 13 in foldable spike on the base that could be locked at an angle before being pushed into the trench wall – this meant the observer's hands could be free. Not only was steadiness important to get a meaningful view but it also reduced the chances of being spotted by the enemy.

The Mk I was made by Adams & Co. and R. & J. Beck. The Trenchscope Co. held a patent (GB 12,523/15) for the Mk II, the application for which was filed at the end of

The Lancashire Fusiliers at Messines using the No. 9 periscope fixed to the side of the trench with its spike, January 1917. (IWM)

A No. 9 camouflaged with a sandbag, early 1918, but note that the observer's bayonet is visible above the parapet. (The Illustrated War News)

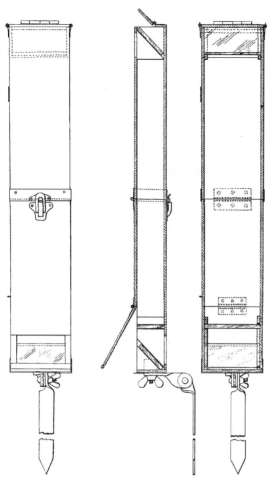

The No. 9 Mk II box periscope as patented by Soul and Howe. It has a door at the top to access the top mirror and a door at the bottom to access the lower mirror and glass screen above it.

The No. 9 Mk II folded. Although shorter, it is still bulky and not nearly as compact as the lazy-tong periscope.

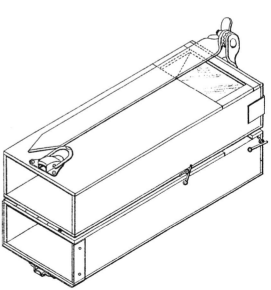

August 1915. Trenchscope was owned by Sydney Soul and Charles Howe, the inventors. The device described in their specification is essentially the same as the Mk I but with a number of differences, including a horizontal glass screen inside the periscope above the lower mirror to catch splinters instead of the shutter. However, because the specification also draws specific attention to a means of replacing the mirrors, a feature of the Mk I as well as the Mk II, the specification may in fact refer to both marks. There is another patent, GB 121,329 (application filed in December 1917), which describes a device that could be a variation on the No. 9. One feature of this was that the top mirror could be repositioned to enable the user to see behind him instead of in front, although quite what the advantage of this might have been is unclear. Externally it looked much the same at the No. 9.

An artillery observer at Salonika in early 1916, using a camouflaged magnifying periscope fitted with a wooden handle, possibly the No. 14. (The Illustrated War News)

The No. 14 was issued at the same time as the Nos 9 and 18 but, unlike these, it was intended for use by artillery observers to locate targets and note the fall of shot. The No. 14 was a magnifying prismatic instrument with a magnification of ×10 (achieved with two or more lenses) and a 4° field of view. It was fitted with graticules (cross-hairs) to aid the location of targets. It was made by Ross Ltd who, like Adams and Beck, manufactured many different optical instruments including various periscopes, under government contracts. The periscope was 17.5 in tall and in its leather case weighed 5 lb 8 oz. It had a ball-and-socket joint with a 'screw coupling . . . for screwing rapidly into wood' so that it could be fixed to 'any convenient baulk of wood or tree trunk, and clamped in position'. There was also a wooden handle to which it could be attached if 'no such convenience is available'.

In the early part of 1916, GHQ requested 4,500 No. 14 periscopes but there were supply difficulties. Only 3,886 periscopes had been delivered by September and, of these, 1,371 were approved substitutes and 575 were other models of variable-power periscopes, leaving only 1,940 No. 14s. Such problems were almost exclusively due to the inadequate supply of acceptable optical glass. By the summer of 1917, GHQ was convinced of the wisdom of issuing magnifying periscopes to the infantry since these allowed the observer to see much further and more clearly than was possible with ordinary mirror periscopes. It asked London to approve the supply of No. 25 and No. 26 magnifying periscopes on a scale of one for each infantry battalion and each field company and field squadron of Royal Engineers, in addition to those already authorized for the artillery. The No. 25 and

Left to right: *Duerr's Lifeguard periscope with U-shaped links and its carrying case; a private purchase three-draw magnifying periscope (×5.5) with belt hook and metal covers to protect the mirrors; the No. 9 box periscope made by Adams; the No. 25 with extension bar, wooden handle and eyepiece.* (Author)

the No. 26, along with the No. 24 and the No. 27, were 'temporary substitutes for the No. 14'. They were more difficult to make and consequently more expensive than simple periscopes and London advised GHQ that it was not possible to comply with the request. Moreover, these periscopes embodied features designed to meet artillery requirements, not those of the infantry.

London suggested that GHQ might use a magnifying periscope supplied from a Paris manufacturer, designated the No. 1 (it is not clear why it should have been designated the No. 1 this late in the war). GHQ did not have much faith in the French periscope and considered it a poor substitute for the No. 25 and No. 26, although it was, in fact, a perfectly good instrument. But, at a pinch, GHQ was prepared to accept it, or something similar from the same source, for infantry use provided some modifications were carried out first so that it complied with the standard requirements for all infantry periscopes.

An order for 500 No. 1 periscopes had been placed in March 1917 so that the instrument could undergo troop trials. The periscope had a magnification of ×3.2 and a field of view of 8°. The distance between the centres of the two mirrors was 34 in but the instrument was only 24 in long when closed up. It weighed 2 lb 6.25 oz. For infantry use, a periscope had to be more serviceable than the No. 9 and No. 18 instruments which were used as yardsticks. Evidently, the French model was not considered by GHQ to be as good as either of them. The reasoning seems to have been that it required more skilful handling by the observer than either the No. 9 or the No. 18 to get the best out of it. This seems an odd judgement to make considering that GHQ was keen to get magnifying periscopes for the infantry and must have been fully aware that magnifying periscopes required training in their use. The French instruments were considered too complicated for ordinary infantry use and were deemed only suitable for trained observers in 'special circumstances'. GHQ knew that the supply of periscopes was problematical and was being, perhaps, unnecessarily choosy. The War Office also found it hard to accept that the infantry were quite capable of learning how to use a magnifying periscope. More importantly, perhaps, the artillery had a greater need for magnifying instruments which

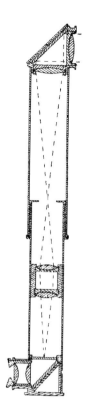

This magnifying periscope was patented (GB 3,439/15) by William Peck, astronomer at the City Observatory, Edinburgh. The mirrors are contained in hermetically sealed chambers to prevent the ingress of moisture and it was designed to have a 'brilliantly illuminated field of view'.

Another magnifying periscope with two powers of magnification invented by Sir H. Grubb and C. Beck in 1914 and patented (GB 22,319/14). It uses prisms as reflectors.

could not be satisfied with simple mirror periscopes and for this reason the artillery always had priority.

There were three variants on the No. 14 Mk I. Because of problems supplying enough of them, two additional manufactures, R. & J. Beck and Watson & Sons, were contracted to produce the periscope. There were slight variations in the instrument depending on who the manufacturer was but these were all concerned with dimensions rather than magnifying power or field of view. Whereas the original Ross model was 17.5 in tall, the Beck was 3 in taller while the Watson was nearly 10 in taller. Both were correspondingly heavier at 8 lb and 8.5 lb. The Watson model was also slightly narrower by 0.5 in all round. There seems to have been no sound reason why they should not have been identical. The likely reason is that imprecise information was supplied to the manufacturers.

Some time later, three new variations on the No. 14 appeared, these being described as the Mk II and designated A, B or C according to who the manufacturer was (Ross, Beck and Watson, respectively). The three Mk Is were now also designated A, B and C on the same basis. The differences between the Mk I and the Mk II were not great. The upper prism mounting of the Mk II was an improved version of that in the Mk I and the upper prism of the Mk II was provided with a shade which was 'attached to the upper prism case by springs covered with leather which hold the rayshade closely round the body of the periscope when not in use'. In addition, the upper prism had a leather cap to protect it when the instrument was not in use.

The Nos 24, 25, 26 and 27, the temporary substitutes for the No. 14, were all different from the No. 14 as well as from each other, their only commonality being their use of prisms. The No. 24 had a magnification of ×7 and a field of view of 6°, the No. 25 a magnification of about ×5.5 and a field of view of about 6.5°, and the No. 27 a magnification of ×10 and a field of view of about 3°; the No. 26 did not magnify. All were intended for the artillery, not the infantry. The No. 24 had an 11 in trench spike like the No. 9 and was 19 in tall, weighing 2.5 lb. The No. 25 was quite different. It was tubular and thin; its height could be varied from 15.5 in to 21.5 in because the upper part of the periscope was a narrow extension bar on the top of which was the small upper prism. This presented a very tiny target and yet the field of view was good. A wooden handle screwed into the base of the periscope. The periscope was fitted with graticules and, an added refinement, clips on the upper prism holder to enable tufts of grass or similar camouflage to be attached. Beck was one of the manufacturers.

The No. 26 was made up of 'a square tapered tube in two pieces' and the 'small end of the upper tube fits into the lower tube'. There was a mirror at the top of the upper tube and a prism in the lower tube, the distance between them being 18 in. A monocular eyepiece was positioned in front of the prism. Different monoculars of differing powers could be used. Like the No. 24, the instrument had a trench spike and to camouflage the top of the periscope a canvas hood was provided. Altogether, the periscope, monocular and their carrying cases weighed about 5 lb. The eyepiece was about 5 in long while the periscope was about 20 in tall. Of the four substitutes, the No. 27 appears to have been the most like the No. 14, complete with wooden handle and means for fixing it to the parapet, but it was not fitted with graticules.

Although the No. 9 was regarded as the ideal infantry periscope, while the No. 18 was viewed as an acceptable alternative, these was not the only instruments to be manufactured and issued specifically for infantry use. There were at least three others: Nos 22 Mk I, 22 Mk II and 30. None of these were magnifying periscopes and all were fitted with mirrors rather than prisms. Without doubt, prismatic instruments were superior to mirror periscopes. The disadvantages of mirrors is that they do not reflect all the light that falls on them; some light rays are internally reflected between the two faces of the glass. The more mirrors that are used in an optical pathway, the more light that is lost. For this reason, no periscope was ever fitted with more than two mirrors. Prisms, on the other hand, take advantage of this phenomenon to produce total internal reflection. In the simplest form, this means that light rays hitting the vertical face of the prism pass through it to hit the inclined face at the back where they are all totally reflected inside the glass to pass through the horizontal face below without loss, providing the prism is made of good optical glass and has no defects. The precision of the prism's dimensions as well as its mounting in an instrument were equally important to ensure that the light was reflected parallel to the sides of the box or tube enclosing the optical pathway. This, of course, made prismatic periscopes more expensive to make.

Expense and complexity were increased when magnifying lenses and graticules became part of the optics. The number of lenses could be anything from two to more than six and these had to be precisely made and precisely mounted. The graticules, which were also made from optical glass, had to be no less precisely made and mounted. Consequently, although mirror periscopes were inferior to prismatic magnifying periscopes, their relative cheapness meant that the infantry were supplied with these rather than any other sort. They could be produced more quickly, more cheaply and in larger numbers. Moreover, they required minimal training.

Some of the prismatic magnifying periscopes made by Beck and similar firms were patented. Whether these became service instruments is difficult to ascertain without examining the optics of the service instruments and comparing them to the descriptions and drawings in the specifications. GB 22,319/14 granted to Sir H. Grubb and C. Beck resembles, for example, the No. 27, but so does GB 20,215/14 granted to C. Beck and H.C. Beck; the optics of these two patented devices are not the same, however. On the other hand, GB 115,925 granted to C. Beck and H.C. Beck (application filed in June 1917) may well describe the

In the centre is a British periscope with a spike for fixing to the trench and loops round the top mirror for fixing camouflage to it. On the left is a No. 30, made by Adams & Co. in 1917. The label tells the observer to look through the small aperture in the shutter at the bottom to avoid falling glass if the top mirror is hit by a bullet. (Author)

No. 25. An interesting feature of the invention was that the narrow arm or extension bar on which the prism was mounted was intended to be the weakest part of the instrument, in terms of physical strength, so that if it was hit by a bullet it would snap off. An alternative to the externally clipped extension bar was a narrow, hollow tube that fitted inside the main body of the instrument. This tube was described as intentionally narrow 'so as to provide a fragile connection'. No doubt it was easier and cheaper to make an extension bar than a tube.

The No. 22 periscope had 'a harp-shaped wood body with a mirror mounted at each end', the distance between the centres of the mirrors being 17 in. The Mk II had a metal shutter in front of the lower mirror to protect the user's eyes if the top mirror was shot out by a sniper. The shutter had two holes covered by glass to look through. The shutter

An Australian officer at Messines in 1917, using the periscope illustrated on the previous page. (The Illustrated War News)

could also be raised to allow the observer to use binoculars. Both mirrors could be replaced if necessary, a hinged door at the bottom allowing access to the lower mirror. The top part of the periscope was covered with canvas 'made to look like a sandbag'. A wooden case containing a spare upper mirror was clipped to the back of the periscope. The Mk II was 25 in tall, 16 in wide at the top but only 8 in wide at the bottom. At 11 lb, the No. 22 was much heavier than other periscopes, doubtless because of the extra wood and the wide mirror at the top. Apart from the lack of a shutter in the Mk I, the earlier model used thinner mirrors (⅛ in thick opposed to ¼ in), was 2 in shorter and lacked the case for a spare mirror.

Unlike all the other periscopes, the No. 30 was adapted from a machine-gun hyposcope, the periscope part of a device for firing a machine-gun from below the parapet. It was a metal tube with short right-angled pieces on the ends, rather like pipe joints which, in effect, turned the tube through 90° at the top and at the bottom. Opposite each was a mirror set at 45°, the mirrors being 16 in apart. In front of each aperture was a metal disc, the lower one having a glass screen, the discs protecting the mirrors, while the screen with the lower disc protected the user's eyes from glass splinters. A label was stuck on the front to remind the user to look through the small aperture in the lower disc. This was another instrument made by Adams. Like most infantry periscopes, the No. 30 was provided with a trench spike. It was 20 in tall, weighed about 4.25 lb and came in a canvas case for carrying it about.

An apparently similar device was tested in late 1915 both by the Royal Engineers at Chatham and the School of Musketry at Hythe. This was a periscope fitted with a prismatic compass for surveying, the invention of H.E.B. Daniell. Daniell filed a patent application for his device (GB 16,483/15) in late November 1915; the Chatham and Hythe tests had been carried out some weeks earlier. The periscope described in GB 16,483/15 was made up of two tubes rather than one and the mirrors were oval (the ends of the pipe joints on the No. 30 are oval, where the mirrors are fixed in place). The reason for having two tubes, with the top one fitting over the lower one, was to enable the periscope to be lengthened or shortened according to circumstances. A clamping ring secured the two tubes at the desired length. A small platform, on which was mounted the compass, was attached to the lower aperture and this was mounted on a support to enable the device to be set up in a trench. Spirit levels were provided to ensure that the accurate bearings could be taken.

Capt Todhunter believed that the device was 'perfectly satisfactory' and likely to meet a need. The total errors likely to arise from all causes would not exceed 1°, a displacement of only 5 ft in 100 yd, which was not a serious error in a mine tunnel. Obviously, the device was meant to be used above ground to ensure that the tunnel ended under the position the mine was intended to destroy. It is quite clear that the device was intended for such a purpose rather than infantry use. Todhunter suggested that better mirrors ought to be used and that the periscope ought to be slightly larger. It would appear that a version of this invention became the No. 31 periscope, which was similar to the No. 30. Although the No. 31 did not include a prismatic compass it did use 'azimuth and angle of sight scale plates, graduated in degrees so that by estimation angles can be read off to the nearest quarter of a degree'. The instrument could be traversed through 80° and elevated or depressed by 10°. And like the Daniell device, it was provided with a spirit level to enable it to be set up properly. In its wooden box, the whole thing weighed 15.5 lb.

Although the periscope described and illustrated in Daniell's specification bears a strong resemblance to the No. 30, his device was clearly not a machine-gun hyposcope. The inclusion of a description of the periscope in Daniell's specification suggests that the instrument illustrated was invented by him. However, the periscope described was a variation on something that already existed, probably the No. 30. There is another specification, GB 4,900/15, which describes a sniperscope, and the No. 30 or its predecessor is shown in the drawings. The inventor, Herbert Cahusac, filed his application at the Patent Office in April 1915. But he did not invent the periscope. The most likely inventor of the machine-gun hyposcope from which the No. 30 was derived was William Youlten. A 'Tubular hyposcope for machine guns' was tested at the School of Musketry in January 1915. In his report on this device and two others submitted by Youlten, Todhunter suggested that 'it might possibly be developed as a more complete form of periscope'. This is the best candidate for what became the No. 30.

There were many other service periscopes, the majority of which seem to have been prismatic devices, including the No. 5 which appears to have been through a number of modifications as there was a Mk VIII. There were many commercial devices, the majority of which were mirror periscopes. Maj Crum, who ran a sniper school in France, noted that the periscope was essential to the sniping team of shooter and observer. In particular, he emphasized the importance of the magnifying periscope and made the point that prisms were superior to mirrors. He recommended several commercial devices, including one called the Piccolo, made by Graham and Latham, and another called the Una, a prismatic device made by Sinclair. He also suggested that a metal tubular periscope made by Ross was good; this may have been the No. 30. According to Crum, the box periscope and the Vigilant bayonet periscope were unsuitable for sniper teams and better suited to sentries.

Both the 2 in toffee-apple mortar and the 3 in Stokes were equipped with periscopes to enable the crews to lay their weapons without exposing themselves to enemy fire. The

No. 4 Mk I and Mk II were designed for the 2 in mortar. These were tubular brass instruments with three lenses in the Mk I, four in the Mk II, and a prism that had a magnification of ×1.5 and 20° field of view. The Mk I was much shorter than the Mk II, which was made up of three tubes, 17 in as opposed to 42.25 in. They were fitted with a brass diaphragm just above the lower lens. This had a pointer to help locate the position of targets. The mortar had a post on its side for attaching the periscope. The post was later modified to include two steel pins for the Mk I to ensure that it was more securely fixed to the mortar. The Mk II periscope was subsequently withdrawn from service.

The 2 in toffee-apple mortar fitted with the No. 4 Mk II periscope. (The Illustrated War News)

A persistent problem with all enclosed periscopes was the ingress of moisture which condensed on the optics and was very difficult to remove. No matter how airtight the seals might be, moisture had a way of getting in. Condensation rendered a periscope useless. This was the reason their cases were always made of waterproof material. But the conditions of the trenches were such that it was inevitable that moisture would find its way into devices that were in regular use. Mirror periscopes suffered less from this problem than magnifying periscopes because the mirrors tended to be exposed but the lenses of magnifying instruments were usually enclosed in airtight sections. However, no seal was 100 per cent effective. The No. 33 magnifying prismatic periscope seems to have been the only one adapted to cope with this problem. It had 'a stopcock which can be connected to a desiccating apparatus by means of which dry air can be passed slowly through the periscope to remove any moisture which may have condensed on the prism and lenses'. This, of course, could not be done in the line and had to be carried out in a Royal Engineers workshop. However, it was acknowledged that this might not be enough to deal effectively with the problem and in the event that the instrument became unusable 'all the optical parts must be returned to Woolwich for refitting to new periscopes'. This was also an acknowledgement of the scarcity of good optical glass. Woolwich had the final word on periscopes, deciding what was fit for service in France and what was only suitable for commercial sale, which only meant that the instruments found their way to France by a different route.

Periscopes were never quite as simple as a couple of pieces of mirror although, as far as the infantry was concerned, that was about the level of sophistication of the instruments supplied to them. Nevertheless, they did remarkably well in the circumstances. Without periscopes the infantry and the artillery would have been severely hindered. Unglamorous though the periscope was, it was an essential item of equipment for fighting in the trenches. It saved lives and helped to dominate the enemy parapet.

CHAPTER 6

Shooting with Heath Robinson – Sniperscopes

It was all very well using a periscope to observe the enemy and his wire from below the parapet but there was still the problem of how to shoot at him without getting a sniper's bullet in the head. The fixed trench shield went some way to solving the problem but there were times when it was not the answer. To be effective, the shield had to be fixed in place and camouflaged, and some sort of light excluder placed behind the loophole so that it did not immediately show up like a beacon when the shutter was opened. It could not be moved to a more convenient location if a potential target was not visible from the loophole. Moreover, it was principally a tool of the sniper.

The answer was the sniperscope, a device that enabled a rifle to be fired from below the parapet; but it was not quite as simple as it sounds. Despite its name, this was not a device that was restricted to snipers. And, despite its name, rifles fixed to sniperscopes were never fitted with telescopic sights, the essential tool of the sniper. Nor was it restricted to being fitted to rifles; it was also fitted to machine-guns. The sniperscope was known by a variety of other names, including periscope rifle and machine-gun hyposcope, partly because, as a new device, there was no recognized term for it.

A Belgian sniperscope with auxiliary trigger, 1915. Although this appears to be a simple, robust device, it does not allow the shooter much cover. (The Times History of the War)

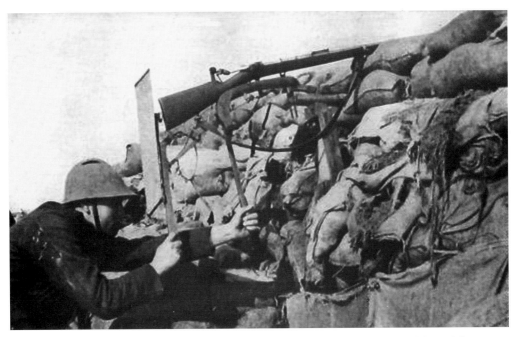

A rather odd-looking Belgian sniperscope, 1916. Note the Belgian helmet. (The World War 1 Document Archive)

Sometimes the terms were applied to just the periscope part and sometimes to the complete device with or without the gun attached. The terms were always loosely applied. Although invented before the war and occasionally used again in the Second World War (for example, the Germans used, if only rarely, an MG 42 fitted with a mirror periscope, and auxiliary trigger and butt), this was a weapon peculiar to the First World War. This was Heath Robinson inventiveness in response to the demands of the trenches, which is not to imply that they were hare-brained, impractical contraptions. They worked. But some complex and bizarre mechanisms were proposed.

It is not certain which side was first to use the sniperscope although it is clear that they were in use in the last few months of 1914. The Belgians, the French, the British, the Australians, the Canadians and the Germans all used them on the Western Front. The British, the Australians and the Turks used them in the Dardanelles. Neither is it clear just how effective they were. No doubt they were a nuisance to the enemy but whether they ever constituted a serious threat, like the telescopic-sighted rifle in the hands of a trained sniper, is open to question. The sniperscope could not be used to shoot at the longer ranges simply because it was too difficult to see a target clearly enough with a mirror periscope at more than about 100 yd, especially when it was in view for only a moment, although the Germans could shoot effectively from 400+ yd with a sniperscope. There were problems with accuracy because the periscope and the rifle could not be precisely aligned. Without the benefit of a zeroed-in telescopic sight, a sniperscope could never be as effective as the sniper's usual tool which was a precision instrument. The sniperscope was not.

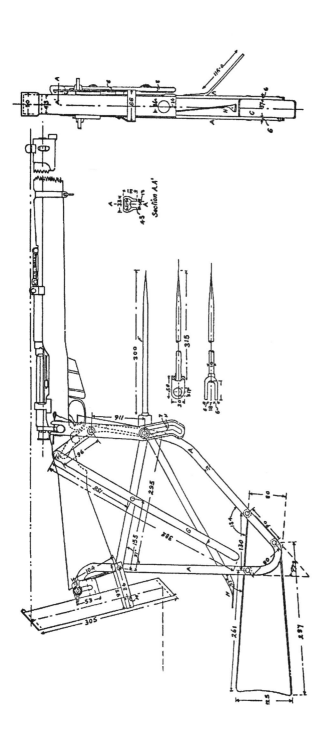

GENERAL ARRANGT OF A SNIPERSCOPE RIFLE | DRG Nº 198.

E. IN C. DRAWING Nº 5262/6.
Drawn by T. Bazley, Sap. R.E. in E. IN C? office.

Iᵀ PRINTING COY, R.E. G.H.Q. (2,616-5.)

IIⁿᵈ **ARMY WORKSHOPS**

A Second Army Workshops design of sniperscope, complete with bolt-operating mechanism, auxiliary trigger and spike for fixing it to the trench wall. It is all steel apart from the butt, essentially a U-shaped frame with simple lever mechanisms. Compare this with the complex devices proposed by civilian inventors. (Newton)

There were practical problems with operating the trigger, coping with recoil and operating the bolt to reload the rifle because the butt could no longer be shouldered and the trigger and bolt mechanism could not be reached easily. But whatever the difficulties, sniperscopes were used in large numbers throughout the period of trench warfare. A lot of research was devoted to developing them, both in France and in Britain, but no sniperscope turned out to be entirely satisfactory. In France, the Royal Engineers made sniperscopes to a number of designs of their own and more of these were used than any other. In 1915, the Royal Engineers Workshops at Béthune, known as the Bomb Factory because its original function was to manufacture grenades, was making sniperscopes 'in considerable numbers'. At the same time, the Second Army Workshops, set up and commanded by Capt Henry Newton, turned out forty sniperscopes a day, which amounted to more than 1,000 a month, and demand outstripped supply. Despite the shortcomings of the sniperscope, it was always regarded as a fundamental tool of trench warfare.

The Second Army Workshops pattern sniperscope, designed by Newton, was simple yet quite sophisticated, certainly a lot more straightforward than many of the devices proposed by civilians. It included trigger and bolt-operating mechanisms – basically levers – and, uniquely, a long spike for fixing the device to the side of the trench, presumably to help the absorption of recoil and to steady the device. Apart from the auxiliary butt, it was an all-metal construction, a slightly distorted U-shaped jig that could be quickly clamped to a rifle or removed. Newton had an engineering background, albeit electrical rather than mechanical, but devising a jig would have been a simple matter. The design had all the hallmarks of engineering experience, which is more than can be said for many sniperscopes.

One of the Royal Engineer designs was one of the simplest of all the sniperscopes and was among the first to see service on the Western Front. It was probably devised at the Experimental Section set up in October 1914 at St Omer under the command of Lt E.S.R. Adams. In 1916, he was posted to the Design Department in the Ministry of Munitions to represent the views of GHQ on the production of trench warfare devices. Although there were a number of local variations of the sniperscope, the device was basically a wooden rifle holder made from two parallel slats connected to an auxiliary stock beneath it via two side-by-side X-shaped pieces, the backward sloping arms of which held the butt. The rifle was strapped between the slats. A simple mirror periscope was fitted at the back and the whole thing was bolted together. The most complicated part was the auxiliary stock, which was shaped like the SMLE's, and this could be shouldered to fire the rifle. A Bowden wire was connected from a trigger on the auxiliary stock to the rifle's trigger so that the weapon could be fired but there was no means to operate the bolt so the device had to be lowered again in order to reload. The idea of using a Bowden wire on sniperscopes appears to have originated with a Maj R.A. Campbell, an idea tested successfully by Capt Todhunter at Hythe in late 1914. Before then, rifle pull-throughs were sometimes used for the same purpose.

An even simpler version used in the Dardanelles consisted of an inverted A-frame, a simple mirror periscope forming the rear, upright leg of the A against which the butt was held. The other leg, which formed the apex of the A where it joined the base of the

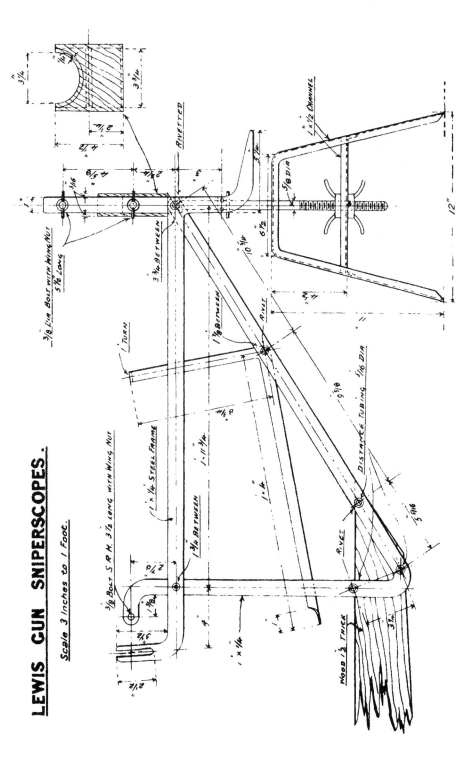

The engineering drawing for a Lewis gun sniperscope designed and made by Royal Engineers. It is similar to the rifle sniperscope made by the Second Army Workshops, including the wooden butt and the auxiliary trigger: the two are clearly related. (Institution of Royal Engineers)

A British sniperscope designed and made by Royal Engineers, 1915. This simple device was made in large numbers throughout the war. Although it has an auxiliary trigger, there is no bolt-operating mechanism. (The Times History of the War)

An even simpler Royal Engineers sniperscope used in the Dardanelles. The periscope forms the back of the device. The trigger is pulled by a wire. The man behind the shooter is observing with a locally made periscope. (The Times History of the War)

periscope about 12 in below the butt, was connected to the rifle stock just behind the trigger. The strut of the A crossed the rear of the butt, one end of which was screwed to the forward leg with the other end screwed to the top of the periscope. The periscope was no more than two pieces of mirror slotted into the upright leg. There was no auxiliary stock or trigger, simply a Bowden wire connected to the rifle's trigger. Recoil must have been a problem as there was nothing to absorb it. When Ion Idreiss, an Australian in the Dardanelles in 1915, described the sniperscope as 'an invention of ingenious simplicity' he was, no doubt, referring to this device. Nevertheless, it was a clumsy instrument to handle, as were many sniperscopes.

By mid-1917, GHQ was fully aware of the sniperscope's limitations and concluded that 'Sniping at individuals is more satisfactorily carried out by means of a telescopic rifle in the hands of a sniper.' It also felt that 'use of the periscope rifle would tend to discourage men from firing over open sights'. Curiously, these conclusions related to its use in open warfare, not trench warfare, where it was obviously redundant. These conclusions were a response to an enquiry from the War Office about the sort of sniperscopes GHQ wanted. The matter of open warfare was evidently raised by London.

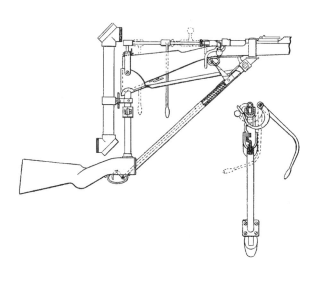

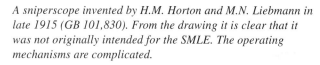

A sniperscope invented by H.M. Horton and M.N. Liebmann in late 1915 (GB 101,830). From the drawing it is clear that it was not originally intended for the SMLE. The operating mechanisms are complicated.

One of the most pointless inventions of the war. This was not the only patented device for firing a pistol from cover, a totally futile pursuit. Drawing from GB 102,410 which dates from February 1916.

Nevertheless, the conclusion that sniping was best conducted by snipers with telescopic sights applied equally well to the trenches. It is clear, however, that GHQ was anxious to make the best use of the instrument where circumstances allowed and was at pains to emphasize this. It drew up recommendations for two types, one suitable for open warfare and one for use in the trenches.

(2) In certain circumstances, however, a pattern of rifle periscope specially designed for portability, and capable of being quickly attached to the Service rifle without alterations, would be of value. For this periscope the auxiliary trigger mechanism and bolt action could be dispensed with in favour of increased simplicity and portability.

(3) For use in fixed positions existing patterns of periscope rifle have not proved entirely satisfactory, and samples of improved patterns are required for practical trial in the trenches.

As far as is known, nothing came of the suggestion in paragraph (2), although various sniperscopes of that type were tested but not because they were considered as potentially suitable for open warfare.

Many of the 'existing patterns' were inventions submitted to the War Office or the Ministry of Munitions by members of the public, some of which had been under evaluation since late 1914. Many of these were tested under the supervision of Capt

Todhunter at the School of Musketry and those that had performed well had managed to be supplied in limited numbers to GHQ for troop trials. Not all the devices were jigs with optical components. Some were periscopic devices without any sort of jig. William Youlten was one of the most prolific inventors of this type of optical apparatus for machine-guns and rifles. His periscopic sighting inventions went back to 1900. Between 1900 and 1904 he was granted five patents for such devices. Curiously, he appears to have made no further applications until 1914 and the outbreak of war. Although he described himself in the later patent specifications as an architect, he was clearly no mere amateur when it came to optics. Despite Youlten's early patents in the field (indeed, his seem to be the only ones until after the outbreak of war), it would appear that none of them was considered by the army

One of William Youlten's machine-gun hyposcopes fitted to a Vickers in the Dardanelles, late 1915. It has two mirrors; the lower mirror is just above the crook of the shooter's right arm. The gun's trigger is operated by an auxiliary depressed with the thumb. (The Illustrated War News)

until late 1914. In January 1915, Youlten visited Todhunter at the School of Musketry 'to explain the use of his hyposcopes. He brought with him 3 patterns.'

The three patterns consisted of a tubular hyposcope for a machine-gun (the device from which the No. 30 periscope was developed), another device that Todhunter called an ordnance hyposcope, and a rifle hyposcope described as 'prismatic 1904'. This last one was patented by Youlten in 1904 (GB 15,531/04); ten years later he improved on it and filed another application in October 1914 that was subsequently granted as GB 20,439/14. It comprised a single prism with six faces, the two side faces being trapezoidal. It was mounted in a casing with hinged covers for the faces through which the light entered and exited. The casing could be moved on a bar that was fixed to the side of the rifle so that the prism was directly behind the rifle sights. Todhunter thought that this device was worth sending to France for troop trials as 'it might enable men in a trench to take accurate shots at snipers without exposing themselves to rifle fire'. Youlten then proceeded to simplify the optics by proposing a triangular prism or even mirrors, no doubt because he discovered that prisms were in short supply, and improved on the clamp for attaching it to a rifle. The clamp was no more than an open metal band that went round the rifle butt with a wing nut to tighten

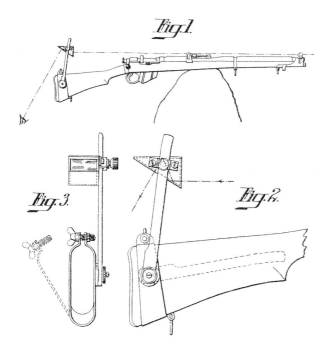

William Youlten's rifle hyposcope described in GB 24,687/14. It uses a single prism and is simple to attach to the rifle but devices like these make it awkward to fire the rifle.

it. The upright bar was attached to the band with a nut that could be loosened to allow the bar to lie flush along the butt when the periscope was not in use, the prism mount having been removed first.

Youlten applied for a patent for this in December 1914 (GB 24,687/14). In his specification, he described various other similar devices that already existed. These included 'a hyposcope comprising mirrors or prisms mounted in tubes', one of which had a hook that fitted 'into a groove in a hinged clip' that was fitted to the butt by a method different from Youlten's. There was also 'a hyposcope comprising a horizontal tube having a mirror or prism at one end coming behind the sights and one or more mirrors or prisms at the other end coming on one side of the rifle and in front of the marksman's eye'. The first device may well have been the one invented by someone called Kingsford, while the second appears to be a device known as the Percival, although Youlten may have been referring to a device invented by Thomas Willson, a Canadian, but patented in Britain by Edward Marks. The Kingsford and the Percival were both tested by Todhunter who generally favoured Youlten's devices over almost everyone else's. Youlten and Todhunter seem to have had a close professional relationship.

Youlten's improved prism device was tested at the School of Musketry in early June 1915. Todhunter found that it was possible to shoot accurately with it and he approved of its simplicity. Its major drawback was that 'the firer is in a constrained position and it would be necessary to supply a trigger release such as Major Campbell's . . . to avoid the hands being exposed.' This was a serious problem with many jig-less devices and one of the main reasons why none of them found much favour at the Front. Todhunter also noted that although it was the most portable of the devices he had tested, a shortage of prisms was likely to be the biggest obstacle to sending examples to France for trials, so he proposed to continue testing the inferior mirror devices.

Of the other two Youlten devices tested in January 1915, the ordnance hyposcope had been tested at Hythe before. This may have been the device described in GB 4,334/15, a variation on the hyposcope in GB 24,687/14, which allowed it to be clamped to one of the handles of a Vickers or Maxim machine-gun. However, it is more likely to have been the device described in GB 480/15 which also concerned a prismatic hyposcope and its method of attachment to a machine-gun. This was more complex than either GB 24,687/14 or GB 4,334/15 as it used a trapezoidal prism and a more complicated mounting that fitted on to the tangent sight. Todhunter believed that a hyposcope of this sort might be useful on a machine-gun because of the reduced ranges that had come about as a result of trench warfare. It had the advantage of requiring no modification to the gun and was small and light but he added that 'the best test for it would be actual use in the field'.

The third pattern, the tubular hyposcope, 'is a heavier and more elaborate affair . . . probably too cumbrous for use with machine guns on modern mountings'. Nevertheless, Todhunter recommended that numbers of both should be sent out to France for trials. The machine-gun hyposcope had the potential to be more useful than the sniperscope because machine-guns did not need the accuracy required of a sniper rifle in order to do damage, and neither was recoil a problem. Youlten's machine-gun hyposcopes were tried in France and by mid-1916 a machine-gun hyposcope with a firing lever extension, which meant that the operator did not have to reach up to the trigger, had been adopted – but it was not one of Youlten's devices. His machine-gun hyposcope, along with many of his other inventions, could be bought in department stores, however, and it is likely that some of them found their way to the Front by this route.

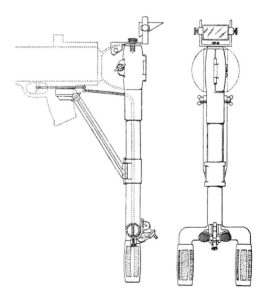

Youlten's later inventions included a hyperscope for the Lewis gun, based on the triangular prism of his earlier rifle hyposcope. This device was not meant to be fitted to the standard infantry Lewis gun, which had a wooden butt stock, but to the Lewis that usually equipped aircraft; this had a handle in the butt's place. The device consisted of

One of Youlten's machine-gun hyposcopes. Although this illustration from GB 112,058 shows a Lewis, the device could also be fitted to the Vickers. An alternative to the single prism is a two-mirror arrangement.

a handle extension on the bottom of which was a double spade grip and an auxiliary trigger that was connected to the Lewis's by a Bowden wire. A forked arm connected to the extension and the back of the gun's pistol grip ensured that the device was rigidly fixed to the weapon. By this time, Youlten was involved with Periscopes & Hyperscopes Ltd, a company that had been set up specifically to manufacture military optical devices. Both the company and Youlten were named as inventors of the Lewis gun hyposcope described in GB 112,058 which was filed at the Patent Office in January 1917. This device was also adapted to be fitted to the Vickers but with double handle extensions and an unenclosed two-mirror periscope instead of the prism. It appears to have been used in the Dardanelles but it is unclear whether it saw operational use in France.

The machine-gun hyposcope that was adopted by the army in France had been tested at the School of Musketry in February 1915. This device was known as the GHQ pattern and was probably designed at the Experimental Section in St Omer. It was a very simple, almost crude, device that incorporated a very basic box mirror periscope and an auxiliary trigger, all of which were attached to the handles of a Vickers or a Maxim machine-gun with a metal band or clip. Because of differences between the two machine-guns, each type needed a different clip, the one for the Maxim being more complex and consequently less satisfactory than the one for the Vickers. To demonstrate that silly mistakes could happen, the original test samples sent to Hythe from London were wrongly marked so that those marked 'Vickers' were in fact meant for the Maxim and vice versa. Todhunter expressed doubts about the lack of safety features on the hyposcope and suggested that a spiral spring should be used to pull the firing lever back

The GHQ-pattern machine-gun hyposcope. A metal band fixes the device to the gun's spade grips. The operator is resting his hands on the auxiliary trigger. (IWM)

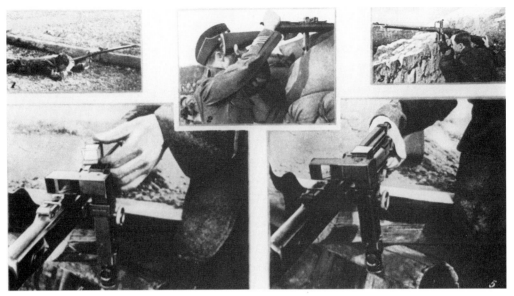

An early rifle hyposcope, dating from late 1914. There is no auxiliary stock or trigger and the rifle has to be fired with the left hand while the right holds the butt. Moreover, the periscope uses more than two mirrors. The amount of cover it affords is minimal. This was the sort of device that Capt Todhunter was continually rejecting. (The Illustrated War News)

against the box 'to allow the safety catch to engage'. The Chief Inspector of Small Arms also suggested that the firing lever should be fitted with 'a bolt and keeper nut, which could be adjusted so as to bear on the double button' of the trigger. Any alterations to the shape of the periscope were rejected as unnecessary complications; it had been mooted that the top and bottom of the periscope should be sloped. Despite the fact that Todhunter felt that this device 'serves its purpose in a satisfactory way' he expressed the opinion that Youlten's hyposcope was more portable and would be preferable to the GHQ device but for the fact that it did not include a firing lever, something which Youlten included in later devices.

The Percival was one of several hyposcopes that were supposed to enable the infantryman to shoot round corners rather than simply over the parapet. Todhunter tested it in March 1915 but judged it too fragile and too complicated for trench use, while offering no advantage to the sniper. The device used four mirrors which significantly degraded the image due to light loss at each mirror, and they needed constant cleaning if a meaningful image was to be produced. The Percival did not compare favourably with Youlten's single-prism hyposcope. The capability to shoot round corners was a dubious advantage anyway as there was no call for it. Todhunter suggested that in the event that a demand for such devices did arise, Youlten should be asked to make a similar device for a comparative trial. Nothing came of it. A similar device using only two mirrors was patented by L.E. Snoeck in 1916 (GB 106,420) but nothing came of that either.

Unlike Youlten's and Percival's devices, the Kingsford device included simple means for operating the trigger without having to reach up to it. In April 1915, Todhunter noted

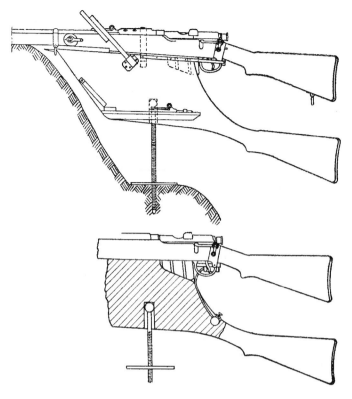

A pivoting sniperscope patented by T.C. Tomlinson in March 1915 and illustrated in GB 3,454/15. Such a device would have been difficult to fit and the trenches did not lend themselves to the way it was intended to be used.

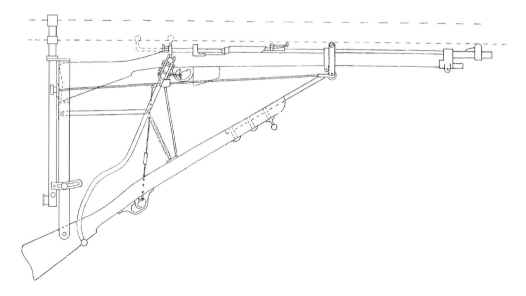

William Peck's patented sniperscope with hinged auxiliary stock as illustrated in GB 107,717. This would not have been good at absorbing recoil. It is unlikely that the bolt-operating mechanism would have been a success. Peck's previously patented periscope is fitted to the device.

that 'Mr Kingsford attended with his periscope', an improved version of a device that had been modified in accordance with Todhunter's suggestions following earlier tests. In essence, the device was a telescoping periscope, the upper tube of which was fitted with trunnions connected to a plug that slotted into the butt trap of the rifle, the trap's open cover locking it in place. Originally, a pull-through was used to operate the trigger but on Todhunter's advice Campbell's Bowden wire was substituted. The original device had several major defects. The periscope mirrors had to be perfectly aligned to avoid getting a distorted image. The position of the top mirror was not adjustable and there was no means of adjusting the position of the whole periscope to ensure that the top mirror was correctly aligned with the rifle sights. The field of view was small but Todhunter doubted that a bigger periscope would be an improvement as it would present a bigger target for enemy snipers.

Kingsford took the advice and criticisms to heart and modified the device accordingly. Todhunter thought that the improved model was good enough to recommend that 'a small supply of these might be sent for trial in the field' but added the proviso that clear fitting instructions, preferably accompanied by a photograph, should accompany each one. However, Todhunter was not completely satisfied with the means for making adjustments to the position of the periscope and he suggested a number of improvements that needed to be implemented before the devices were sent out. Nevertheless, the device was judged to be superior to the currently most favoured sniperscope which had been invented by a Mr Eshelby. It was small and light, making it more portable, and it could be used in a trench up to 7 ft deep. When the rifle was fired using the Bowden wire, accurate shooting was possible. To fire the rifle, the butt had to be held in the left hand above the head. The periscope could be used simply as a periscope when it was not attached to the rifle. Todhunter suggested that an equal number of the periscopes without the attachment trunnions and plug could be sent out with the others to be used by the observers who accompanied snipers.

Edward Marks was an engineer residing in London but his hyposcope was clearly intended for the Canadian Ross, unlike other rifle periscopes which were principally designed for the SMLE, although many could be adapted to fit the long Lee Enfield and Kingsford's could be fitted to the Ross. The reason for this was that, although Marks was described in the specification as the inventor, the invention had been communicated to him 'from abroad by Thomas Leopold Willson, of Ottawa'. The device described in GB 4,992/15 was a tubular periscope suitably bent so that the upper part was parallel with and above the barrel, while the lower part extended below the level of the trigger. It was rather too complicated for easy manufacture, however, as it consisted of three parts, the middle one having a lateral bend as well as a downward one, necessitating the use of three mirrors. Correctly aligning the three reflecting surfaces would have presented something of a headache, as this required positioning in two planes rather than one. Various methods of attaching the periscope to the rifle were described in the specification, including a clip to fix it over the rear sight, a slotted guideway fixed to the side of the rifle that engaged a pin on the periscope and was clamped in position with a screw, and an elastic strap.

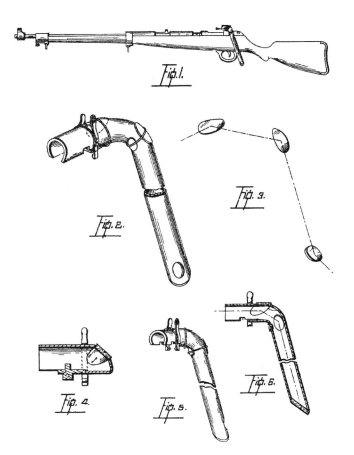

Fig.1.

Fig. 2.

Fig. 3.

Fig. 4.

Fig. 5.

Fig. 6.

Thomas Willson's Ross hyposcope, patented in Britain by Edward Marks (GB 4,992/15). The optics were too complex for the device to be seriously considered. Note the three mirrors and the lateral and vertical bends in the tube.

A similar hyposcope invented by Capt W.E. Napier was tested at Hythe in June 1915. This used two prisms and was difficult to adjust; it needed to be fitted as accurately as telescopic sights. Its field of view was too small and it was tricky to use. Cheaper commercial periscopes performed just as well. It was rejected. A rather odd device, a triangular mirror fitted to the rifle butt so that 'the rifle can be sighted from cover' required the rifle to be turned upside down to fire it; when the mirror was not in use, it fitted into a recess in the butt (GB 8,017/15). This one sank without trace.

The Eshelby was more along the lines of what could be termed a true sniperscope rather than an optical device that allowed a rifle to be fired from cover. It was a metal holder for the rifle butt with a vertical wooden arm that had an adjustable pistol grip, a Bowden wire mechanism at the bottom and two mirrors, one at the top to view the backsight and one aligned below to see the image in the top mirror. The bottom mirror had 'a range finding device based on the apparent height of a standing figure'. Capt Todhunter was quite enthusiastic about this device as it offered a number of advantages over others. A rifle could be fitted into the holder and loaded in the trench, then raised above the parapet without exposing the shooter's hands. It also allowed accurate shooting, no doubt helped by the fact that with the pistol grip it was easier to control the recoil. But Todhunter was sceptical about the range finder and reckoned that it had no practical value. He also felt that making the pistol grip adjustable was unnecessary. 'Mr Eshelby attended on one day and the defects of the appliance, as submitted by him, were pointed out to him.' This was in April 1915. It took until August for Eshelby to return with an improved model that had dispensed with the range finder and no longer had an adjustable pistol grip. The holder had been improved and strengthened and would now fit the SMLE, long Lee Enfield, P14 and Ross rifles. Todhunter recommended that a small number should be sent out to France for trials but suggested that proper instructions should accompany each device. Unfortunately, it was expensive to make.

It would appear that this idea was taken a stage further by John Chandler of Cheltenham, who filed a patent application for a device like Eshelby's in September 1915 (GB 2,582/15), but with a mechanism for operating the bolt from below cover. It is

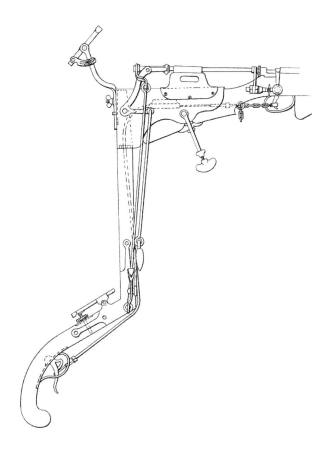

A truly Heath Robinson device invented by John Chandler in 1915. The operating mechanisms are complicated arrangements of levers. Apart from anything else, the device would not have been easy to manufacture. Compare this with the Second Army Workshops design.

Chandler's device seen from the back, again illustrating the complexity of the mechanisms. Both drawings from GB 2,582/15.

likely that Chandler either knew Eshelby or his device because of the close similarity of the two, the major difference being the bolt-operating mechanism. Because Chandler's invention still incorporated an adjustable pistol grip, it is possible that he developed his device before Eshelby made the modifications in the light of the trial at Hythe. The mechanism was something of a Heath Robinson affair. Two sets of rods and levers, both connected to a single spindle and a ball-and-socket joint fixed to the end of the turned-down bolt handle, enabled the bolt to be rotated, pulled back, pushed forward and rotated again to extract a cartridge case and chamber another round. A handle on the end of one set rotated the bolt while another handle on the end of the second set pulled or pushed it.

After Eshelby had brought his sniperscope to Todhunter in the spring of 1915, all other devices were measured against it. A device submitted by a Mr Robertson in June 1915 failed to compare favourably. Interestingly, it was fitted with an auxiliary butt that Todhunter thought 'unnecessary and prevents the firer adapting his position to any height of cover'. Another device that failed to measure up, despite being more portable because it was foldable, was a device invented by a Mr Husband, also submitted in June. Apart from not fitting any rifle, what let it down was the trigger release mechanism, 'a long lever actuated by a Bowden wire', which, although it was 'neat', tended to catch on whatever the rifle was resting on, causing it to fire prematurely. Moreover, the prismatic periscope, though inconspicuous, was unlikely to be a viable proposition because of the difficulty of obtaining prisms. An alternative mirror periscope supplied by Husband was too short and the mirrors of too poor quality to be of much use; this was a commercial instrument. Nevertheless, Todhunter thought it had some merit and recommended that Husband get together with Kingsford, as Husband's device combined with a Kingsford periscope promised to make an excellent sniperscope.

Many inventors believed that the best way to retain proper control of a sniperscope-equipped rifle was to provide the sniperscope with a cranked or set-down auxiliary butt so that it could be shouldered in the same way as a conventional rifle. There were advantages to this approach but it tended to add complications, not least of which was how to attach the device to the rifle. In the end, it came down to one of two methods: either clamp the device to the rifle or saw off the rifle butt and attach the device to the truncated stock in its place. The second method gave rise to a specialized weapon that could no longer be used like a conventional rifle and could not be reconverted. Such specialized sniping weapons could not be made in the field. This was a serious drawback as it not only meant that the weapon had to be manufactured elsewhere but it had to be supplied through the same channels as the SMLE, which would inevitably cause delays. Such a device was also bulky and far from easy to transport in the trenches. But of all sniperscopes, they were the most stable and consequently the most accurate.

One of the earliest sniperscopes of the war was of the clamped auxiliary stock type, invented by Wilfrid Boult, an engineer. He filed a patent application at the end of October 1914 and another a few weeks later; these were joined to become GB 21,318/14. It was a simple device except that the auxiliary stock would have been too complex a shape to manufacture easily if it had been made of wood. It would have been no easier if made from Duralumin, a suggested alternative, especially if Boult's suggestion that it

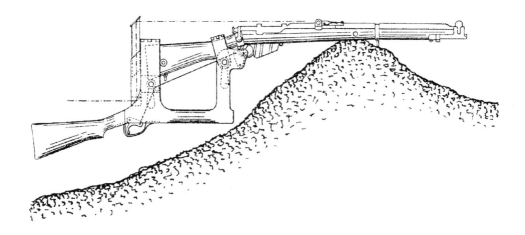

Wilfrid Boult's sniperscope of October 1914.

could double as a water canteen was taken up. He was not specific about how the device was to be fitted to the rifle and herein lay its biggest fault. A simple and secure attachment was essential. Judging from Todhunter's remarks about other sniperscopes, it is clear from Boult's specification that there were other potential problems and it is doubtful whether it would have performed very well. However, Boult was clearly aware of the problem of recoil because he provided a foregrip to help steady the whole thing when the rifle was fired.

A similar device was invented by Mr Walker of the Birmingham Small Arms Co. for his son who was serving with the 6th Warwicks in France. It was strapped to the rifle with leather or webbing bands and a metal box periscope was fitted into a metal holder screwed to an extension of the auxiliary stock against which the heel of the butt was held by one of the straps. One end of the auxiliary abutted the small of the rifle stock and was held there by the other strap. The periscope also sat in a recess in the auxiliary stock. Its position could not be altered unless the periscope was telescopic, as suggested in Boult's specification. Walker's device had no auxiliary trigger so the rifle trigger had to be operated with the left hand. It is doubtful whether the straps would have held a rifle securely enough and the device did not afford the shooter much cover. From a practical point of view, it was not a viable proposition.

While experiments were under way in Britain, both the Belgian and the French Armies were looking at sniperscopes of their own. In September 1915, the Experimental Section at Hythe evaluated a sniperscope of the modified stock type for the Belgian government. This was invented by a Belgian artillery officer, Lt Gérard. To fit the device, the rifle stock first had to be removed at the small of the butt. The auxiliary stock was a butt-shaped piece of wood with a vertical extension, the top of which was screwed to the rifle stock in place of the piece that had been removed. A metal brace was fixed between the vertical extension and the rifle fore-end and a Bowden wire mechanism operated the

An early sniperscope constructed by Mr Walker of the Birmingham Small Arms Co. for his son who was serving in the 6th Warwicks. Although from the way the shooter is holding the auxiliary stock, it appears to be fitted with an auxiliary trigger, it is not. The rifle's trigger has to be operated with the left hand. Again, the device offers only minimal cover but the recoil was reported to be less than expected. However, the muzzle jumped by about 1.5 in. (The Illustrated War News)

trigger. This was like other Bowden wire mechanisms used on numerous sniperscopes but had the disadvantage of being much more difficult to adjust. The trigger mechanism of the device supplied to the School of Musketry for tests was set up 'to give a hair trigger, consequently the bolt sometimes failed to cock and sometimes went to half cock', a far from satisfactory arrangement. In view of the fact that the modified stock turned the rifle into a specialized weapon, Todhunter told Gérard that he would be well advised to add a bolt-operating mechanism to the sniperscope so that it did not have to be lowered for loading. Todhunter was not altogether impressed with it. It lacked the portability afforded by Eshelby's and Husband's devices, provided less cover and turned the service rifle into a specialized weapon that could no longer be used in the conventional way. Nevertheless, it offered more cover than other sniperscopes of the type and accurate shooting was possible with it, despite the fact that Gérard used a commercial tubular periscope at the trial, which did not impress Todhunter either.

Gérard applied for a patent in Britain a few days before the tests at Hythe. His specification (GB 13,091/15) described the periscope as being fitted with two pairs of trunnions which engaged in two pairs of slots in metal plates bolted to the upright extension of the auxiliary stock. These allowed the periscope to be raised and lowered according to the height of the raised backsight. The lower pair of slots were curved so

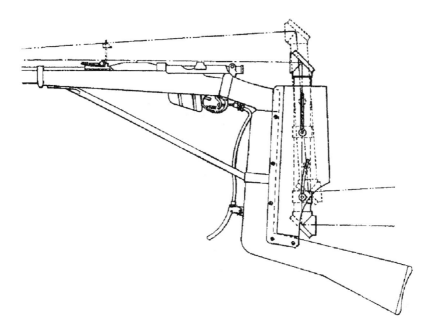

Lt Gérard's sniperscope tested by Capt Todhunter. Drawing from GB 13,031/15.

that the periscope rotated slightly forwards as it was raised to allow the upper mirror to be aligned with the backsight. This was an unnecessary complication. The only reason for raising the backsight was in order to shoot at ranges above about 400 yd, greater than those at which sniperscopes were generally considered useful by the British; at 100 yd or less, the backsight did not need to be raised. By 1917, GHQ was favouring another Belgian sniperscope called the Visoscope but nothing is known about it other than it underwent troop trials.

Capt Todhunter was never very keen on sniperscopes that could only be fitted by modifying the rifle stock. He tended to reject them almost as a matter of course. A typical comment in his early reports was 'unsuitable for present use as it involves changes in the rifle butt . . . a rifle so fitted would not be capable of being used in the ordinary way', a remark he made about Louis Vergue's 'rifle device' in January 1915. This was hardly surprising. The service rifle was the main tool of the infantryman and anything that interfered with its conventional use was considered unfavourably. The School of Musketry was a bastion of conventional usage. The infantryman was viewed as naked without rifle and bayonet. This was to change, however. Although many pre-war soldiers decried the inability of New Army volunteers and later conscripts to handle a rifle, the influx of such men who had no background in 'proper' rifle shooting and the growing emphasis on grenades meant that the rifle was no longer the first weapon of the infantryman. These changes had already made an impact by 1917 and with them came a change of heart about the value of special sniperscopes that necessitated the modification of the rifle stock. By the summer of 1917, GHQ was positively in favour of them, despite

Haig's preference for an infantryman to use his rifle as it was originally intended. The realities of the trenches showed that it was all very well having a device that could be fitted quickly but there was no substitute for what in a later age would be called a dedicated weapon system.

It was this change of attitude that gave rise to both types of sniperscope undergoing trials in the trenches on an equal footing. No doubt the greater respect being shown by senior field officers by about 1917 for the necessarily specialist sniper rifle had an effect. In the early days, snipers often had to make do with rifles that were used as ordinary infantry rifles which did nothing for accuracy. It took the concerted efforts of men like Hesketh-Pritchard to bring about a change in attitude. Nevertheless, the majority of sniperscopes were still of the type that could be removed to allow the rifle to be used conventionally. By 1917, GHQ was much more interested in getting hold of effective weapons than it was with preserving tradition at any cost. And the search for the perfect sniperscope was no nearer to resolution than it had been two years earlier. What was needed was a device that combined the best features of those that had promise while at the same time eliminated all the defects. This was not an unreasonable goal and demonstrated that GHQ was not content just to make do.

By mid-1917, several sniperscopes had undergone successful troop trials with the British Army. Of these, one was a French design already in use with the French Army. This was of the detachable type but it is unlikely to have been removed once it had been set up as it would have been too fiddly, especially if the bolt-operating mechanism was also fitted. The rifle holder without the mechanism was designed first and was in use with the French by the middle of 1915. The auxiliary stock was attached to the rifle by a large, metal, U-shaped bracket, the rearward arm of which looped over the end of the rifle butt to come down the other side so that the arm also formed a U but an inverted one. The forward arm was in two parts that came up either side of the small of the butt, above which it was clamped tightly by a lever mechanism. The auxiliary wooden stock was fixed between the two sides of the bracket at the base of the U. It was fitted with an auxiliary trigger that was connected to the rifle's with a stirrup and cross pin on the end of an adjustable rod. The periscope, a simple box and mirror affair, was mounted by a dovetail slide on the back of a socket shaped to take the butt of a rifle, and fixed at the top of the rearward arm of the U. A spring catch secured the periscope in place. This method of mounting the periscope in the holder was the subject of GB 124,771, which had three patentees, G. Espitallier, L. Roman and A. Bellard, all three of them French. The specification was filed at the British Patent Office in March 1916 but the invention predated this by as much as a year. Although it is likely that all three were the designers of the whole apparatus, the British knew the device as the Espitallier. The method for attaching the auxiliary trigger to the rifle's was described in GB 124,771.

By spring 1916, Alfred Bellard, a Paris engineer, had devised a bolt-operating mechanism for this sniperscope. This was a far simpler mechanism than that proposed by Chandler. It had fewer parts and there was consequently less opportunity for the mechanism to jam or come apart. The rifle holder in combination with this apparatus underwent troop trials with the British Army in 1916 and by late 1917 it had become the

The Espitallier sniperscope fitted with the Bellard bolt-operating mechanism (the dark inverted Y), June 1916. Note his observer with a No. 9 periscope. Although this is supposed to be a shot of a front-line position, these New Zealanders appear very relaxed. (IWM)

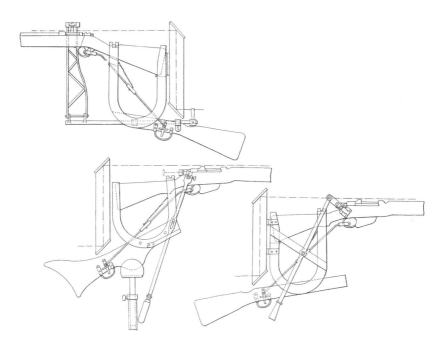

The Espitallier sniperscope fitted with the Bellard bolt-operating mechanism from GB 104,790. The arrangement illustrated on the top left is the version that was adapted for the SMLE and used by British and Empire troops although it was originally intended for the Lebel.

standard pattern. It remained in use with the British until the end of the war. Bellard applied for two British patents in May 1916 and these became GB 104,790 and GB 113,044 (the latter was an addition to the former although it was filed at the patent office a week earlier). The specifications described a number of mechanisms adapted for the SMLE, Belgian Mauser and Lebel (although the French had replaced the Lebel with the Berthier in 1915). The sniperscope operated by the British used the Lebel mechanism rather than the one intended for the SMLE, perhaps because it was the simplest and the most robust, and possibly because it was the only one of the several described in the specification to have been shown to work.

It was ingeniously simple. An auxiliary bolt mechanism that mirrored the rifle's was mounted on the auxiliary stock. The auxiliary bolt, a long spindle mounted in collars that allowed it to be moved back and forth as well as rotated, was connected to the rifle's bolt handle by an arm with hinges top and bottom, the bottom hinge joining the arm to the spindle and the top one joining a simple clamp to the knob of the bolt handle. Such an arm and its hinges were likely to suffer considerable stress during constant use which could distort the mechanism and render it unusable. To avoid this, the arm had an inclined side piece that connected the top of it with the spindle at a second point; this prevented twisting stresses from damaging the mechanism. To operate the mechanism all the user had to do was use the auxiliary bolt as he would the bolt on the rifle. This was a vastly superior method to practically any other proposed for a sniperscope. Although Bellard's specifications described other, more complicated, mechanisms involving what were in effect auxiliary bolts set at an angle to the axis of the barrel, none of these seem to have been used on any version of this device. The disadvantage to these mechanisms and others like them was that they required the shooter to execute an unfamiliar set of movements to operate the bolt, apart from the fact that they were more complex mechanical arrangements.

Of the sniperscopes sent out to France for trials, three emerged during 1917 as the most favoured by GHQ. The Belgian Visoscope has already been mentioned. The other two were British designs evaluated by the Munitions Inventions Department. The older of the two, dating from the spring of 1915, was known as the Cahusac after its inventor, Herbert Cahusac. Although in many ways simpler than the French sniperscope, the Cahusac design required the removal of the rifle butt, thus converting the rifle into a specialist weapon. However, because of the way in which this was achieved, the conversion was reversible and the process could be completed very quickly – at least, in theory. The auxiliary stock was constructed by unbolting the rifle's butt from the fore-end and bolting it to a short wooden auxiliary fore-end. A vertical arm joined the auxiliary stock to the rifle where the butt had been using a shortened bolt. A second arm from the auxiliary was clamped to the rifle's fore-end with a metal band that could be tightened with a wing nut, making a rigid framework. The periscope was clamped to the vertical arm and could be adjusted to align the top mirror with the rifle sights or even removed entirely.

Although this was fitted with a simple Bowden wire type trigger mechanism, it had no bolt-operating mechanism and had to be lowered each time the shooter wanted to reload. But Cahusac did address the problem of recoil. By shaping the clamping band in such a way that when tightened it was inclined towards to the shooter, he ensured that a large

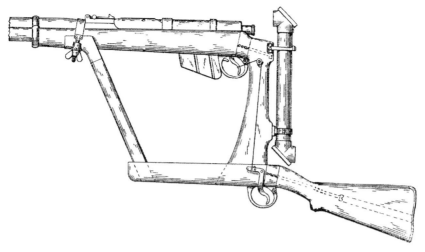

Herbert Cahusac's sniperscope as illustrated in his patent, GB 4,900/15. The rifle's butt is removed and fitted to the auxiliary stock which is fitted to the rifle in its place. This device was used on the Western Front.

proportion of the rifle's kick was transmitted down the forward arm of the auxiliary stock, into its fore-end and subsequently the shouldered butt. It was helped by having the auxiliary stock parallel with the barrel rather than angled downwards as it was on some sniperscopes. The auxiliary stock of William Peck's sniperscope, for example, was hinged from the rifle's fore-end and sloped downwards towards the shooter to form a triangular frame with a vertical arm at the butt end. Such an arrangement was not well suited to absorbing recoil and it was necessary to fit 'recoil stays' to prevent the device falling apart or being jerked out of the shooter's grasp. The Cahusac did not need stays. Absorption of the recoil was aided by ensuring that the forward arm sloped towards the muzzle.

A particular advantage of the Cahusac's construction was that the whole weapon was no longer than the normal rifle. Most other sniperscopes were considerably longer when fitted to a rifle and therefore needed more space to shoot which could prove to be a problem in the sometimes confined space of a trench. The Cahusac was also only slightly heavier than the service rifle and the periscope was positioned closer to the backsight than on many other sniperscopes, more or less where the shooter's eye would have been had he been using a conventional rifle, so that aiming was more like aiming with a conventional rifle.

Herbert Cahusac filed a patent application in April 1915 and this subsequently became GB 4,900/15. In between filing the provisional specification in April and the complete specification six months later, Cahusac was made aware of Boult's sniperscope and had to amend his specification accordingly. But Cahusac's sniperscope was vastly superior to Boult's in every respect. And there was a slight twist to this. The firm of patent agents who drafted and filed Cahusac's specifications was called Boult, Wade and Tennant. Wilfrid Boult, inventor of one of the first sniperscopes, lived within walking distance of the firm's offices in Hatton Garden and he had drafted his own specification, written in the language used by patent agents. It was not unusual for inventors to write their own specifications

(William Peck wrote his own) but those who did were not usually well versed in the language of patents in the way that a patent agent was, something that only comes with tutelage and experience. It is highly likely that Wilfrid Boult was not only a patent agent but also drafted Cahusac's specifications. Since Cahusac was a 'Secretary to a Public Company' it is not unreasonable to assume that the firm did patent work for Cahusac's company and that they knew each other. The reference to Boult's patent in Cahusac's complete specification may have been Boult's sly attempt to draw attention to his own invention.

In early 1917, GHQ was supplied with another quite different sniperscope for trial. This was an adjustable metal skeleton butt with a separate pistol grip that could be fitted to and removed from the service rifle. The strip-metal pistol grip was clipped to the small of the butt while the skeleton butt was attached to the rifle's with bands. A metal strip connected the front one with the back one along the top of the rifle's butt and a small tubular periscope was fixed to this via a ball-and-socket joint. A telescopic front link pivoted from beneath the front band while the pivoting rear link slid in a bracket on the end of the front link. The butt plate was connected to this bracket. The device was invented by Jack Sangster who applied for a patent on 28 February 1917 and this became GB 113,337. This lightweight framework would have been simple to attach to the rifle but it provided less cover than the Cahusac. Nevertheless, GHQ considered that it had enough merit to recommend it to London as one of the most favoured sniperscopes. Jack was related to Charles Sangster (possibly his brother) who invented the Pitcher hand grenade and the No. 25 rifle grenade as well as a wire-cutter (*see* Chapter 8). They lived and worked in Birmingham and Charles was a director of a number of engineering companies. Although it is not certain, one of them may have been Decimals Ltd. There

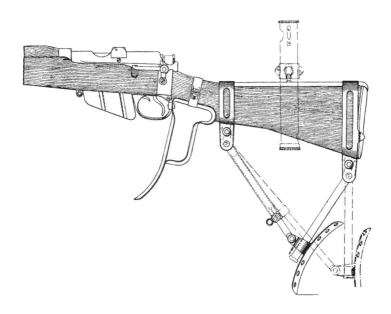

Jack Sangster's skeleton stock and pistol grip for the SMLE, as illustrated in his patent GB 113,337.

was a connection between him and the company because it made all of his patented devices. However, Charles Sangster was involved with many engineering businesses during his career and Decimals was not mentioned in his obituary when he died in 1935 at the age of sixty-three. He was better known for his contribution to the cycle and motor industry in the area than he was for his military inventions.

At much the same time as GHQ was corresponding with London about sniperscopes, a German sniperscope and a leaflet explaining how to fit it to a rifle were captured (*see* p. 126). Examination of the device by the Royal Engineers Experimental Section persuaded GHQ that it was in some respects superior to anything that the British had so far proposed or tried. Whether this was an entirely unbiased assessment is open to question – enemy equipment was often judged to be better than equivalent Allied stores. But it had features that were absent from British designs and it looked less like something that Heath Robinson could have dreamed up than most British sniperscopes. The captured example, along with a translation of the leaflet, was sent to the Munitions Inventions Department which was asked to design a sniperscope based on the German apparatus. The MID was impressed with it and immediately asked for more examples. Whether raids were organized to achieve this object is not known but it is not outside the realms of possibility. It is not known whether the Munitions Inventions Department got their additional sniperscopes.

The German device, the *Spiegelkolben* BAF, could be fitted to the Mauser 88 and 89 rifles as well as to the carbine. It was collapsible, the metal holder acting as the housing for the folded-up auxiliary butt and periscope. The auxiliary butt was attached to the holder by a bolt, around which it pivoted. After it was swung out, a pin was put through the holder to prevent the butt from moving. The top of the holder clamped over the rifle butt which had to be hard against a recoil bolt in the holder. A wire or lanyard, much like a Bowden wire, was passed from the auxiliary trigger over a pulley at the top of the holder and clipped to the rifle's trigger. The mirrors of the tubular periscope could be replaced if they were broken but they were paired so both had to be replaced at the same time to ensure that a clear image was obtained. To avoid confusion over which was the top and which the bottom of the periscope, the top protective cap was painted green while the bottom one was painted black. The assembly instructions stated that to fit the periscope into the holder it was essential to engage

the two ribs on the [periscope] in the corresponding grooves in the [holder], taking care to note the following:-
(i.) The end of the periscope (which is painted black) to be held downwards, i.e., inserted first, so that the toothed rib is to the right.
(ii.) Press the spring catch on the holder outwards so that the toothed rib can slide down the groove . . .

The line of sight was checked by raising or lowering the periscope. When in the right position for the range, the catch was released to engage the toothed rib to keep it at the correct height. When the sights were set at 400 m, which was a considerably longer range than the British seemed to think a sniperscope could be used effectively, the periscope

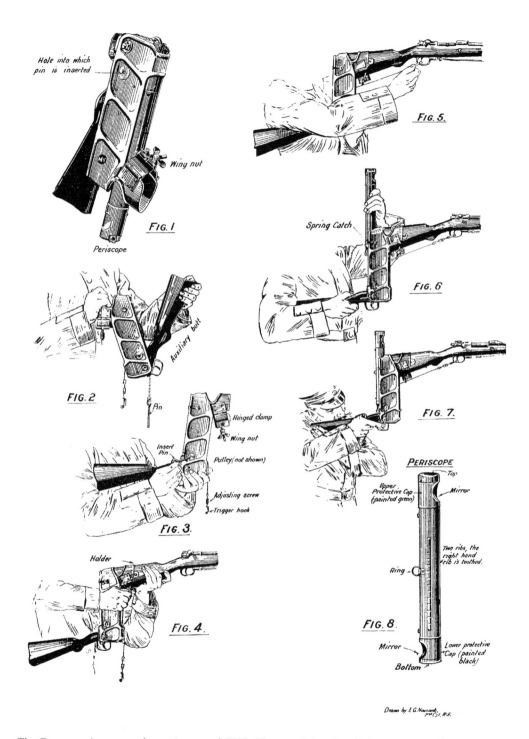

The German sniperscope that so interested GHQ. This set of drawings is from a captured German document explaining how to fit the device. The sniperscope is more compact than many British devices but probably no better. (MUN 4/3589)

was pushed all the way down the holder so that the catch engaged the top tooth.

By December 1917, the Munitions Inventions Department had devised their own version of the German device and GHQ wanted samples sent out for troop trials. Four examples of the new sniperscope had been made, one of which was fitted with a bolt-operating mechanism designed by Edgar Duerr, the jam maker. The sniperscope was foldable like its German parent and lighter and more portable than the Espitallier, as well as more efficient. The four examples were passed over to the Controller of Munitions Design who recommended a number of minor modifications. When these had been carried out, the four sniperscopes were sent to France for troop trials in the new year. It is not clear whether all four had now been fitted with the Duerr mechanism.

From his success with lazy-tong periscopes, commercially if not militarily,

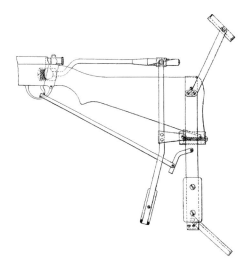

Edgar Duerr's device for firing the SMLE from cover. It has two mirrors and a double pistol grip instead of an auxiliary butt. There is an auxiliary trigger and a bolt-operating mechanism. This mechanism was adapted to be fitted to the Munitions Inventions Department sniperscope based on the German device. Drawing from GB 109,236, which dates from 1917.

Duerr was inspired to turn to sniperscopes. In early 1916 he came up with a very simple device which, like his periscope, he proceeded to patent. GB 103,382 describes a metal stirrup-like attachment for the end of the butt which was clamped and wedged in place. The lower extension of the stirrup was fitted with wooden blocks that acted as hand grips. A mirror was hinged to a 'swinging link' at the top, so that its position could be adjusted (but not clamped) and another was similarly connected to the bottom via another swinging link. A very simple auxiliary trigger was joined to the rifle trigger by a rod. By May 1917, he had developed a bolt-operating mechanism for this device and he patented this too (GB 109,236). Like the butt attachment this was a very simple affair, far simpler than many such mechanisms, and judging by the interest taken in it by the Munitions Inventions Department, it must have been very effective and easy to use. A cranked rod was attached to the knob of the rifle bolt. Cut into the other end was 'a steep-pitch screw' thread to take a peg connected to the top of a rod or lever that extended downwards, parallel with the stirrup. The lever was joined to the stirrup by a pivot. By pivoting the lever up or down the rifle bolt was actuated. It was like a gear change lever.

It was this mechanism that was fitted to the Munitions Inventions Department's sniperscope developed from the German device. Unfortunately, there is no record of what became of the department's sniperscopes. Around the time they were being evaluated, the Germans launched the first of their breakthrough offensives and the British Army lost interest in sniperscopes as it was fighting for its life.

CHAPTER 7

Dark Terrors –
Shot, Stabbed and Clubbed

Night in the trenches could be a dangerous time. It was now that patrols went out into no-man's-land, to gather information about the enemy and his wire, to repair their own entanglements or to attack enemy patrols and wiring parties. And by early 1915, the prospect of a raid had become a very real danger. Raids in the early days could be brutal brawls rather than organized fights, as indeed could encounters between patrols in the black, restricted space of unfamiliar trenches. Under these circumstances, fighting became an instinctive struggle for individual survival in which any action was justified. They were close up and frightening, so close you could smell the breath of your enemy. The night was pitch dark as there were no lights anywhere near the front-line positions, the only illumination coming from star shells that burst intermittently above the lines or Very lights fired from the trenches. Ears had to be finely attuned to distinguish genuine threats from insignificant sounds. Night could be very stressful.

Not surprisingly, it was practically impossible to fire properly aimed shots at night. Even when you knew the enemy was in front of your trench, it was hard to know where precisely to shoot as sound was the only indicator. One approach to dealing with enemy raids and patrols was to set up one or more fixed rifle batteries to fire in predetermined zones where, for example, a passage had been cut through the wire entanglements to entice the enemy to enter. A tripwire was sometimes used to fire them. This could have unexpected results, as Capt Dunn noted in October 1914: 'It wasn't altogether unknown for a bullet-riddled farm animal to be seen beside a tripwire by daylight.' A rifle battery was a frame designed to hold one or more rifles set up to fire into the predetermined zone. Although these were sometimes referred to as devices for night sniping, this was not how they were used. When fired, either individually or in a fusillade, it was not usual for the operator to see the enemy unless illuminated by a star shell or a flare. Most batteries were made at the Royal Engineer Workshops, or later by the Workshop Companies following a reorganization in the summer of 1917 'to do away with the large number of small workshops established by each and every unit of R.E., which were unavoidably extravagant in personnel, and wasteful of material'.

It is not clear if any designs originated from the inventions departments in Britain. Some of the batteries dating from 1915 were 'rough and ready improvisations', one design, for example, consisting of 'a packing case with slits and a sandbag over it'. Robert Graves described an incident in October 1915 in which a rifle battery was improvised to deal with an enemy machine-gun that had been firing on the 2nd Royal Welch Fusiliers at night. He and another officer called Owen devised a way to pinpoint

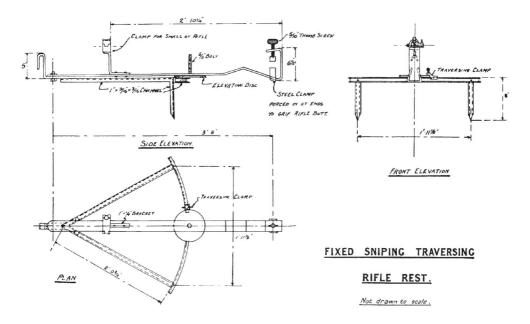

The Royal Engineers rifle rest, a simple but effective device. This is the engineering drawing from which it was made in the Workshops. (Institution of Royal Engineers)

the gun using lengths of string, each a yard long with a cartridge case tied to each end. As the gun traversed the British line, sentries down the trench pegged out the string towards the gun and they

> got a pretty accurate line on the machine-gun. When we had about thirty or more of these lines taken on a single machine-gun, we fixed rifles as carefully as possible along them and waited; as soon as it started again we opened five rounds rapid. This gave a close concentration of fire and no element of nervousness could disturb the aim, the rifles being secured between sandbags.

According to Graves, Division asked for a report on the effectiveness of this system but he omitted to mention what they thought of it.

There were also properly made rifle batteries, frames that held twelve rifles. A design for a single rifle, called a fixed sniping traversing rifle rest and originally manufactured at the Béthune Bomb Factory (the First Army Workshops) in 1915, was produced in very large numbers. It consisted of a triangular frame made from 1 in $\times$ $\frac{3}{16}$ in $\times$ $\frac{3}{16}$ in channel-section, with the traversing arc as one side of the triangle, and a sheet steel rest running up the centre line, long enough and shaped to take a rifle butt, with two clamps to hold it, one at the small of the butt, the other enclosing the shoulder. There was an elevating disc that ran up a $\frac{5}{8}$ in bolt to change the angle of elevation of the central rest, and two 8 in spikes, one at each end of the channel-section arc, to secure the device to the ground.

Capt Henry Newton (left), commanding officer of the Second Army Workshops, with two fellow officers from the 5th Sherwood Foresters, 1915. (H.A.B. Newton)

The device was just under 4 ft long and about 2 ft wide. It was very simple but effective and easy to make. It was not difficult to change the direction and angle of fire without disturbing its position.

Capt Henry Newton designed one of the earliest rifle batteries and this was produced by the Second Army Workshops in large numbers. It was an altogether more sophisticated device than the fixed sniping traversing rifle rest, could accommodate six rifles and allowed elevation and traverse to be finely set. Before the creation of the Second Army Workshops, the battery was constructed in a blacksmith's shop at Kemmel near Ypres by Newton and men of his company who had previously worked at Newton Brothers in Derby; they all served in the 5th Sherwood Foresters, a Territorial battalion. It was a fine piece of engineering. The success of this battery led Maj-Gen Furse, II Corps commander, to order Newton to set up the Workshops to serve the whole of the Second Army. Newton, now with the title of Chief Engineer, located the Workshops at the École Nationale at Armentiéres which had machine tools, wood-working facilities and sheet and hot metal shops. Originally, he had only forty-five tradesmen from the 46th Division, formerly infantrymen, but soon more tradesmen were sent to the Workshops, along with a couple of officers and about twenty local civilians. In time, more than 200 civilians were employed at the Workshops which, due to the shelling, were later moved to Hazebrouck.

The Mk I rifle battery, a three-rifle device, was supplied under contract during the early part of the war. It was intended for the long Lee Enfield rather than the SMLE. The battery had a wooden frame as a base on which was a square iron frame with a traversing plate to which the rifles were clamped. It had the refinement of running on bearings. By turning hand wheels that worked through elevating and traversing screws, the aim of the rifles could be adjusted. Because the thickness of the rifle butts was not always the same, it was sometimes necessary to pare down the butt to make it fit into the clamps. When the SMLE was fitted, the sling swivel had to be removed. To stabilize the battery, loose wooden boards were placed inside the frame and soil and stones piled on top. Steel spikes and 'picketing pegs' fixed the battery to the ground. Finally, an armoured shield could be mounted on the front of the frame. This was used in large numbers.

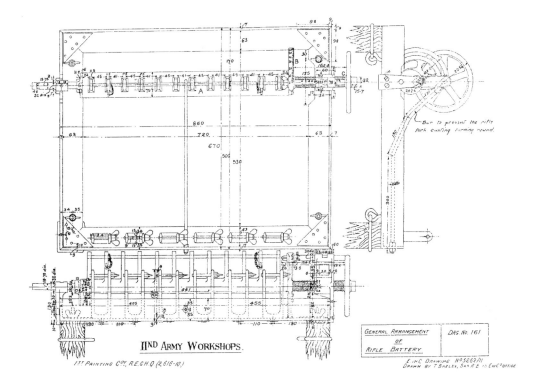

IIND ARMY WORKSHOPS.

GENERAL ARRANGEMENT OF RIFLE BATTERY. DRG. No. 161

The rifle battery designed by Henry Newton and made at the Second Army Workshops but originally made in a blacksmiths in Kemmel, near Ypres, by men of his battalion, the 5th Sherwood Foresters, who had originally worked at the Newton family business in Derby. Up to six rifles could be clamped into the device but often only one was fitted. Looking at the plan view, the rifle pointed up the page. (Newton)

The School of Musketry evaluated a rifle rest in October 1915, submitted by its inventor, a Mr King. Capt Todhunter reported that it gave no better results than the improvised packing case affair and was cumbersome. He was of the opinion that rather than experimenting with new devices the better course of action was to supply instructions on how to improvise such rests. Nevertheless, several inventors attempted to produce the perfect rifle battery. In late 1916, William Youlten invented a device similar to the traversing rifle rest made by the Royal Engineers. This was also a simple apparatus, an extensible metal frame with a rifle mount that could be traversed and elevated, and several short spikes to secure it to the ground (GB 113,294). A more complex aiming rest was invented by W.R. Ellison and H.L. Cole in early 1915 (GB 12,195/15) which included a toothed traversing 'arcuate guide' and a small shield (*see* Chapter 1). This could also be used with machine-guns. There was J.M. Crannidge's folding rest (GB 102,285) from early 1916 and W. From's 'inclined plate', which had no means for attaching a rifle to it (GB 121,555). And most complicated of all, not to say outlandish, was O.J. Lund's rifle battery with ten rows of barrels contained in a metal box, complete with automatic firing mechanism actuated by the impact of enemy bullets

A rifle battery improvised by the French, late 1915. It holds six Lebels which appear to be clamped in place. Note the wedges used to alter the elevation. (The Illustrated War News)

on rows of 'shield-plates' connected by gears and levers to the guns (GB 16,662/15). Perhaps he had never heard of the machine-gun.

Night shooting was a problem because of not being able to see the rifle sights let alone the target. The Experimental Section at Hythe evaluated more than thirteen luminous sights in the first year of the war. Between December 1914 and November 1918 there were thirteen patents concerned with luminous sights and sighting accessories to aid night shooting. Todhunter's reports on these devices were rarely favourable. He commented that the night sight submitted by J. Blanch & Son was 'weak and fragile' and went on to say that 'It is necessary for a sight of this kind to be luminous.' Which makes you wonder what J. Blanch & Son's night sight was. Hill's 'Electric Sight' was 'tried at night without favourable results. It was not possible to pick out a man at 50 yards whereas the enemy at the same range has no difficulty sighting on the user who would be shot as a result.' Hill's device was similar to Paterson's 'Spot Light Attachment', which was supposed to direct a beam of light on to the target. It was tried in August 1916. That too was rejected with the comment 'Others have been tried before and this is no better.' There was Wise's 'Spot Light Attachment' which was meant 'to assist night attacks and bombing parties or wood fighting'. It was a torch clipped to the right-hand side of the SMLE and was supposed to automatically stay in register with the barrel axis. An S-shaped filament could be focused between 3 ft and 20 ft in front and when the light was correctly aligned the bullet passed through the centre of the 'S'. The beam was switched on and off by a lever worked with the index finger of the left hand. Trials in France in the summer of 1917 indicated that it had the potential to be of value in patrol work and GHQ wanted it supplied on a scale of twelve per infantry brigade. Although this device never managed to enter service, it was not dropped because of its impracticality but rather because of manufacturing difficulties.

Night sights were tried out on the Lewis and Hotchkiss machine-guns, including one in August 1916 which Todhunter commented was acceptable in failing light but was not much good in complete darkness. Several luminous night sights were adopted for use with the SMLE during the course of the war, however. The first, the No. 1 Mk I was a flat metal plate that went behind the foresight. A recess in the rear face had a horizontal strip of luminous material with two short vertical bands that went either side of a notch that framed the foresight when sighting. The backsight was seen against the horizontal strip. To fit this device, it was necessary to remove the rifle's nose cap screw, put the night sight in place and insert the device's fixing screw through the sight's arm to hold it in place. It was invented by Sgt J.E. Martin, a well-known manufacturer of optical sights and telescopic sights with offices in Glasgow, Edinburgh and Aberdeen. Martin patented it in December 1914 (GB 23,433/14).

He visited Hythe in the spring of 1915. Todhunter was not altogether impressed with Martin's night sight, noting that it was not easy to use because it required deliberate aim, and that the luminescence was not very good. Nevertheless, the sight saw widespread use. A later patent, GB 6,451/15, which Martin applied for in April 1915, was for 'an electric or other torch for revivifying the luminous nightsight described in specification 23,433/14'. Evidently, the sight's luminosity degraded with time. The torch was designed to make a light-tight seal round the sight when it was fitted on the rifle so that it could be used at night without being seen by the enemy.

Rather confusingly, another luminous sight was also called the No. 1 Mk I, although admittedly it was termed 'sights, luminous' rather than 'sight, night'. This one came in two parts, one for the foresight, the other for the backsight, and required specialist tools for fitting. The blade of the foresight had to be removed. This was replaced by a new one with 'Projecting arms . . . formed at the rear end in which a frame, bored vertically to receive a glass tube filled with radio active material, is pivoted'. The replacement foresights came in three sizes. The backsight was 'a frame with a square sighting gap in the top at the centre' with a horizontal hole containing a glass tube of the same radioactive material each side. This was fitted over the leafsight and could be folded down for daytime shooting, as could the luminous foresight. The device appears to be an invention of A.H. Atkinson, who applied for a patent in September 1915, subsequently granted as GB 13,428/15, although the luminous material is not contained in glass tubes. This aspect of the device may have been derived from GB 12,270/15, granted to a G. Panerai. The pivoting tube frame of the foresight evidently caused problems. It sometimes jammed against the metal cap at the end of the wooden fore-end, just aft of the foresight protectors when it was folded down for daylight shooting. The first solution was to cut a slot in the front of the cap but this was not entirely successful and the upper part of the cap had to be filed at 45° to ensure that the frame cleared it.

Robert Graves was not alone in looking into ways to locate enemy machine-guns at night. There were serious investigations of curious devices to pinpoint the positions of machine-guns using sound location, triangulation from bullet impacts or other means, all of them imprecise and unreliable. Todhunter evaluated Capt Wauchope's 'Position Finder' in 1915. This worked by encouraging the Germans to shoot at the device and, with the aid of a prismatic compass, it was supposed to be possible to determine where the shots had come from. Todhunter was not impressed and remarked that it was too impractical for the trenches, even supposing that it worked at all, which by all accounts it did not. A 'machine-gun position finding instrument' favoured by GHQ in the first half of 1917 worked by locating the sound of the gun with a bearing. Two bearings were necessary and the location of the gun was where the lines intersected. It was found to be accurate to 0.5° which amounted to an error of 10 yd at a range of 1,000 yd. According to GHQ, 'It was considered that an apparatus of this nature would be of great value, and arrangements were made accordingly to construct some of these instruments in France for further trial by Armies.' However, it evidently did not work as well as anticipated and GHQ requested that one of the inventions departments look at it. By the end of 1917, GHQ had changed its opinion. The device proved to be especially unsatisfactory in hilly or 'accidented' country.

Maj Hesketh-Pritchard devised a simple device for determining the position of a machine-gun. It consisted of three sheets of tin spaced apart by several inches and mounted on a frame that allowed the device to be raised above the parapet. Once in position, all that was required was for a bullet from a machine-gun burst to penetrate the plates. By lining up a periscope with the holes

the observer found himself looking down the course along which the bullet had come, directly at the spot from which it was fired.

This was rather a clumsy and uncertain device, but it was used in a dozen other forms. Had it been invented earlier, before the issue of [German] light machine-guns . . . it might have been quite valuable, but it came too late, and was soon discarded.

Locating enemy machine-guns was important not only for forthcoming offensive operations but also for raids and patrols. Knowing where they were meant that, in theory, they could be dealt with but as Hesketh-Pritchard commented this could only work for the fixed positions of Maxims; light machine-guns did not have permanent positions. Patrolling and raiding were crucial if dominance over the enemy was to be established and maintained. These activities were unlike anything the pre-war regulars had been trained to do. The techniques had to be learned by trial and error and they did not suit everyone. Raiding in particular required aggression and strong nerves. Although raiding later took on the nature of small battles involving artillery preparation and whole companies, the early raids were made by much smaller parties, no more than a few men, with the intention of getting in and out of the enemy trenches quickly, irrespective of whether the purpose was to take prisoners or to kill Germans.

Both patrolling and raiding presented unusual problems. Stealth was often fundamental to success and that meant that the enemy sometimes had to be killed as quietly as possible. This was especially true when it came to ambushing an enemy party in no-man's-land. And to kill quietly meant being up close, what is disengenuously referred to as hand-to-hand or close combat, made worse by the deep darkness. It was bloody and violent. Instinct rather than training was what counted, partly because there was no training for this sort of thing. The rifle and bayonet were not suited to such fighting. It was reported that on some raids men had discarded their rifles and had taken to using their hands and feet. Although this was deplored by higher authorities too far away from close fighting to understand its nature, it was the basic survival instinct that made men do it, not lack of training in bayonet work. Although hand grenades were usually taken on raids and revolvers were often more use than rifles because they were small, something suitable for close combat was needed. The inevitable result was that soldiers took up all manner of knives, daggers, knuckledusters, clubs, maces and other killing implements, even entrenching tools when desperate. Dunn once noted a couple of raiders carrying billhooks. This was a different world. Stephen Westman, conscripted into the German Army in July 1914, served on the Western and Eastern Fronts as an infantryman for a year and described how in 1915 he was forced to kill a French soldier with an entrenching tool hitting 'him so deeply between the neck and shoulder with the sharp edge . . . that I had difficulty in extricating it'. His uniform was splattered with blood.

During a raid in which Ernst Jünger was participating, the British were alerted by a noise and he described what it was like to lie in wait for the British to come and find them. His breath came in 'gasps and it is all you can do to suppress the noise of it . . . The fray will have to be short and murderous. You are aquiver with two violent sensations – the tense excitement of the hunter and terror of the hunted.' The British soldiers gradually came closer through the long grass and Jünger could hear their whispers. He 'heard Parthenfelder, a Bavarian, bite on the blade of a dagger'. But the British did not see them and the German party retreated silently and undetected.

Robert Graves commented that 'If a German patrol found a wounded man, they were as likely as not to cut his throat. The bowie-knife was a favourite German patrol weapon because of its silence.' But the British and French were just as brutal. And the Canadians in particular had a fearsome reputation. Hesketh-Pritchard described a Canadian ambush patrol that went out night after night to jump German patrols; it was known as Silent Death because the patrol was armed 'with trench daggers, and its members killed as silently as possible. This soon made the Germans very shy of taking their evening crawl.' On the other side of no-man's-land, Ernst Jünger described the tension of crawling about in front of enemy trenches as 'unforgettable'. Stephen Graham described a raid in which the raiding party of six were armed with clubs. When they came upon a sentry and his relief they

flew at them and pounded their heads with the clubs and down went one Fritz in a heap. One was killed, the other bruised and overwhelmed . . . I was told this type of raid was introduced by the Canadians who had the instinct and the idea of it from the North American Indians.

Trench knife issued to the Austro-Hungarian Army. It has a single-edged 8 in blade. (Author)

Frank Richards remarked on the death of an officer killed by 'a dagger . . . driven up to the hilt in his belly'.

The British preferred the club, or knobkerrie as it was usually called at the time (Capt Dunn referred to it as a cosh), so that when they came upon an enemy they could, as Graves put it, 'beat in his skull'. Nevertheless, many British soldiers bought knives when on leave in Britain or from shops in France and Belgium; Graves bought one in Béthune before Loos in 1915 'for use in the battle'. The preference for the club seems to have been a deep-rooted prejudice against the blade which was viewed by some soldiers as an assassin's weapon. According to Graves, the attitude of the British soldier later changed from regarding 'as atrocious the use of bowie-knives by German patrols. But after a time, he learned to use them himself; they were cleaner killing weapons than revolvers or bombs.' The British Army never adopted a knife, unlike many Continental armies during the war, but manuals were issued to troops later in the war explaining how to disarm a knife-wielding assailant. However, it is doubtful that the lack of an 'official' knife was due to prejudice. It was probably more to do with the fact that a knobkerrie could be made more easily by Royal Engineers. Moreover, there were far more pressing things that needed to be manufactured in both Britain and France for the army, such as grenades and mortar ammunition. Knives were not a priority. *The Training and Employment of Bombers* issued in 1916 made it clear that knives were to be taken on raids because they were useful for close combat. Had there been official disapproval of knives they would not have been mentioned.

It is clear that many British soldiers did not like the knife but this may have had nothing to do with supposed national characteristics but more to do with the intense personal nature of killing another man with a knife, despite Graves's assertion that it was cleaner. In late 1915 there was correspondence in *The Times* about the lack of knives for the troops and the apparent refusal of the army to supply them. It appears to have been started by Sir John Macdonald, a retired brigadier-general, who was keen to remedy the situation. His first letter was published on 29 November in which he pointed out that he had been calling for the knife to be issued for more than a year. He argued that the rifle and bayonet could not be used effectively in the confined space of a trench and cited examples of men who had removed the bayonet to use it as a knife and others 'resorting to their fists'. He went on to say that

Everything points to the advisability of a short knife or dirk being at instant command . . . not for thrusting forward as in striking a blow, but for back-handed action, the arm being swung with the blade projecting – a dagger action in fact, which is much the quickest and most effective way of dealing with an enemy who is close up to you.

Macdonald described a dagger which he claimed had been recently adopted by the French Army. It had a metal 'loop handle . . . the point [of the blade] projecting from the back of the knuckles'. By his reckoning this was 'not a good arrangement'. It is not clear how Macdonald came by his knowledge of knives and fighting with them but he had strong views on the subject. He advocated that the knife should be swung 'into the face of the nearest man, and as rapidly as possible into the faces of as many men as can be reached – no stabbing at the body'. He believed that stabbing a man in the face was more effective than stabbing him in the body because it was more of a shock and rendered him incapable of offering further resistance. Mind you, being stabbed in the belly was very disturbing, not to say disabling.

Macdonald's letter prompted two vigorous replies, one of which was published the following day, the second on the day after. Both correspondents were serving officers who chose to remain anonymous. The first made it plain that knives were being supplied to the men in his brigade on the initiative of the brigadier. From his description of the knife in question it would appear to have been one manufactured by Robbins of Dudley. The second correspondent questioned the 'real fighting value' of such weapons, stating that 'From what I know of the dirks at present on the market I should be very sorry to depend on any of them in an emergency. They seem specially designed to infuriate the enemy and make him more dangerous.' Although he had a point about what was available to buy, his other comments seem more to do with a fear of using a knife than anything else. This was a very real fear for many. Using a knife is not like using any other weapon – it is profoundly personal.

In February 1917, the *Journal of The Royal United Services Institute* published an article by Macdonald in which he expounded at some length on the trench knife, castigating the army for not formally adopting a suitable weapon, by which he meant a weapon according to his specification. He did not entirely approve of the 'tradesmen [who] have found it profitable to design knives for trench use, and offer such for sale, exhibiting them along with other military accessories in their shop windows'. According to him, some of them were 'very badly designed', including the Robbins punch or push dagger which he singled out for criticism without going so far as to actually name it. Evidently, the view that the knife was 'un-English' and 'distasteful to the British character' was still prevalent in some quarters. This argument had been used whenever Macdonald lobbied for the army to adopt the knife. It was also argued that the rifle with fixed bayonet would always beat a man armed with a mere knife. Unfortunately, Macdonald never indicated who held these views because they were clearly not shared by GHQ but it is doubtful that he had contact with those who were responsible for what was supplied to the army in France.

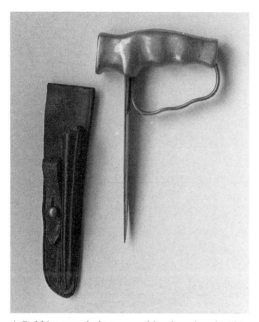

A Robbins punch dagger and leather sheath. This example has lost its original dark finish. Another dagger made by Robbins used the same blade and hilt but the blade projected from the thumb rest on the top of the hilt like a normal dagger. (Author)

The firm of Robbins was just one of many 'tradesmen' who produced trench knives during the war. The business had gone through a number of changes since its beginnings in 1880 in Fountain Street, Dudley, Worcestershire. Originally, it had manufactured baths and ironwork. Later it described itself as a grate and fender maker. In 1906, it started to produce art metalwork and in 1910 Robbins dropped all other business to concentrate on this. The firm must have seen the war as an opportunity to change its business once again and switched to making knives of its own design, most of which betrayed its previous incarnation as an art metal works. Robbins produced at least nine patterns of knife. All had alloy hilts and all but two had knuckle guards. Two designs were push or punch daggers in which the blade was attached to the grip in such a way that it projected between the fingers when grasped in a fist. The shortness of the blade tang in these designs was a weakness and it might well have snapped during a violent fight. One of the punch daggers was especially popular and sold well. There was even what has been termed a ring dagger which slipped over a finger with two curved wings fitting over the adjacent fingers. This, too, was a punch dagger and could be purchased from the Civil Service Co-operative Stores in Regent Street; no doubt it stocked all the Robbins daggers. Although many of the surviving examples are now shiny and well polished, the hilts and blades were originally blackened to be inconspicuous at night. Most knives and daggers were blackened for this reason, irrespective of their country of origin. Robbins blades varied in length from 5 in on the popular punch dagger to as much as 12 in on a dagger that was more than 16 in long and weighed 1 lb. Robbins survived the war but went out of business in 1928.

Knuckleduster knives were popular with British soldiers, perhaps because they could kid themselves that they had bought them for the knuckleduster rather than the blade. Neither the French nor the Germans found any use for them. A number of manufacturers produced similar knives in which the blade was riveted to the side of a knuckleduster grip. The grip was usually made of aluminium, although some were of brass. Many of these knives are marked with the Sheffield cutler who made the blades but some are marked with the retailer, such as Charles Clements of Southampton Row. It is probable that knives were mostly bought by officers rather than other ranks. Some officers went so far as to purchase a job lot of knives for their men. Others even went to the trouble of having weapons designed and made specially. One such officer was Lord Howard de Walden who served in the 9th (Service) Battalion Royal Welch Fusiliers and the Westminster Dragoons, fighting at Gallipoli and in France.

The 8th Baron Howard de Walden, Thomas Evelyn Scott-Ellis, was a writer, sportsman (he was an accomplished fencer who participated in the Olympics of 1906) and antiquarian with an interest in armour. He built up an important collection at his Scottish home, Dean Castle in Kilmarnock, and through this interest came into contact with Félix Joubert, a well-known and knowledgeable dealer and restorer of arms and armour. The 8th Baron was a generous man and when, as a major, he took command of the 9th Battalion Royal Welch Fusiliers he decided to provide a weapon that was both useful in the trenches and at the same time celebrated the battalion's Welshness. He decided to give them a sidearm. And who

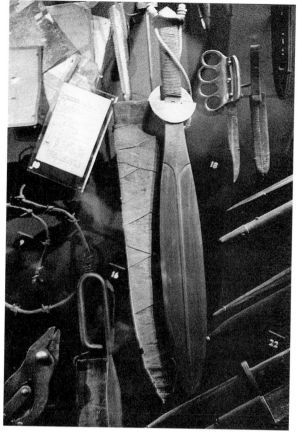

The Joubert sword issued to the 9th (Service) Battalion Royal Welch Fusiliers. The folding hilt, the cord-bound grip and the skull-cracker pommel can be clearly seen. Behind is its scabbard. To the right of it is a British knuckleduster knife and its leather sheath. (Author)

better to design this weapon than Félix Joubert who had already devised a form of overlapping steel armour for trench use, although it does not appear to have been used.

No doubt Howard de Walden discussed with Joubert what form this sidearm might take and between them they came up with the idea of a weapon based on an ancient Welsh sword, the *cledd* – on the face of it, a less then promising one. Joubert duly designed the weapon, set up a company to make it (some of the swords are marked Joubert et Cie, suggesting that it was made in France rather than Britain) and Howard de Walden had his Welsh sword. It was a fearsome weapon, quite unlike any other used in the trenches of the First World War, 2 ft long with an elliptical blade that was 17.5 in long and 3 in wide at its broadest. Some blades were inscribed *Dros Urddas Cymru*, 'For the Dignity of Wales'. The weapon was not manufactured in large numbers but exactly how many were made is unknown. There is also very little known about when it was introduced or its use in battle, although it has been claimed that the sword played a part

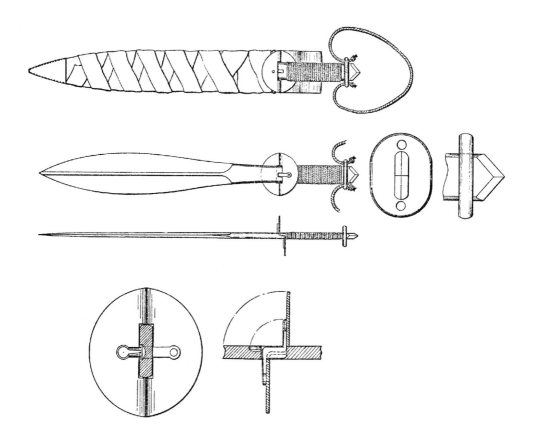

Joubert's Welsh sword, with its folding hilt. Drawing from GB 108,741.

at Messines in 1917. It was given to machine-gunners and bombers of the battalion and would appear to have been issued from trench stores according to circumstance rather than being worn all the time. The weapon had a novel feature, a folding hilt to enable it to be worn in its scabbard without the oval hilt digging into the owner's side. Because of this feature, Joubert decided to apply for a British patent in August 1916 which was granted as GB 108,741 a year later. He probably applied for a French one as well. Curiously, the specification describes Joubert as a sculptor. If the application date is anything to go by, the weapon dates from mid-1916.

Joubert's weapon was not the only dagger to be patented. Maj Eugene McNary, serving in the Service of Supplies of the American Expeditionary Force, applied for a British patent in October 1918 for a knuckleduster knife that the American Army had already adopted as the Model 1918 Mk I. This became GB 127,777 in June 1919. None of the knives was made in Britain, however; they were either made in France (marked *Au Lion* on the blade) or the US and were produced in large numbers. There were at least four manufacturers and the knives all seem to have been made in 1918. This was a vicious-looking weapon with a weighty brass handle, the whole thing weighing 17 oz. The double-edged blade was identical to that of a French trench knife. When the Americans returned to the US after the war the Mk I was taken back into store, redesignated the Trench Knife Mk I, and reissued when the US entered the Second World War, although not for long as it was not an ideal fighting knife. It was also supplied to the Algerians serving with the Free French. This weapon, like many other trench knives, including the Welsh sword, had a skull-cracker pommel that was clearly a functional part of the weapon. The very fact that so many of the trench knives in Allied hands had knuckledusters shows just how vicious close combat was. None of the knives carried in the First World War was meant to be used in the way that Second World War Commandoes were trained to use their stiletto-bladed daggers. The First World War knife was more of a close-in brawl weapon of last resort rather than a swift silent killer.

One or two inventors of knives were perhaps a little optimistic. Mr P. Baker devised a way of attaching a knife to the crown of the steel helmet, which could be used much like an Elizabethan buckler (a small shield held in the left hand and which sometimes had a spike projecting from the centre for punching in the face of an adversary). Baker patented it (GB 103,241) in 1916 but no one shared his vision. An idea with a little more practicality was Capt Pritchard's bayonet for the Webley service revolver, the idea being to combine the benefits of a small firearm and a blade for close-in trench fighting. The invention clearly

The US Trench Knife Mk I patented in Britain by Maj McNary in 1918. This has lost its original dark finish and the maker's logo, L.F. & C. (Landers, Frary and Clark), has been filed off the brass hilt. The guard opposite the blade is circular. (Author)

came from his experience. The gunmaker W.W. Greener thought the bayonet had commercial potential and manufactured a few hundred. It used a cut-down blade from the obsolescent French Gras bayonet. The hilt was machined from brass or steel to grip the body of the revolver and the upper part of the crossguard gripped the muzzle, held there with a spring clip. The revolver needed no alterations for the bayonet to be fitted. Pritchard filed a patent application in November 1916 and this was duly granted as GB 111,526. The

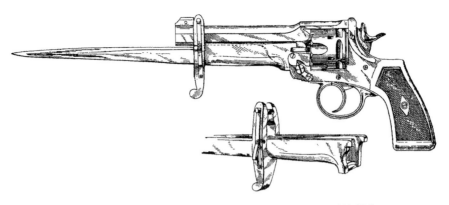

Pritchard's pistol bayonet made by W.W. Greener. Drawing from GB 111,526.

The US Model 1918 trench knife with its hard leather scabbard. It has a 9 in triangular blade. The metal parts are black except the blade which is blued. (Author)

hilt of the bayonet was marked with the maker's name and the word 'patent', along with a number. However, the number was not the patent number, it was the application number. This was one of the numerous tricks used by manufacturers to kid others that something was protected by a patent – protection only happens if the patent is granted.

The Americans entered the war having taken note of the nature of trench warfare, although that did not stop them from repeating the mistakes made by the British and the French in the early years, that of using the same infantry tactics that had been such a failure in the face of machine-guns and artillery. However, they were fully prepared to arm the troops with trench knives. Weapons besides the Mk 1 were issued to US soldiers. In 1917, the Ordnance Department asked a number of knife-makers to submit designs for trench knives to equip the American forces going to France. A design submitted by Henry Disston & Sons of Philadelphia was selected for manufacture. This became the Model 1917 and Model 1918 trench knives, although the latter was also made in 1917. They were identical but for how the projections on the knuckleduster guard were formed, the Model 1917 having pyramidal knobs while the Model 1918 had flanges like the plates on a stegosaurus. The blade was triangular so could only be used for stabbing. These were made in large numbers by four US companies during 1917 and 1918. They were declared obsolete in 1922.

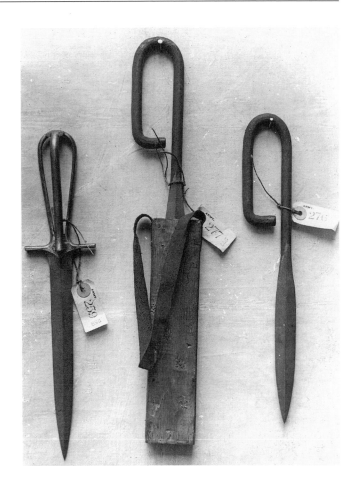

Trench knives. Left to right:
French dagger, its 8 in blade
inscribed Le Nettoyeur de
Tranchées *(The Trench*
Cleaner) and Compagne
1914–15–16–17, *with belt loop;*
two British daggers made from
wire entanglement pickets by
Royal Engineers, one of which
has a crude wooden scabbard
with leather belt loop. (IWM)

The British probably used more improvised knives than any other combatant. The majority of these were made by Royal Engineers but a number seem to have been made by individual soldiers according to what they had to hand and their talents. Broken bayonets, files, barbed wire pickets and scrap metal were all turned into trench knives, some with knuckleduster guards, others without. A very simple but no doubt effective weapon was made from a section of barbed wire picket. The dagger was simply a metal rod looped at one end to form a handle while the other end was hammered out into a sharply pointed blade. Although these have been called French Nails, there is nothing to suggest that they had anything to do with the French. They were, in fact, made at Royal Engineers Workshops; when one of them was handed over to the Imperial War Museum from the Weedon Ordnance Depot in May 1920, it was catalogued as 'Knife, Jabbing. British Pattern'. The French had a wide range of trench knives with wooden handles and double-edged blades as well as an all-steel loop-handled dagger and a variety of weapons made from French bayonets with cruciform-section blades. With the one exception, they all had similar wooden handles. Some of the French weapons had slogans like *Le Nettoyeur de Tranchées* ('The Trench Cleaner') or *Le Vengeur de 1870* (referring to

Trench clubs. Left to right: *moulded lead head; rope wrist-loop and head of looped metal; wrist-loop, hobnails hammered into a lead-filled head; wrist-loop, moulded head, designed and made by Royal Engineers to fit the entrenching tool handle; weighted head with thick metal band.* (IWM)

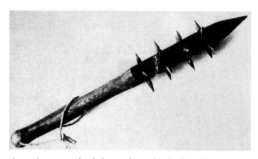

Austrian trench club used on the Italian Front. Although the spikes make this weapon look fearsome, it is likely to have been less practical since the spikes would tend to stick into whatever was struck. (The Illustrated War News)

France's defeat in the Franco-Prussian War) engraved on them. However, these may well have been added after the war, since dates like 1914–1918 are often part of the engraving.

The British had a knack for devising weapons suitable for trench work. Frank Richards remarked on two old sweats 'fixing knives on to a couple of broomsticks . . . [with] some sticking-plaster' borrowed from the Aid Post for a raid. Robert Graves thought they were 'a useful addition to bombs and revolvers' even if his comment was tinged with a touch of sarcasm. On the same raid, 'Some of the officers were going to carry clubs with spikes on, which were very handy weapons at close quarters in a trench.' Frank Richards agreed with the sentiment. Knobkerries came in all shapes and sizes but they all shared one characteristic: weighted heads on wooden shafts. The business end had to be heavy enough to get the momentum to cause damage. Sometimes the head was weighted with lead inside the shaft and hobnails were driven into the outer face. Others had spikes of steel protruding, although these may have been something of a disadvantage since the spikes would have had a tendency to stick into things. Siegfried Sassoon talked of picking up his 'nail-studded knobkerrie' ready for a raid. From all the references in the memoirs written by soldiers who had served in the 2nd Royal Welch Fusiliers, the spiked club must have been the tool of preference when it came to raids. In the Imperial War Museum, there is one with heavy-gauge wire wound in a spiral from a wooden handle to a large square block of metal. Presumably, a rod-like core runs up inside the spiral, to which the head is attached.

Some had lead heads that were cast in moulds. These were clearly made in large enough numbers to warrant the making of moulds from which a great many heads could be produced very quickly. Not all these weapons are British. The Germans, the French and the Austrians all used these crude but deadly weapons in the trenches.

The flanged mace head was a speciality of the Royal Engineers who produced them in thousands. This would appear to be yet another design originating from the Second Army Workshops. It may even have been designed by Newton. The cast head was push-fitted on to the handle of the entrenching tool which already had a metal cap to take the more customary spade. It was a simple but ingenious solution, typical of the way in which the Royal Engineers solved practical problems. Production began in the spring of 1915 and continued into 1918. It is difficult to put a figure on how many were made but the daily output was considerable and they were widely used. In one week in March 1918, the Hazebrouck Workshops had 3,294 in store.

According to Stephen Graham, who served in the Guards, clubs were still being issued in 1918 for men to go out on raids 'like savages'. These were produced by Royal Engineers from 'the iron part of Mills hand-grenades clamped to entrenching tool handles', by which he presumably meant the segmented casing. Graham was impressed with their ability to do damage since 'One sharp blow on the head from one of these' was usually enough to render a man senseless, if not kill him. The knobkerrie was a highly

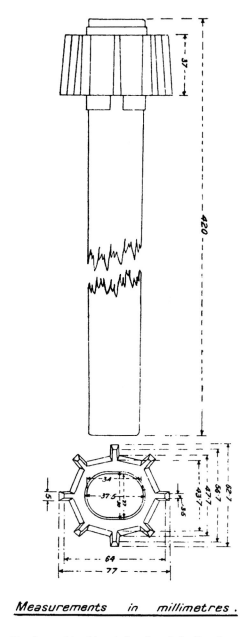

Measurements in millimetres.

The flanged knobkerrie head made by Royal Engineers and fitted to the entrenching tool handle. (Institution of Royal Engineers)

effective weapon, even against soldiers wearing helmets. The mace's ability to inflict injury to the head of a man wearing a helmet may have been the real reason why the British preferred it to the knife. This medieval weapon, which in times past had come to signify authority and status, now represented the brutality of trench warfare.

CHAPTER 8
Mud and Wire

Mud was a pernicious enemy. It got into everything. The trenches were almost a breeding ground for the stuff. A combination of feet, shells and rain turned soil into brown misery. Frank Richards remarked of a German attack in late October 1914 that 'continual rain had made the parapet very muddy and the mud had got into the rifle mechanism'. Already hot from constant shooting the bolt inevitably jammed. The rain had been heavy for a couple of days and Capt Dunn noted that:

> Rain and mud were by now causing a lot of trouble with rifles; and the supply of oil had given out. There was nowhere to lay or clean a rifle without its getting clogged with mud, or a plug in the muzzle, which caused the barrel to bulge or burst when a shot was fired.

The barrels had to be cleared by ramrod and there were only two of these between a couple of hundred men. The situation got so bad that the support company's rifles were brought forward, leaving the support company impotent.

This was but a foretaste of what was to come in later years. Mud hindered movement in the trenches to such an extent that supplies could not be brought up through communication trenches. And when it rained, trenches filled with water, sometimes knee deep, which mixed with the mud to make a glutinous mess. It rotted feet, rusted rifles and jammed anything mechanical. Capt James Jack described the mud as 'glue-like'. Ankle-deep liquid mud was common in winter. Some of the British trenches were in ground where the water table was so near the surface that trenches were continually wet. Under such conditions, trenches had to be part hole in the ground, part sandbagged wall. This was a major problem in low-lying Flanders. With the effects of heavy shelling, the situation was made much worse.

Water and mud was no less a problem for the Germans, despite having entrenched on higher ground. Writing in November 1914, Rudolph Binding recorded that 'hardly a shell bursts on contact, but is imprisoned by the soft, sticky mud'. In December 1915, he observed that 'In the trenches and dug-outs the men are literally lying in the water'.

The only solution to mud getting into rifles and rendering them unusable was regular cleaning and regular inspections to ensure that mud and rust were being kept at bay. In the course of a firefight, there was not much that could be done to prevent the ingress of mud but at other times, when the danger of a firefight was absent, the breech and muzzle could be protected by special covers. These did not become available until 1915. The basic design of the breech cover remained much the same throughout the war although there were some modifications to try to prevent it slipping back over the breech. This problem was never satisfactorily resolved and Todhunter noted in late November 1916 that it was 'unavoidable'.

A breech cover was invented by W.C. Hammond in late 1914 and was intended to protect the breech and magazine from dust and dirt but leave the trigger guard exposed. It was a split sleeve made of waterproof material 'which is wrapped round the breech action and secured by snap-fastenings' with an overlap at the join. According to the specification (GB 23,895/14) filed in December 1914, the cover was supposed to be permanently attached to the small of the butt and could be

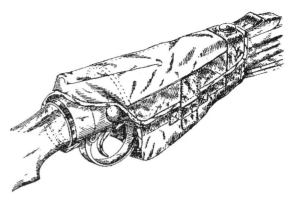

W.C. Hammond's breech cover, GB 23,895/14. This did not cover the trigger.

rapidly removed from the breech by pulling a tab. Whether this became the basis of the Cover, breech, Mark I, which was entered in the List of Changes in June 1915, is difficult to

A pair of British corporals at Beaumont Hamel on the Somme, November 1916. They wear the original Brodie helmet with the unprotected rim. The rifle of the man on the left has a No. 1 Mk I breech cover. The man on the right has protected his rifle with the Mk II rifle cover. (IWM)

A metal muzzle cap taken from a Turkish rifle in the Dardanelles, summer 1915. (The Illustrated War News)

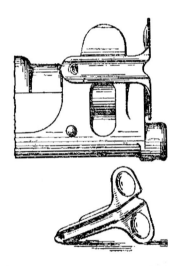

A.S. Purdey's spring clip muzzle cap, GB 3,188/15.

tell but it is likely as it is the first patent for this type of cover and the application would probably have been refused had the Mk I already existed. It was later redesignated the No. 1 Mk I. It was 'made of double-texture waterproofed drill' and had three press studs that fastened on the left-hand side of the rifle. There were two eyelets 'for a lace which is knotted on the inside to retain it in position'. The entry notes that 'If the lace is not tied tightly, or is drawn too far back, it may fall over the front of the cartridge way in the body and obstruct the closing of the bolt.' This cover was intended for all the rifles in service with the British and Empire forces except the P14 for which a modified cover was later introduced. Before the introduction of the Mk I there had been a couple of experimental covers made of canvas with only two press studs but these saw very limited use before being withdrawn. The Cover, short rifle (Mk II), which dated from the early 1900s, was similar to the kind of case used by sportsmen. It covered most of the rifle from the muzzle to the small of the butt where a lace tied it in place (the Mk I was for the long rifle). It was made of canvas and was originally fastened by a strap with a buckle.

Although the No. 3 Mk I muzzle protector was only entered in the List of Changes in January 1917, the device had been in service some time before then. It replaced two experimental muzzle protectors, the Nos 1 and 2. It is unclear what form the earlier protectors took but the No. 3 used a screw to hold it in place. It consisted of a top plate hinged to a side plate and was 'fitted with a . . . spiral tension spring'. The top plate had a cupped depression in it that fitted into the muzzle. The plate extended in front of the foresight so that if the shooter should attempt to fire with the protector still in place he would be unable to aim, the idea being that this would remind him of the protector over the end. Whether this worked in practice, especially in the heat of the moment, is debatable. The side plate had a 'positioning nib' that fitted into the recess of the nosecap and a hole for the fixing screw that replaced the rifle's nosecap fixing screw, and the spring held the two plates together.

The protector was clearly intended to be used only when the rifle was in transit and nowhere near the fighting. The protector was designed to fit all rifles except the P14 for which it was modified and issued as the No. 6.

A simpler protector was invented by A.S. Purdey in early 1915 (GB 3,188/15). This did not need to be screwed to the muzzle, using instead 'rearwardly projecting spring arms' to clip it to the muzzle. It, too, had an extension that projected in front of the foresight but, unlike the No. 3, the rifle could be fired with it still in place because the bullet would knock the protector off. It was made in one piece and would have been simpler to manufacture than the No. 3. However, the spring arms may not have been strong enough to withstand rough treatment and it may have fallen off too easily. An even simpler protector was a rubber cap complete with ventilation hole (C. Liddiard, GB 12,087/15) but this was not designed for the SMLE and rubber was unlikely to have been available for such a device had the cap been suitable for the service rifle.

A different but no less daunting problem was entirely man-made – barbed wire. This invention, the first patents for which dated from 1867, saw widespread use in America after 1874 when the first machine for making it was invented. Thousands of miles of it stretched across the plains to keep cattle in. By the First World War, it had long since ceased to be a purely agricultural fencing material and had acquired a military use. It served much the same purpose, except that it was no longer cows that were to be contained. Whenever trenches were dug, barbed wire was laid in front. At first, only a few strands were erected. In October 1914, sappers 'put up three strands of wire' to keep nearby cows out of the Royal Welch trenches but this was typical of the strength of wire obstacles to keep the enemy at bay. It was quite inadequate and by early 1915 the wire had blossomed into belts 'several yards across, fixed on stakes'. The 6 January issue of *The Illustrated War News* described a barbed-wire entanglement as 'from sixteen to twenty feet wide, of intricately interlaced spiked wires, forming a web spread on stakes from three to six feet tall'. But even this was not enough. A year later and great rolls of concertina wire and seas of criss-crossing wires formed belts 30–60 yd deep, and there was usually more than one belt. These belts were often laid with cunning to funnel men into killing zones. Around strong points it could be even thicker. These presented impassable obstacles.

The most effective way to cut wire was with high explosive but artillery shells tended to bury themselves before exploding, which created craters and added to the obstacles that had to be crossed. The instantaneous artillery fuse was not developed until 1916 – a modification of a fuse invented by Henry Newton for trench mortar bombs – and did not start to see widespread use until the later stages of the Battle of the Somme. Before the Somme, high-explosive shells were not as plentiful as they might have been. The British were left with shrapnel balls with which to cut wire but this method was unreliable and often unsuccessful; whole sections of wire could be left undamaged while neighbouring areas were well cut. Inventors turned their minds to special artillery shells that could cut wire: shells with extending blades (for example, GB 7,102, filed in May 1915); shells with lengths of chain inside and designed to separate into two parts with the chain linking them (for example, GB 7,652/15, filed in May 1915); and paired shells linked by

A group of French artillerymen pose with ancient cannon used for firing the grapnels that are displayed in front of them, summer 1915. The grapnels, attached to ropes or chains, are fired into wire entanglements then reeled back through the entanglement to clear a path – at least, in theory. (The Illustrated War News)

chain and fired from double-barrelled guns. The first patent for a twin gun was granted to A.L. McKelvey who filed an application in February 1915. Downs and Bedford filed the last application in March 1918. None of these special shells was truly original, as similar sorts of things had been used at sea in the eighteenth century to shred sails and rigging.

It is very doubtful that any of these shells would have been as effective against barbed wire as high explosive, even supposing they worked. Their complexity would have also mitigated against their manufacture, especially as until early 1916 the Ministry of Munitions was having enough trouble supplying conventional ammunition without squandering resources on mechanical shells. There was at least one British patent for ammunition with a grapnel (GB 106,853, filed in June 1916). The French certainly used ancient wheeled cannon to fire grapnels into wire entanglements; these were pulled back through the wire by ropes or chains, hopefully destroying the wire on the way. But it is unlikely that this was widespread and even more unlikely that grapnels achieved very much. It would have been a labour-intensive and time-consuming task, even supposing that it was possible to pull a gap in the wire rather than making a worse tangle.

And there were other more exotic devices, strange mechanical contraptions that were supposed to precede the advancing infantry and chew up the wire in their path. The tank was a much better idea. Some of these inventions were, in effect, tanks of a sort. Others were odd little contrivances, wire-cutters operated by gears and cams intended to be attached to the front of vehicles. From the patent drawings, it would appear that some of them were actually built. They were not practical.

When artillery or trench mortars firing high explosive were not available or circumstances made them unsuitable for cutting wire, there were only two realistic alternatives – mechanical, hand-operated wire-cutters and hand-laid explosive charges. The Bangalore torpedo was intended to destroy enemy wire entanglements to enable raiders to get into enemy trenches. Torpedoes were manufactured at Royal Engineer Workshops in considerable numbers. Cumbersome and difficult to manoeuvre, the Bangalore torpedo was not quite the solution to cutting wire that GHQ hoped it would be. Sometimes it failed to explode. The 2nd Royal Welch Fusiliers used one for the first time on a raid in April 1916 and it did not go off because the 'detonating gadget . . . failed to explode it'. Frank Richards recalled that it had to be retrieved the next night because it was still top secret but the Germans beat them to it, removed the contents of the torpedo and replaced the empty tube. According to Capt Hitchcock, 'The torpedoes would only be used as a last resort, and they were always cumbersome articles to work, and if used, the chief element in the raid, "surprise," would be lost, and the Boche put on their guard'. He described Bangalore torpedoes as 'aluminium tubes about 6 feet in length, filled with ammonal, and were worked by an ordinary fuse'. They usually came in 10 ft lengths of 2 in steel tubing but it is not impossible that Hitchcock could have come across aluminium torpedoes.

Hitchcock claimed that the Bangalore torpedo was invented by an artillery officer in Bangalore, India, although others reckoned it was a Royal Engineer. The first mention of the Bangalore torpedo was in *The Royal Engineers Journal* of March 1913. By early 1915, the device was well known to the French and the Russians as well as to the British.

Captured German Bangalore torpedoes, early 1918. (The Illustrated War News)

Whereas the British version consisted of a tube of steel containing packets of explosive and a shorter, wider second tube that fitted over one end of it (the second tube appears to have been a connector to allow several tubes of explosive to be joined together), the French used a long, flat piece of wood to which explosive charges were tied. The French device had a pair of tiny wheels at the front to help it along the ground and a separate pole to push the torpedo into place. The Russians used a variation of the French device and another of their own design. The French torpedo was apparently fired electrically but the British torpedoes never were, making do with a safety fuse or some other timer mechanism. The Bangalore torpedo was evidently introduced on the Western Front in early 1915 but memoirs often describe it as something new introduced in about spring 1916.

The French overcame the problem of manhandling the cumbersome torpedoes by devising a pulley system. A man carried an anchor with the pulley out to the wire and hooked it on to a picket. A light cable fed through the pulley could then be used to haul the torpedo out to the wire. GHQ was enthusiastic about this development and in the summer of 1917 a series of trials were carried out but these showed that the device was no better than the usual method of carrying torpedoes into position and the British abandoned the idea. The British continued to use their own design of torpedo until the end of the war.

Various other ways of cutting wire were tried, including machine-gun fire. In June 1916, Hythe evaluated a smooth-bore Maxim, firing at a range of 150 yd into an entanglement 30 yd deep. A lane was cut with 250 rounds of Mk IV ammunition but this was no better than what could be achieved with a conventional barrel. A Vickers firing 220 rounds at the same range and at the same obstacle was, in fact, better. In October 1916, Capt Hitchcock reported that for several nights in a row a machine-gun fired off a couple of belts that 'may have killed some Boches, but at any rate . . . cut a lot of the enemy's wire entanglements . . . one could see the sparks flying from the enemy's wire'.

The alternative to explosives and machine-guns was hand-operated wire-cutters, although these were supplemented with devices attached to rifles. Guy Chapman drew a distinction between the various types, listing 'wire cutters, wire shears, wire breakers' as part of the ever-increasing inventory of new equipment the infantryman was expected to cart about with him; it also emphasized the importance of wire cutting. James Jack referred to them as hand pliers. Hand-held wire-cutters were nothing new, of course, and the army had used them long before the outbreak of war in 1914. But it had only a few and these were the preserve of Royal Engineers. With the coming of trench warfare and the ever-thickening barbed-wire entanglements, wire-cutters became an essential item for the infantryman. Not to mention the indispensable 'hedging gloves' to protect the hands, some of which may have been made from Mr Lynch's patent 'puncture-proof material'. By late 1914, each company of a battalion was supplied with large numbers of wire-cutters, while many officers bought their own while on leave. These devices were no substitute for artillery bombardment of wire, neither were they indestructible and they were often lost, but they were crucial for patrolling and raiding. Robert Graves complained that British issue wire-cutters would only cut British wire; presumably German wire was of a heavier gauge. In late 1916 he bought 'a pair of insulated wire-cutters strong enough to cut German wire'.

Sassoon agreed with Graves's assessment of British issue wire-cutters, often cursing 'the savage bluntness of our Company's wire-cutters', and claimed that 'we hadn't got a decent pair of wire-cutters in the Battalion'. While in the Army & Navy Stores before the Somme, he bought two pairs of wire-cutters with rubber-covered handles. Rubber was put on the handles because it was believed that wire entanglements might be electrified. Using these for the first time, he noted 'that cutting tangles of barbed wire in the dark in a desperate hurry is a job that needs ingenuity'. He and several other men spent more than three hours 'snipping and snatching' at the wire and shredding their leather gloves in the process. The results looked far from impressive in daylight and Sassoon wondered if the effort had been worth it. Nevertheless, one of his co-workers remarked that the Army & Navy wire-cutters worked 'a fair treat'. Returning to the task in daylight, better progress was made now that they could see

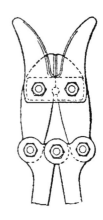

The head of the hand-operated wire-cutters invented by R. Pengeot, illustrated in GB 13,202/15.

what they were doing. After ninety minutes, 'the gaps were real good ones'. Cutting wire by hand was hard work. Although this was in preparation for the Manchester attack on the Somme, wire-cutting parties regularly went into no-man's-land to ensure that passages through the entanglements remained open for patrols and raiders – and the enemy did his best to go out and repair the gaps. Wire cutting was a never-ending job.

Sassoon's wire-cutters could have been those invented by G.F. Pittar in early 1915 (GB 2734/15); these had rubber-covered handles but so did many others. Pittar's invention had a toggle link between the blades and a hook-shaped frame to increase the leverage as the cut progressed. Other commercial wire-cutters were also patented. The device invented by R. Pengeot, dating from September 1915, was described in the specification (GB 13,202/15) as 'shears for cutting wire &c'. A pair of blades were pivoted about a pair of diverging horns. The handles pivoted about the lower ends of the blades and were joined to each other at another pivot between the blades. A pivot roller engaged in recesses in the blades between the blade/horn pivots and beneath the cutting edges. 'When the shears are open, the horns form forward extensions of the blades and serve to guide the wire to them.' It would seem that these were the first hand-held wire-cutter to make use of diverging horns; others had nothing to feed the wire to the blades, making the job of cutting wire much harder. Pengeot's shears were heavy duty tools with long wooden handles and were used on the Western Front. The longer the handles, the greater the leverage that could be applied to the wire and the easier it was to break it. The leverage was increased by the pivots. Other wire-cutters relied purely on the physical strength of the user.

In August 1917, William Lea, an engineer, filed a patent application for 'an improved cutting device which is more efficient and more readily operated than such devices heretofore constructed'. It was also foldable. His specification described two other types of wire-cutter on which his invention was supposed to improve. One had two jaws

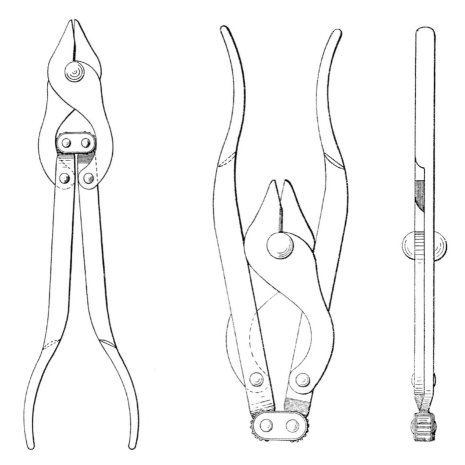

Left: *folding hand-held wire-cutters invented by William Lea in 1917, illustrated in GB 112,111.* Centre and right: *Lea's wire-cutters folded.*

mounted on a common pivot, the jaws having crossed 'tail pieces pivotally connected to operating levers at points below the common fulcrum' of the levers (or handles). In the other type, the tail pieces did not cross and the levers were geared together and connected by links, their pivots being above those of the links and levers (handles). The idea in each case was to increase the leverage. Lea's invention had two jaws mounted on a common pivot, the crossed tail pieces of which were joined by pivots linked to the operating levers. The ends of the levers at the pivots had gear teeth that meshed together. This linking piece was the key to the extra leverage Lea's cutters could theoretically achieve. The leverage increased as the cut progressed and he claimed that his cutters would cut wire 'with less pressure than that hitherto required'. However, surviving examples of his wire-cutters do not have the link, the levers being joined at a single pivot.

The idea of combining a wire-cutter with the service rifle dated from at least 1909. The army had, in fact, adopted the No. 1 Mk I and the No. 2 Mk I wire-breakers a few years before the war, the former for use when the bayonet was fixed to the SMLE and the latter for when it was not (a rather unwieldy arrangement that must have seemed logical to someone at the time). A single strand of wire was guided to the muzzle by a V-shaped groove and a round was fired to sever it. No doubt these were used on the Western Front but they can hardly have made much of an impression. Another version, the No. 3 Mk I, was issued after the start of the war and was designed to be used with the 1888 Pattern bayonet fixed to the long Lee Enfield. But these devices were not considered to be adequate for the task and alternatives were sought.

The type of wire-cutter meant to be attached to the rifle (or bayonet) evoked considerable interest during the first eighteen months of the war. The devices were mostly mechanically operated, some worked by hand while others were 'automatic' and did not require the infantryman to take his hands off

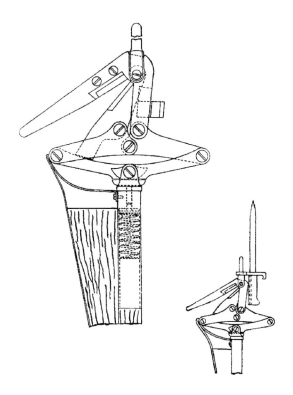

Wire-cutters used by the Italian Army, invented by P. Malfatti, operated by toggle levers. The cutter was attached to a pole and was fitted with a pin and lug for fixing a bayonet. Drawing from GB 106,334.

the rifle. But even this was an old idea. None of these devices was proposed as an alternative to the hand-held wire-cutters. They were hardly practical alternatives for discrete night-time cutting and those that required a round to be fired certainly were not. They were meant to help infantrymen in an attack, to snip passages through uncut wire without having to put aside the rifle to use hand-held cutters.

More than twenty-five wire-cutter attachments were patented during the war, fourteen of which date from 1915. There were others. Inventors saw these devices as important additions to the infantryman's equipment, essential for his survival, and better than hand-held cutters. Hythe was keen to find suitable devices that could be quickly supplied to the army in France. One of the first devices to be tested, in late 1914, was invented by a Capt Dunn (this was not the same Capt Dunn of the Royal Welch Fusiliers). Todhunter thought that the device, which had to be attached to the bayonet, would be too expensive to make but recommended that it ought to be seriously considered anyway because of the shortage. However, there is no evidence to suggest that Dunn's wire-cutter found its way to France.

Many of the inventions were wire-cutters that worked in combination with the bayonet. T.R.R. Ashton's device, dating from September 1914, was fitted over the bayonet adjacent to the crossguard and was worked by the infantryman pushing the device against a strand of wire, an action that forced the pivoting blades to turn, slide and cut the wire. He had already patented a couple of similar cutters a few years earlier; GB 20,241/14, an improvement on his earlier cutter, was published but not granted because he failed to pay the sealing fee. None of his designs was taken up. A viciously toothed wheel which rotated eccentrically to cut the wire against a stationary disc is described in GB 5,904/15, dating from October 1915. It, too, was fitted to the bayonet. And there was Sir Ernest Moir's invention, which again fitted over the bayonet but the cutting blade was pushed down by firing a round (GB 7,442/15). This dated from May 1915. Moir was head of the Munitions Inventions Department at the time but his device was not adopted. Even though he was in a position to know what was practical and desirable he failed to invent something useful.

There were cutters that were operated by hand and simply fixed to the side of the rifle as a convenient place to put the device. None of these was a success. Herbert Cocks, engineer, filed two patent applications, the first in June 1915, the second in January 1916, for such a device and these were subsequently joined to become GB 8,457/15. It was similar to the hand-held wire-cutters but offered no advantage at all. It was clamped to the fore-end of the rifle and operated by a long handle that reached back as far as the magazine; this would have been a considerable hindrance to shooting as not only would the handle have got in the way but the clamps partly obscured the fore-sight. It is clear from his specification that some of the hand-operated cutters attached to rifles were extremely awkward to use as the handles were not in easy reach, so the infantryman had to perform a sort of juggling act. This was made worse when the handle was operated by a cord. This was all too much for an infantryman to deal with under pressure. Such devices were impractical and conventional hand-held cutters were superior. However, by late 1915, a different sort of wire-cutter had been developed. This was of the 'automatic' type, in itself nothing new, but the blades were operated by pins moving in curved slots, a significant improvement.

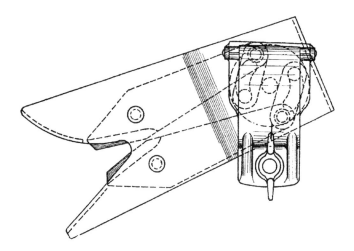

Charles Sangster's wire-cutter attachment showing the jaws open. Note the curved slots, on the right, in which the jaw pins turned. Drawing from GB 3,761/15.

The first of these was a Russian invention. Stanislas Korsak of Petrograd (present-day St Petersberg) devised a mechanism in early 1915 where the blades were mounted on pivots in a casing that rotated. Horns on the casing guided the wire to the open jaws and made the casing turn. This closed the blades on the wire and cut it. The device was fixed near to the muzzle of the Moisin Nagant rifle and in the open position faced downwards and towards the butt, a spring returning it to this position after a strand was cut. The wire was, in effect, pulled into the device. The subject of GB 7,154/15 and GB 8,596/15 (the method of clamping it to the rifle), it was adopted by the Imperial Russian Army. In September 1915, Charles Sangster applied for a patent for an improved version of this wire-cutter (GB 3,761/15). It is likely that Decimals manufactured the Korsak design; it certainly manufactured

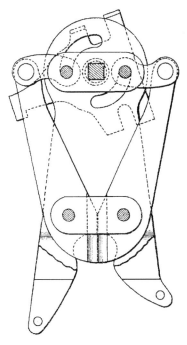

The wire-cutters invented by George Bull of Charles H. Pugh Ltd, showing the jaws closed. This is a refinement of Sangster's cutter. Drawing from GB 17,886/15.

Sangster's. Like Korsak's invention, his device was used by the Russians.

Another Birmingham company, Charles H. Pugh Ltd, devised a further improvement. It is probable that this was a development of the Sangster wire-cutter and may even have been devised with the full cooperation of Sangster. The Korsak, Sangster and Pugh wire-cutters follow a clear line of development. The Pugh wire-cutter was the subject of GB 17,886/15. The company and George Bull, its managing director, were named as the inventors. The application was filed in December. Pugh's improvement consisted of a modification 'to relieve or equalise the levering or bending strains which are imposed upon the actuating pins [which moved in the curved slots] when the appliance is in use'. From this it is clear that the pins of the previous devices had a tendency to bend or break. If this happened while the wire was in the device, the whole rifle would have been useless as the weapon would have been attached to the wire. In such a situation, the wire-cutter would have to be removed from the rifle, a far from simple operation when under fire.

The Pugh wire-cutter was adapted to fit the SMLE, P14 and the Ross and became the Cutters, wire, SA No. 1 Mk I, No. 2 Mk I and the No. 3 Mk I. It was fitted to the right side of the rifle near the muzzle, projecting 'diagonally upwards, and to the rear, when in position'. The wire-cutter was operated by the infantryman drawing back the rifle as the wire contacted the fore-end:

Muddy conditions on the Somme, summer 1916. The soldier on the right has a No. 1 Mk II wire-cutter attached to his rifle. (The Illustrated War News)

the wire entering between the jaws of the cutter [which] rotates it, causing the rear levers of the shear blades to be opened and the jaws closed, at the same time winding up a coiled wire spring which, when the wire is severed and pressure on the cutter has ceased, expands and returns the cutter to position with jaws open.

Some time later, the No. 1 Mk II and the No. 4 Mk I were introduced, the former for the SMLE, the latter for the P14. These differed from the earlier cutters in having longer horns and being operated by a push forwards instead of a pull backwards. They were attached in the same position as the earlier cutters but projected diagonally upward and towards the muzzle with the longer horn overlapping and nearly touching the blade of the bayonet. Most of the components were common to all the devices. About a year later, Bull and a colleague, E.W. Starkey, filed a patent application for a variation on the theme, modifying the wire-cutter to be a hand-held device (GB 104,627); it is not known whether this found its way to France but it seems likely.

In May 1916, Todhunter evaluated a wire-cutter invented by Lt J.M. Brewis. This was yet another variation on the same theme and Todhunter did not think it was an improvement. The bayonet got in the way with the push version and the opening for the wire was too narrow on the pull version. He rejected it. He also rejected a wire-breaker of the same type as the No. 1 and No. 2 wire-breakers that required a round to be fired through the wire to break it. Although Henry Johnson's device was more easily fitted and removed from the rifle than the Nos 1 and 2, it suffered from the same basic problem inherent with all such devices: its success or failure was more dependant on the type of ammunition used than it was on the design of the breaker. Johnson's device was already the subject of a patent application when Todhunter tested it (GB 13,621/15). It was a piece of sheet metal shaped to fit over the muzzle cap with a guideway that centred strands of wire in front of the muzzle, the lower arm of which engaged the top edge of the bayonet blade. It was held in place by fixing the bayonet. The first shot cut three of six strands of 0.25 in wire but four more rounds failed to sever the remaining three and

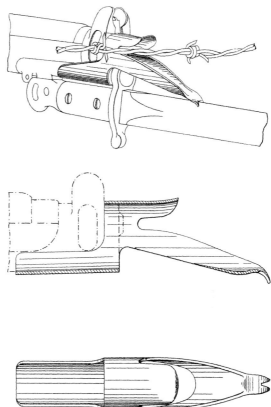

This design of wire-breaker, by Henry Theophilus Johnson, a member of the Institute of Mechanical Engineers, was tested by Capt Todhunter and rejected. Drawings from GB 13,621.

two-strand wire needed two shots to cut it. It was the shape of the bullet nose that determined how well wire was cut with small arms ammunition; pointed bullets were much less able to cut wire than round-nosed bullets. This basic flaw in all such wire-breakers ensured that they were unpopular with everyone. Todhunter sealed the fate of Johnson's device by pronouncing it expensive to make and dangerous to use. It was not firmly held in place and could therefore fall over the muzzle and be hit by a round. He noted that although there were various bayonet wire-cutters in service with the British and French armies which were easily attached to the bayonet, there was only one effective cutter of wire: artillery.

This did not prevent some odd ideas from taking hold. In early 1915, suggestions that soldiers could cross wire entanglements using what were in effect mattresses thrown over it gained some credibility. Quite how the 'mattresses' were supposed to be manhandled to the wire without those carrying them being shot down is something of a mystery. And 'blankets' of Lynch's barbed-wire-proof material could also be used similarly. This approach to crossing wire was taken seriously, so seriously in fact that in January 1917 the Leinsters were issued with 'special mats' for a raid near Loos so that the company-strength raiders could negotiate uncut wire. This was desperate stuff.

CHAPTER 9

The Way Ahead

The Farquhar-Hill automatic rifle was tested by the Experimental Section at the School of Musketry on 15 May 1915. It was neither the first nor the last time this weapon was tested at Hythe. According to Capt Todhunter's report, the rate of fire was about equal to the highest attainable with the SMLE. His explanation for this was that most of the time was taken up with aiming at the target. This was calculated to be 40 seconds of a minute's worth of shooting. Little time was saved by the automatic loading and ejection system. The Farquhar-Hill could not fire more than twenty-five rounds in 1 minute whereas it was possible to fire thirty to thirty-five rounds with the SMLE in the same time (not, it has to be said, by many infantrymen). The Farquhar-Hill was thrown more off target by the recoil than the SMLE 'and the firer has in consequence more to do in recovering his aim'. So much for the automatic rifle.

The automatic rifle was more than two decades old by the time of the First World War. Capt Todhunter did not like it and always rejected it in tests, irrespective of whose it was. He was of the old school when it came to musketry and firmly believed in the shooting skills displayed so effectively by the BEF at Mons and Le Cateau: aimed rapid fire. No other army before or since could match the shooting skills of Britain's small pre-war regular army. In theory, an infantryman could fire fifteen to twenty individually aimed shots in 1 minute (the so-called 'mad minute'). All that died at Mons and Le Cateau. The New Army raised from Kitchener's volunteers never even came close to developing the same expertise, not least because it took years of sustained practice. And with the advent of trench warfare the rifle gave way to the hand and rifle grenade as the principal means by which the infantryman killed his enemy, despite exhortations from on high to use the rifle more, especially in defence. It was a vicious circle. Old soldiers like Frank Richards were scornful of the new soldiers' lack of expertise with the rifle and reliance on the bomb.

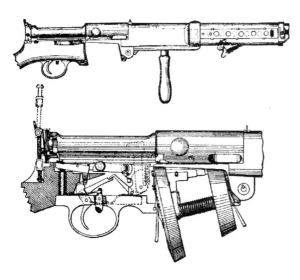

One of many patents for the Farquhar-Hill automatic rifle, GB 126,055, dating from 1916.

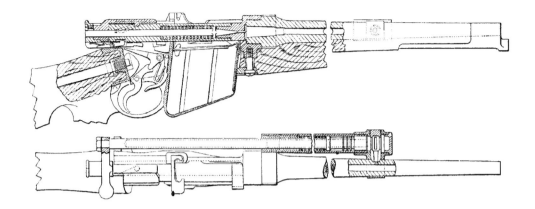

A conversion of an SMLE into 'a gas-operated rifle by providing a gas cylinder attached to the barrel and communicating with the bore by a port, and a piston connected to a longitudinally-slidable sleeve which first rotates the breech-bolt and retracts the cocking piece and then retracts the breech-bolt', as shown in GB 128,395, dating from June 1918. This was invented by Sir A.T. Dawson and Sir G.T. Buckham, who were responsible for a large number of inventions concerned with automatic weapons.

The truth was that the bolt-action rifle had had its day. It took the British Army another forty years to recognize this. In fact, the British Army was just about the only army in the Great War not to use an automatic rifle at the Front, if only experimentally. However, none was a resounding success. The French tried the St Étienne, the Germans a gas-operated Mauser, the Americans the Browning Automatic Rifle – all in 1918 – while the Russians tried a Federov design in 1916. Of these, only the BAR went on to see widespread use but as a light machine-gun. The others all had serious shortcomings such as excessive recoil and fouling of the gas ports, the former making automatic rifles unpopular with infantrymen. The United States Army was the first to adopt a semi-automatic service rifle, the M1 Garand in 1936. Significantly, the M1 failed British trials; British intransigence over the usefulness and workability of the automatic rifle was unchanged in the 1930s. However, the automatic rifle was never intended by inventors to be used in the way that the pre-war army had been trained to use the SMLE. Todhunter and those of like mind nevertheless viewed the automatic rifle as merely an SMLE in which the burden of loading and ejecting by hand had been replaced by automation. They did not recognize that automatic rifles were all about volume of fire not shooting skill of the old school.

The Farquhar-Hill was tested again in August 1916. Four hundred rounds were fired after which the gun began to develop problems due to fouling. Moreover, it stopped feeding properly. Todhunter noted that these same faults had been in evidence in the previous trials. The inventors, M.G. Farquhar and A.H. Hill, held at least thirteen patents related to automatic rifles, the first dating back to 1909; they filed their last application in 1922. It availed them nothing. The British were opposed to the automatic rifle, regarding the automatic mechanism as an unnecessary weight burden. The Farquhar-Hill was not the only British automatic rifle of the period, of course. The Griffiths and Woodgate, for example, dated from 1894 and was one of the first successful automatic rifles. It was tested but turned down.

The First World War saw the emergence of the sub-machine-gun. This weapon was unlike other automatic weapons. Lightweight and firing a pistol cartridge with a consequently limited range, it was neither machine-gun nor rifle although it was as a light machine-gun that the Italians first used the double-barrelled Villar Perosa, protected by a small shield. The British had a demonstration of the Villar Perosa (also known as the Rivelli after its inventor) in October 1915 at the School of Musketry. Todhunter believed that it would be a serviceable addition to the infantry on the Western Front but was only suitable for short ranges. There were problems with ejection, however. Tested again a month later for accuracy and penetration power, Todhunter noted that the weapon ought to be fitted with a stock so that it could be fired from the shoulder. A patent specification dating from March 1917, an addition to a patent from two years earlier, specifically describes a stock for a single-barrelled weapon (GB 133,090, addition to GB 16,362/15) but it was not built until after the war. The Villar Perosa was the first operational sub-machine-gun and was used by the Italian Army. Despite Todhunter's apparent recommendation of the Villar Perosa, as well as other favourable trials carried out by the Royal Small Arms Factory at Enfield, GHQ did not want it, stating that the army had a wide enough diversity of weapons as it was and did not need another one. The British rejected the sub-machine-gun until the Second World War when it was forced to adopt it.

The Italian firm of Beretta developed a sub-machine-gun with a wooden stock, the Model 1918, under instructions from the Italian government. It entered service before the

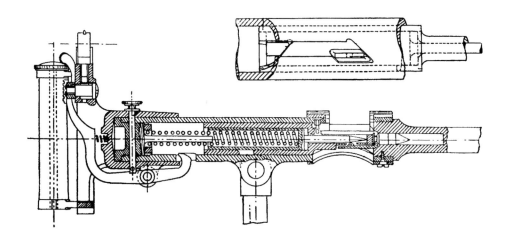

Drawings from the first Villar Perosa sub-machine-gun patent, GB 16,362, dating from September 1915.

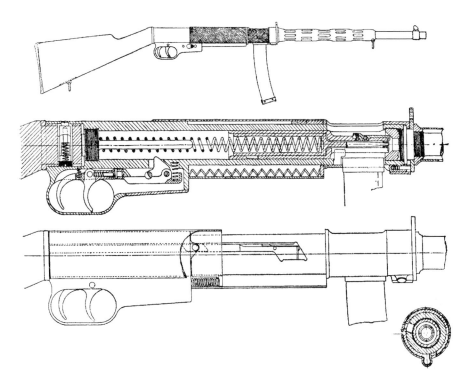

The Villar Perosa adapted to take a stock described in GB 133,090 of 1917. A version of this weapon was made after the war and was still in use with the Italian Army at the start of the Second World War.

better-known Bergmann MP 18 entered service with the German Army in the summer of 1918. Following tests of a captured Bergmann in September 1918, GHQ was again asked if a weapon of this type was wanted. It said no, citing among other things that a weapon that could penetrate body armour was essential to deter the enemy from wearing it. The sub-machine-gun bullet did not have the same power of penetration as a rifle or machine-gun bullet.

The German Army had little idea at first how to exploit the MP 18 (*Maschinenpistole* or machine-pistol Model 1918). For one thing, the ammunition for it was supposed to be brought forward on handcarts during an attack which severely hampered its mobility. But they soon learned, although by then the Germans were in retreat. Unlike the magazines of later sub-machine-guns, the MP 18's was a snail drum, holding thirty-two rounds, which came from the Luger pistol as, indeed, did the weapon's barrel. By the end of the war, 35,000 MP 18s had been manufactured. The Versailles Treaty specifically forbade the postwar German Army from using the Bergmann or any other sub-machine-gun.

Of all the devices developed for trench warfare discussed here, the automatic rifle and the sub-machine-gun emerged as two of the most significant for the future of warfare. The effectiveness of the sub-machine-gun was demonstrated in the closing months of the war and the automatic rifle, although imperfect, was clearly the way forward for small arms. By

The Bergmann MP 18. Note the snail drum magazine. (The World War 1 Document Archive)

the 1920s, the sub-machine-gun was recognized by most armies as a means of dramatically increasing the firepower of the infantry. Despite the British Army's refusal to see the merits of the sub-machine-gun, it had come to stay. Although the United States adopted a semi-automatic rifle in the mid-1930s and the Soviet Union soon followed, it took until the last years of the Second World War and the emergence of the assault rifle (for example, the German StG 44) for the automatic rifle to begin to supplant the manual bolt action.

As far as many of the devices developed for trench warfare were concerned, they were products of the time and disappeared with the end of the war. Devices like the sniperscope and the trench periscope had been devised to cope with the peculiar conditions of the trenches. As soon as trench warfare gave way to open, mobile warfare, such things became redundant. With the development of armoured fighting vehicles, warfare again assumed a mobility that it was hoped could never be stopped. Nevertheless, trenches remained a crucial feature of warfare even in the Second World War where conditions were just as bad as anything in the First, the only difference being that warfare did not remain static. Similarly, wire-cutter rifle attachments disappeared from the battlefield. None of these had been an unqualified success. They had served a purpose but they were a short-term measure and never intended as a substitute for the only effective cutter of wire, high explosive. Nevertheless, the wire-cutting gadget re-emerged in the 1960s with the Kalishnikov AKM's bayonet/scabbard wire-cutting slot and lug arrangement. There have been other similar bayonet/scabbard cutters since then.

The Bangalore torpedo, despite its unwieldiness, was more useful for cutting lanes in wire than either hand-held or rifle attachment wire-cutters. Because of its effectiveness, it not only survived the war but went on to see service in the Second World War.

The trench club was never used again. The trench knife disappeared only to be reborn as the fighting or commando knife. But the British commando knife of the Second World War was quite different from the trench knife of the First. Designed in 1940 by Capts Fairbairn and Sykes, formerly of the Shanghai International Police, the weapon was the result of their experience of Chinese fighting styles and was intended for quick silent killing rather than as a weapon of last resort. It had a closer relationship to daggers of the seventeenth century than to those of the Great War. A man armed with a knife was acknowledged by the fencing masters of the sixteenth and seventeenth centuries as more dangerous than a man armed with a sword. But this was only true if the man knew how to use the weapon. None of the soldiers of the First World War had such knowledge and it may have been because of the difficulties of using a dagger effectively that so many took up the club instead which required far less skill. That is not to diminish the danger posed by a knife-wielding man bent on killing you but injury rather than death was the likely outcome. There are no statistics for deaths caused by knives in the First World War but the number was minute.

Body armour never vanished from the battlefield. The sudden rise in its popularity during the First World War was an expression of frustration and impotence born of mutual siege rather than a sudden recognition of the value of some form of ballistic protection for those in the front line. The siege conditions that prevailed for most of the time persuaded both GHQ and London, as well as inventors, that some practical means of protecting soldiers was necessary. Body armour was a symptom of siege mentality and casualties had become too high to turn aside any means of preventing them from increasing any more than was necessary. This was as much political as it was practical. Politically, the ever-growing casualty lists were a real problem as the war progressed. In the last years of the war, Lloyd George withheld troops from Haig because he felt that Haig was incompetent and squandered the lives of his men. The shortage of fighting men in the spring of 1918 was a consequence of this. The demand for body armour sent a political message that Haig was concerned for his men. It is not clear that he saw it in this way, however, as Haig was a keen supporter of body armour from the outset, before the question of the cost in lives became an issue. Had not Haig been in favour, there is no doubt that Lloyd George would have used it against him.

Politics aside, there is no question that body armour did play a role in reducing casualties but by how many it is impossible to determine. From a practical point of view, body armour was shown to reduce casualties or at least diminish the seriousness of some injuries. The steel helmet clearly made a difference to the numbers of men suffering head wounds from shrapnel. Of all the forms of body armour to be tried during the war, only the shrapnel helmet became standard equipment for all soldiers. And this process began in less than six months of the outbreak of war, although it was not until mid-1916 that all British troops had helmets. The helmet stayed. In fact, the steel helmet remained in use until relatively recently when steel was replaced by composite materials. It is the only item of body armour to have been retained from the First World War by all soldiers in all armies. Interest in armour to protect the trunk fell sharply by mid-1918 and it did not revive until the 1950s, although that is not to suggest that experiments were not conducted during the Second World War. But it was really only aircrew who wore body armour in the 1939–45 War. It took until the American involvement in Vietnam in the 1960s before the flak jacket, the descendent of the First World War body shield, became widely used by ordinary soldiers. Today, the modern flak jacket made of composite materials is commonplace.

Domination of the enemy was what it was all about. None of these devices would have been given a second glance had they not promised to swing the balance of power. They were attempts at technical solutions to the problems presented by mutual siege – war in the trenches. The steel helmet and the sub-machine-gun had tremendous impact for future wars. The history of the First World War has been dominated by the huge casualty lists and debates over how this could have been allowed to happen. The inventions proposed as solutions to the problems of trench warfare are a part of this complex picture that is often overlooked.

APPENDIX
Patents

Body Armour

Application Date	Patent Number	Inventors	Description
2/11/14	21,863	E.W. Jackson	Combined entrenching tool and shield; detachable spade as breastplate
8/12/14	23,746	M.H. Mörner (Countess Helen Mörner)	Flexible metal bands in leather casings sewn between cotton coverings. No patent granted; sealing fee not paid
8/3/15	3,663	M.A.A. Roux	Rolled steel breastplate
19/3/15	4,376	M.P.J.E. Fontijn	Large portable shield with slots supported on shoulders
6/4/15	5,196 cognate 13,258/15	F. Dayton, E.A. Whitfield	First Dayfield Body Shield
3/5/15	6,585	M.C. Favre	Face shield tried experimentally by French at Verdun; weighed 10 lb
8/5/15	6,900	G. Lynch	Resin-impregnated wadding
29/7/15	10,991	F.C. Lynde	Layer of overlapping steel strips with another at right angles
29/7/15	11,012	F.C. Hunt	Breastplate with spring bands for wearing
16/8/15	11,803	J.L. Brodie	Helmet and liner; the British tin hat
7/9/15	12,765	A.R. Page	Double helmet
10/9/15	12,957	E. Sherring	Composite armour
24/9/15	101,629	F. Della Valle, C. Benazzi	Metal goggles with slits
7/1/16	103,140	D. Anderson	Second Dayfield Body Shield
7/2/16	105,348	Sir R.A. Hadfield, A.B.H. Clarke	Helmet and liner
10/2/16	104,699	W. Hill, J.P. Wilks	Chemico Body Shield
25/4/16	103,915	T.H. Randolph	Wilkinson Safety Service Jacket
21/5/16	104,911	W. Beedle	Third Dayfield Body Shield
31/5/16	105,822	J. Berkley	Berkley's Flexible Armour Guard
23/6/16	103,425	Hawkes & Co., W.C. Bensley	Ventilation of helmets
9/7/16	104,617	T. Roberts	Hinged plates with straps, doubles as loopholed shield
24/8/16	105,699	J. Pullman	Interlocking plates in overlapping pockets
5/9/16	101,957	J. Dunnand	Visor for British helmet
17/10/16	108,244	J. Taylor	Armoured waistcoat with asbestos
26/10/16	105,513	R. Fariselli	Waistcoat with pockets for armour plates
11/11/16	105,785	F.C. Hunt	Additional armour for 11,012/15
14/11/16	111,149	J.H. Fielding	Multiple plates with energy-absorbing layer
20/11/16	109,343	H. Siswick	Composite armour with resin, wadding, wire and fabric
27/12/16	108,801	A. Corelli, Cammel Laird & Co.	Body shield with energy-absorbing layers
14/2/17	110,093	W. Hill, J.P. Wilks	Chemico Body Shield; addition to 104,699
18/4/17	127,321	T.G.H. Burton, J.W. Fawcett, W.H. Hatfield	Small recesses or closed holes in armour plate
31/5/17	115,912	Coir Tyre Co., G.D. Rose	Rubber reinforced with fibres; similar to vehicle tyres
11/6/17	116,362	A.D. Daigre	Body shield with energy-absorbing layers
17/8/17	133,131	Sir R.A. Hadfield	Thin manganese steel sheets suitable for body shields and helmets

continued overleaf

Application Date	Patent Number	Inventors	Description
9/11/17	120,606	J.L. Brodie	Additional armour for 11,803/15
9/11/17	120,607	J.L. Brodie	Helmet and visor
16/4/18	118,251	L. Soren	Helmet with external spring
20/7/18	129,815	W.F. Pamphlett	Armour with energy-absorbing backing
16/9/18	132,600	S. Suderlock	Two layers of hinged plates with metal cloth in between; portable shield and body armour
4/10/18	133,165	Sir R.A. Hadfield, A.G.M. Jack	Shovel blade as breastplate

Mobile shields

Application Date	Patent Number	Inventors	Description
22/2/16	101,827	J.J. Oxley	Hood-shaped with large ball instead of wheel, and pole for pushing it
20/3/16	124,772	W. Bray	Cylindrical shell that rolls
28/8/17	118,335	J.E. Logan	Infantry shield (box) and wire-cutter operated from inside by lever; mounted on two wheels and front castor; man-powered

Shields for rifles and machine-guns

Application Date	Patent Number	Inventors	Description
23/6/14	24,535	C. Levens	Collapsible fan-like shield for rifle
31/8/14	19,281	E. MacAdam	Combined spade and shield
19/11/14	22,767	W. Winans	Small cranked oval shield for rifle muzzle
2/2/15	1,635	J.H.T. Greenwood	Conical shield for rifle
10/3/15	3,801	H.J. Lawson	For rifle. Patent not granted; sealing fee not paid
29/4/15	6,378	W.G. Ward	Shield with rotating aperture plate
21/5/15	100,536	D. Stergianopulos	Shield attached to bayonet for bayonet fighting
20/9/15	13,346	H. Austin	Adjustable pillar mounting with shield for MG
24/9/15	101,630	Officine di Villar Perosa	Shield with ball-and-socket joint for Villar Perosa SMG
8/10/15	14,286	Sir A.T. Dawson, G.T. Buckham	MG shield attached to special mounting; has shelves for sandbags
6/11/15	15,678	W. Bate	Cover for MG on telescopic stand
19/11/15	16,312	A.E. Thorneycroft	Conical shield for rifle
4/1/16	100,652	J.M. Lamothe	Shield with universal ball joint with gun aperture. Also acts as sighting rest
20/1/16	103,178	Sir H. Grubb, Vickers Ltd	Spaced plates with out-of-register apertures and sighting system of glass parallel piped or prism between
25/2/16	103,201	Sir A.T. Dawson, G.T. Buckham	Cap for front of Vickers for protecting MG
12/5/16	101,269	T.J. Gee	Conical shield with hinged locking jaw for rifle
14/12/16	106,786	W. Peck	Attached by rods to rifle
12/7/17	118,132	A.S.F. Robinson	Tripod and shield for MG

Breech & muzzle protectors

Application Date	Patent Number	Inventors	Description
10/12/14	23,895	W.C. Hammond	Shaped split sleeve wraps round breech, held by snap-fasteners
27/2/15	3,183	A.S. Purdey	Metal muzzle-protector with clips
21/8/15	12,087	C. Liddiard	Rubber cap to fit over the muzzle
23/10/14	14,973	H. Senn	Muzzle cap attached to muzzle-ring of bayonet that fits over barrel when bayonet fitted. Application void
6/12/15	17,138	F.H. Sterling	Waterproof breech cover

Knives & bayonets

Application Date	Patent Number	Inventors	Description
25/8/16	108,741	F. Joubert	Leaf-shaped short sword with folding hilt
29/11/16	111,526	A. Pritchard	Revolver bayonet
17/10/18	127,777	J.E. McNary	Knuckleduster-knife; US Mk 1

Night sights

Application Date	Patent Number	Inventors	Description
2/12/14	23,433	J.E. Martin	Luminous screen for backsight
30/1/15	100,050	B.S. Del Borgo	Luminous
30/4/15	6,451	J.E. Martin	Electric torch for revivifying night sight in 23,433/14
25/8/15	12,270	G. Panerai	Glass tubes containing luminous salts
27/8/15	125,082	H. Fenderl	Luminous and screened
21/9/15	13,428	A.H. Atkinson	Luminous auxiliary sights
20/3/16	104,905	G. Panerai	Luminous crystals with incisions
15/5/16	105,812	A.H. Watson, P.H. Watson	Luminous
27/5/16	108,166	C.O. Erwood, H.J. Prockter	Lamps to illuminate sights
13/2/17	126,690	Sir A.T. Dawson, Sir G.T. Buckham	Transparent foresight illuminated by luminous material
8/12/17	116,848	E.J. Hall	Lens illuminated by electric light
19/1/18	122,453	K.J. Pen	Luminous spots
30/3/18	125,052	E.F. Watson	Detachable luminous sights

Periscopes

Application Date	Patent Number	Inventors	Description
26/9/14	20,215	C. Beck, H.C. Beck	Magnifying periscope
10/11/14	22,319	Sir H. Grubb, C. Beck	Magnifying periscope
18/12/14	24,284	D.A. Sunderland	Lazy-tongs
29/12/14	24,743	A.L. Adams	Folding rod with two mirrors
4/1/15	110	W. Youlten	Collapsible; false mirror to draw enemy fire
5/1/15	163	E. Duerr	Lazy-tongs. No patent granted; sealing fee not paid
15/1/15	673	R.J. Cracknell	U-shaped wire frame
13/2/15	2,345	A. Cuthbert	Collapsible wire frame
16/2/15	2,484	A.G. Tottem, J. Wolfe	Telescopic tubes, hinged lower mirror

continued overleaf

Application Date	Patent Number	Inventors	Description
1/3/15	3,282	F.E. Moody	Collapsible bellows with lazy-tongs; mirrors flexibly attached to fall into correct position. Patent not granted; sealing fee not paid
3/3/15	3,407	T. Ovenden	Collapsible
5/3/15	3,549	W. Peck	Telescopic and magnifying
5/3/15	3,563	C. Beck, W.H.S. Marriott	Magnifying
20/3/15	4,397	H.R. Taylor	Telescopic flat boxes
7/4/15	5,239	J.T. MacCallum	Hinged mirrors on metal frame
14/4/15	5,633	R.D. Batten	Lazy-tongs
3/5/15	6,564	A.C. Webster	Extendible, not enclosed, two mirrors
8/5/15	6,926	E. Duerr	Lazy-tongs with U-shaped pieces
24/5/15	9,259	E.E. Fournier-d'Albe	Top mirror attached to sliding support connected to a tube with a top lens and a lower prism
5/7/15	9,779	H.B. Sankey, J.J. Steward	Tubular
31/8/15	12,523	S.C. Soul, C.W. Howe	Hinged; issued as No. 9 Mk II
16/10/15	14,660	H.E. Collins	Telescopic standard of portable semaphore apparatus provided with mirrors to serve as periscope
22/11/15	16,483	H.E.B. Daniell	Tubular; sighting compass
14/2/16	101,826	G. Baker	Mirror attached to bayonet
17/8/16	108,540	G.R.G. Robertson	Portable camera obscura
12/6/17	115,925	C.Beck, H.C. Beck	Right-angled prism in top of cylindrical tube with slidable extension; like No. 25
8/12/17	121,329	H.F. McShane	Box; reversible top mirror; lower part has aperture to see directly ahead

Hyposcopes

Application Date	Patent Number	Inventors	Description
2/10/14	20,439	W. Youlten	Single prism
28/12/14	24,687	W. Youlten	Single prism attached to butt
12/1/15	480	W. Youlten	Hyposcope and attachment
4/3/15	3,496	Periscopes & Hyposcopes Ltd, W. Youlten	Hyposcope
19/3/15	4,334	Periscopes & Hyposcopes Ltd, W. Youlten	MG sight using double-reflecting prism
20/3/15	100,203	J. Walter	Hinged mirror attached to butt
31/3/15	4,992	E.C.R. Marks	Three mirrors in a bent tube with a portion parallel to barrel
31/5/15	8,017	P. Keane	Triangular mirror attached to butt and rifle turned upside down to fire
3/11/15	15,516	F.M. Vonk, J.H. Eradus	Attaching periscope to butt
10/12/15	102,729	J.L. Cameron, L.E. Yaggi	Detachable tubular periscopic sights plus adjustable auxiliary shoulder piece for range and deflection; trigger cord
21/1/16	103,011	J.S. Withers	Hyposcope attached to rifle; adjustable
5/2/16	102,759	Periscopes & Hyposcopes Ltd, W. Youlten	Means of mounting hyposcope described in 4,334/15 to rifle or MG
18/3/16	125,667	G. Espitallier, L. Roman, A. Bellard	Telescopic, tubular with top lid to prevent ingress of water
18/3/16	125,668	G. Espitallier, L. Roman, A. Bellard	Method of fixing 125,667 to rear of Vickers
5/4/16	106,109	G. Prescott	Sighting to one side using mirror; recoil absorber attached to bayonet lug and bayonet bar
10/11/16	106,420	L.E. Snoek	Horizontal periscope

Sniperscopes

Application Date	Patent Number	Inventors	Description
21/10/14	21,318 cognate 22,178/14	W.S. Boult	Auxiliary stock with periscope and auxiliary trigger
17/9/15	2,582	J.E. Chandler	Pistol grip with two mirrors and auxiliary trigger, attached to butt
4/3/15	3,454	T.C. Tomlinson	Set-down auxiliary stock
13/4/15	4,900	H.B. Cahusac	Rifle butt removed and turned into auxiliary stock
8/6/15	8,469	J.B. Evans, W.H. Kelsall	Set-down stock with periscope
11/9/15	13,031	G. Gérard	Set-down stock attached in place of butt, with periscope & auxiliary trigger
9/10/15	14,307	L.L. Richard	Pivotable set-down stock with folding periscope
26/11/15	101,830	H.M. Horton, M.N. Liebmann	Auxiliary stock, bolt and trigger
16/2/16	102,410	R.E. Ellis	Extended magazine for pistol attached to rod resting on trench floor, periscope and trigger cord
13/3/16	103,382	E. Duerr	Two-mirror periscope with handles and auxiliary trigger attached to butt
18/3/16	124,771	G. Espitallier, L. Roman, A. Bellard	Auxiliary stock with periscope and auxiliary trigger; relates to auxiliary trigger linkage and how periscope attached
29/3/16	106,634	A.B. Knotts	Disappearing parapet MG; complex system of gears and mechanics
9/5/16	106,132	G. Ponchielli, G. Pavesi	Two mirrors on rifle, one angled, auxiliary stock, trigger operated by lever
19/5/16	104,790	A. Bellard	Auxiliary stock attached to butt by U-shaped frame, bolt-operating mechanism and auxiliary trigger
24/11/16	107,717	W. Peck	Auxiliary stock, bolt and trigger; uses periscope of 3549/15
13/1/17	115,013	W. Youlten	Tubular frame for MG
2/1/17	111,931	W. Lloyd	Periscope (two mirrors) and folding auxiliary stock with hand grips
5/1/17	112,494	B.F. Seymour	Large, extensible mast with three telescopic legs. Raised and lowered by gears
13/1/17	115,013	W. Youlten	Raising and lowering gun above and below parapet
16/1/17	112,058	Periscopes & Hyposcopes Ltd W. Youlten	Prism on forked bracket attached to Lewis; auxiliary trigger on twin grips
28/2/17	113,337	J.Y. Sangster	Extensible skeleton auxiliary stock; mounting for periscope; separate pistol grip
9/3/17	111,780	C.J. Cooke	Auxiliary stock for automatic pistol attached to magazine channel and mounted on bayonet grip via ring and socket
11/5/17	113,044	A. Bellard	Addition to 104,790; relates to bolt-actuating mechanism
25/5/17	109,236	E. Duerr	Similar to 103,382 but with bolt-actuating mechanism
29/11/17	147,673	H. Pirmez	Disappearing gun mounting

Aiming rests

Application Date	Patent Number	Inventors	Description
24/8/15	12,195	W.R. Ellison, H.L. Cole	Curved track and shield
13/1/17	113,294	W. Youlten	Expanding A-frame with spikes
9/3/18	121,555	W. From	Inclined plate

Wire-cutters

Application Date	Patent Number	Inventors	Description
26/9/14	20,241	T.R.R. Ashton	Combined with bayonet. Patent not granted; sealing fee not paid
20/2/15	2,734	G.F. Pittar	Hook-shaped frame and toggled lever
11/5/15	7,102	T. Emery	Eccentrically pivoted arms; also relates to shells with fold-out arms for cutting wire
12/5/15	7,154	S. Korsak	Attached to rifle; pivoting casing and jaw pins in curved slots
18/5/15	7,442	E.W. Moir	Attached to bayonet operated when bayonet attached to rifle
18/5/15	7,472	E.E. Lindkvist	Attached beneath stock
7/6/15	8,457 cognate 3,15/16	H.G. Cocks	Hand operated fitted to front of rifle
10/6/15	8,596	S. Korsak	Improvement on 7154/15 and clamp
19/8/15	11,984 cognate 14,478/15	T.R.R. Ashton	Hooked cutter and compound lever mechanism
7/9/15	12,766	E. Perks	Attached to bayonet; hand operated
9/9/15	3,761	C.T.B. Sangster	Attached to rifle; pins in curved slots turn jaws in casing; improvement on Korsak
15/9/15	13,202	R. Pengeot	Hand operated, multiple pivots and horns
24/9/15	13,620	W. Threw	Muzzle attachment for pistol to shoot wire
24/9/15	13,621	H.T. Johnson	Muzzle attachment with guides for centring wire over muzzle; wire cut by shot
2/10/15	13,975	W.C. Haigh	Hand operated, attached to rifle or pole
16/10/15	5,904	F.G. Wallis, D.R. Kinghorn	Clipped to bayonet
22/12/15	17,886	C.H. Pugh Ltd, G.F. Bull	Attached to rifle; similar to Korsak and Sangster; adopted by British
22/12/15	17,887	C.H. Pugh Ltd, G.F. Bull, A.L. Green	Similar to 17,886/15
11/1/16	102,995	R.J. Southwood	Garden shears that can be adapted as wire-cutters; hand operated
18/1/16	102,391	G. Caplen	Attached to rifle, blade at mid-stock, operated by hand lever
18/4/16	105,607	F.J. Shenton	Attached to rifle via sling-swivel pivot, operated by handle
12/5/16	101,933	W. Stewart	Attached to bayonet, operated by thrust on wire
20/5/16	106,334	P. Malfatti	Attached to pole, operated by toggle levers; pin for attaching bayonet
27/7/16	104,627	C.H. Pugh Ltd, G.F. Bull, E.W. Starkey	17,886 adapted for hand-operated cutters
1/9/16	109,987	T. Emery	Similar to 7102/15 and attached to rifle or lance
11/9/16	109,473	H.J. Dyke	Cutting wheel attached to bayonet at hilt
29/12/16	110,658	A.E. Turner	Attached to muzzle; pivoted blade actuated by bullet
24/2/17	111,020	J.F. Melling	Three heads pivoting in each other
7/6/17	113,212	J.G. Carew-Gibson	Pivoted cutting levers with toggle

continued overleaf

Application Date	Patent Number	Inventors	Description
30/8/17	112,111	W.C. Lea	Hand operated and foldable
4/5/18	121,894	E. Wilczek	Irregularly shaped cutting wheels attached to bayonet; for Russian Mosin-Nagant
4/5/18	122,104	C. Szfranski	Shearing-type cutter attached to bayonet, operated against bayonet blade by curved lever
21/5/18	138,945	M. Sroke	Bayonet with hand-operated notched wheel

Wire-cutting machines

Application Date	Patent Number	Inventors	Description
9/11/15	15,807	C.L. Burdick	Self-propelled machine with knives, wire-cutters, flame-thrower, gas projector; self-destructs at destination
15/11/15	2,240	A.H.S. Landor	Armoured vehicle with curved bars which cut wire or guide cable over top
15/11/15	16,111	J. Prétot, J.L. Breton	Machine with multiple cutting shears mounted on motor vehicle
3/1/16	124,450	R.F. Macfie	Tank with two sets of tracks; front set has conical hood-like shield for forcing through obstacles; cutters behind shield
17/2/16	127,266	Schneider et Cie	Tank with projections for cutting wire
14/3/16	103,036	J.E. May	Pointed nose on armoured car with reciprocating saws driven from engine
24/10/16	110,582	J.J. Oxley	Armoured car with serrated strip from front to top
19/4/17	116,115	F.W. Golby	Chain with hooks between two vehicles
23/4/17	113,870	T. Marshall	Caterpillar-tracked; spiked endless chains and quillotine

Wire-cutting ammunition and guns

Application Date	Patent Number	Inventors	Description
4/8/15	11,279	T.D. Wanliss	Twin-barrelled gun for firing chain-shot to cut wire. No patent granted; sealing not paid
18/11/15	16,234	J.M. Newton	Projectile with arms that open out to cut wire
22/1/16	103,500	H. Mitchell	Projectile splits longitudinally in flight, sections connected by chain/rope
1/3/16	104,382	A.H.S. Landor	Projectile with radiating arms with serrated discs for cutting wire
4/4/16	104,771	A. Bever	Shell with internal chains
3/6/16	106,853	L.G. Walker, J.E. Hughes	Projectile with grapnel for cutting wire
13/6/16	107,617	D. Samaia	Projectile for multi-barrel gun
27/6/16	107,253	J.M. Murphy	Shell with internal chains
30/10/17	119,316	D.G. Saunders	Shell with chains
2/1/18	117,400	P.C. Rushen	Ammunition for multi-discharge gun
13/2/18	119,387	O.I. Straub	Chain-filled shell
19/3/18	124,818	D.G. Downs, W.S. Bedford	Chain-shot for 124,868
19/3/18	124,868	D.G. Downs, W.S. Bedford	Twin gun for chain-shot
17/6/18	133,360	E.G. Yeates	Shell with weighted chains

Automatic rifles

Application Date	Patent Number	Inventors	Description
2/6/15	8,172	M.G. Farquhar, A.H. Hill	Horizontal drum magazine; cartridges move in circular or spiral grooves
19/10/15	14,747	F. Tittenton	Mechanism to fire SMLE when closing bolt without using trigger
27/11/15	16,758	A.W. Brewtnall	Mechanism to fire SMLE when closing bolt without using trigger
20/3/16	127,642	Soc. Anon. des Etablissements Delaunay Belleville	Gas operated; springs, levers and catches operated by movement of gas piston
20/3/16	131,350	Soc. Anon. des Etablissements Delaunay Belleville	Related to 127,642
1/4/16	124,792	M.G. Farquhar, A.H. Hill	Gas operated
20/11/16	126,055	M.G. Farquhar, A.H. Hill	Relates to breech mechanism in 28587/07, 17211/09, 27972/11 and magazine in 8172/15
1/12/16	127,663	Soc. Anon. des Etablissements Delaunay Belleville	Detail improvements to type of gun in 127,642
6/2/17	127,670	Soc. Anon. des Etablissements Delaunay Belleville	Addition to 127,663
8/6/17	120,741	B.B. Roberts, J.Walters	Gas-operated gun with vertically sliding locking bolt
18/7/17	117,312	E.C.R. Marks	Adapting an automatic gun to semi-automatic
14/9/17	113,805	A.L. Chevallier, O. Lambert	Breech action; spring-controlled inertia weight
29/12/17	121,639	H.C. Scofield	Sheet metal semicircular guard for auto mechanism
5/1/18	119,960	M.G. Farquhar, A.H. Hill	Shallow drum rotary magazine
6/6/18	127,957	M.G. Farquhar, A.H. Hill	Development of rifles in 28587/07, 17211/09, 9118/10, 27972/11, 28792/12, 126055 with inverted breech body and bolt cover, and operating cartridge feed and firing mechanisms from above bolt instead of below
6/6/18	128,165	M.G. Farquhar, A.H. Hill	Bipod for rifle in 127,957
19/6/18	128,395	Sir A.T. Dawson, Sir G.T. Buckham	Conversion of SMLE to gas operation
5/7/18	129,253	W.D. Forbes, T.W. McKenzie	Long recoil; barrel, breech block and bolt-operating sleeve recoil together
27/7/18	133,980	Vickers Ltd, T.K. North	Regulating rate of fire by trigger pressure
30/7/18	130,454	A.L. Chevallier	Fixed-barrel automatic gun; relates to manual operation
9/8/18	133,379	O. Imray (Colt's Patent Firearms Manufacturing Co.)	Relates to BAR; locking mechanism and buffer
9/8/18	133,552	O. Imray (Colt's Patent Firearms Manufacturing Co.)	Adapting to single or automatic fire
19/8/18	131,705	A.L. Chevallier	Development of 130,454

Sub-machine-guns

Application Date	Patent Number	Inventors	Description
8/9/15	16,362	Officine di Villar Perosa	The Villar Perosa sub-machine-gun
8/9/15	101,882	Officine di Villar Perosa	Magazine for Villar Perosa. Void
20/11/16	133,080	Officine di Villar Perosa	Improved firing mechanism
10/3/17	133,090	Officine di Villar Perosa	Addition to 16,363/15; hand slide that covers breech; double trigger. Also describes single-barrelled, shoulder-fired weapon

Miscellaneous

Application Date	Patent Number	Inventors	Description
14/7/15	100,891	A.B. Pratt	Helmet gun fired by blow tube
20/10/15	14,863	W.R. Brown	Pivotable blade fitted in butt. No patent granted; sealing fee not paid
25/11/15	16,662	O.J. Lund	Many rifles arranged in rows in armoured box, fired by bullet striking shield plates connected to firing mechanism
28/4/16	101,517	S.E. Page	Pistol with knife
8/5/16	103,241	P. Baker	Foldable knife attached to helmet
15/5/16	106,461	A.B. Pratt	Addition to 100,891
9/8/18	122,142	M. Lesko	Aiming-rest-cum-dagger – a spike with a rifle fork

Sources

BRITISH PATENTS AND PATENT ABRIDGEMENTS, AUGUST 1914 – NOVEMBER 1918

Classes
> 9 (i) ammunition
> 30 cutlery
> 61 (ii) hand tools
> 63 hats and other head coverings
> 83 (ii) metal articles and processes
> 92 (i) ordnance and machine-gun carriages and mountings
> 92 (ii) ordnance and machine-guns
> 97 (i) optical systems and apparatus
> 119 small arms
> 141 wearing apparel

OFFICIAL PUBLICATIONS

List of Changes in British War Material, 1902–18

PUBLIC RECORD OFFICE, KEW

MUN 4/135 – shields
MUN 4/426 – Munitions Inventions Department reports
MUN 4/2577 – optical stores
MUN 4/2656 – Trench Warfare Department papers
MUN 4/2749 – shields on wheels and body shields
MUN 4/3098 – periscopes
MUN 4/3586 – intelligence on enemy weapons
MUN 4/3589 – intelligence on enemy weapons; 'Notes on Inventions and New Stores'
MUN 4/3590 – intelligence on enemy weapons; 'Notes on Inventions and New Stores'
MUN 4/6878 – Trench Warfare Committee papers
MUN 5/382/1600/8 – 'History of Trench Warfare Supply, Aug. 1914 – May 1915'
MUN 5/383/1600/14 – 'Development of Weapons used in Trench Warfare'

WO 140/14 – Reports on Trials (Experimental Section, Hythe)
WO 140/15 – Reports on Trials (Experimental Section, Hythe)

PUBLISHED BOOKS

Binding, Rudolph. *A Fatalist at War*, Allen & Unwin, 1929
Blunden, Edmund. *Undertones of War*, Cobden-Sanderson, 1928
Chapman, Guy. *A Passionate Prodigality*, Buchan & Enright, 1985

Coe, Michael D. *et al. Swords and Hilt Weapons*, Weidenfeld & Nicolson, 1989

Cole, H.M. *US Military Knives*, Cole, 1979

Dean, Bashford. *Helmets and Body Armor in Modern Warfare*, Pugliese, 1977

Dunn, J.C. *The War the Infantry Knew*, Jane's, 1987

Edmonds, Charles (Charles Carrington). *A Subaltern's War*, Peter Davis, 1929

Gilbert, Adrian. *Stalk and Kill*, Sidgwick & Jackson, 1997

Graham, Stephen. *A Private in the Guards*, Macmillan, 1919

Graves, Robert. *Goodbye to All That*, Cassell, 1957

Hartcup, Guy. *The War of Invention*, Brassey's, 1988

Hesketh-Pritchard, Maj H. *Sniping in France*, Leo Cooper/Pen & Sword, 1994

Hitchcock, F.C. *"Stand To" A Diary of the Trenches 1915–1918*, Gliddon Books, 1988

Hobart, F.W.A. *Pictorial History of the Sub-Machine Gun*, Ian Allen, 1973

Jünger, Ernst. *The Storm of Steel*, Chatto & Windus, 1929

Richards, Frank. *Old Soldiers Never Die*, Faber, 1933

Sassoon, Siegfried. *Memoirs of an Infantry Officer*, Faber, 1965

Skennerton, Ian. *The British Sniper*, Skennerton, 1983

——. *List of Changes*, vol. IV 1910–1918, Skennerton, 1993

Terraine, John. *General Jack's Diary*, Eyre & Spottiswoode, 1964

Westman, Stephen. *Surgeon with the Kaiser's Army*, Kimber, 1968

The Illustrated War News, 16 vols, 1914–18

The Times History of the War, 21 vols, 1914–20

History of the First World War, 8 vols, Purnell/BPC, 1969–71

JOURNALS AND NEWSPAPERS

Macdonald, Col the Rt Hon Sir John. 'The Knife in Trench Warfare' in *Journal of The Royal United Services Institute*, February 1917

Correspondence, *Journal of The Royal United Services Institute*, August 1917

'The Work of the Royal Engineers in the European War, 1914–19', *The Royal Engineers Journal*, 1924–5

Letters, *The Times*, 29 and 30 November 1915, 1 December 1915

Index